Kyoto Revisited

Kyoto Revisited

Heritage Tourism in Contemporary Japan

Jennifer S. Prough

University of Hawaiʻi Press
Honolulu

Paperback edition 2022

Printed in the United States of America

Library of Congress Cataloging-in-Publication Data

Names: Prough, Jennifer S., author.
Title: Kyoto revisited : heritage tourism in contemporary Japan / Jennifer S. Prough.
Description: Honolulu : University of Hawai‘i Press, 2022. | Includes bibliographical references and index.
Identifiers: LCCN 2021056656 | ISBN 9780824888534 (hardback) | ISBN 9780824891688 (pdf) | ISBN 9780824891695 (epub) | ISBN 9780824891701 (kindle edition)
Subjects: LCSH: Heritage tourism—Japan—Kyoto. | Kyoto (Japan) —Description and travel.
Classification: LCC G155.J3 P76 2022 | DDC 338.4/791521864—dc23/eng/20220119
LC record available at https://lccn.loc.gov/2021056656

ISBN 9780824891671 (paperback)

University of Hawai‘i Press books are printed on acid-free paper and meet the guidelines for permanence and durability of the Council on Library Resources.

Cover art: Photos by Jason Mitzner (top) and the author.

To Andy and Emmett, my fellow travelers in this journey

Contents

Acknowledgments

I still remember my first experiences in Kyoto as an undergraduate studying abroad at Kansai Gaikokugo Daigaku; I spent many weekends exploring the city's temple and shrines, markets, and festivals. Two decades later this book sprouted while I was taking undergraduates in my "Urban Japan" seminars to Tokyo and Kyoto over spring break. Conversations with students as we traveled often highlighted the ways that history is palpable in Japan and the ways that it is preserved, evolving, retold, and recreated. My thinking about the ways that heritage is crafted for both domestic and international tourists in Kyoto came out of these experiences, and my first thanks go to the students who traveled with me.

Writing a book is at once creative and insular, but it also requires the care of a community—to carve out the space from teaching and committee work, to act as a sounding board for new ideas and emerging theories, and to keep you engaged when you are spinning your wheels, lost in the details or at a loss for words. I received invaluable support from my communities both here and in Japan throughout the ten years of research and writing. First and foremost, my colleagues and friends at Christ College (the Honors College) at Valparaiso University provided me with interdisciplinary conversations throughout the years that have shaped my thinking in unmeasurable ways; to work with a convivial group of scholar-teachers is a privilege indeed. Special thanks to friends Liz Wuerffle, Allison Schuette, David Western, and Jana Cram for countless nights relaxing after a hard day's writing. Additionally, I was supported with time and resources by three deans—Mel Piehl, Panayiotis Kanelos, and Susan VanZanten. Mel, in particular, nurtured my thinking at all stages of this process; I stand in a long line of scholars whose work he has shaped intellectually.

This book is stronger for conversations both formal and informal with the members of the Midwest Japan Forum. This community of Japan scholars from across the Midwest provides much needed intellectual sustenance and camaraderie for those of us teaching at smaller universities with few other colleagues in our field. Scholarship on tourism was new to me, and I am indebted to Jennie German Molz for chatting with me about the field and providing an engaging lit review at the outset of this project. Anne Allison, Jan Bardsley, Laura Miller, Alisa Freedman, and Kris Troost all helped write letters in support for grants, track down resources, and read chapters; without their encouragement this book would not have come to fruition. Jan, in particular, was a partner in this Kyoto research; her careful read of the full draft and enthusiasm all along was vital. Finally, Hayley Kim provided much needed energy putting together the index.

Fieldwork is best with friends to share the ups and downs, and Catherine Phipps has been an invaluable travel partner. Conversations while traveling, over ramen and beer, helped me process what I was finding. I have benefited from ongoing conversations with Catherine and Noell Wilson throughout the years, and they have watched this project come into its own. And Susan Westhafer Furukawa has been an unwavering writing partner. Our weekly conversations started to keep ourselves on track as we wrote, edited, and published our books, and they developed into a rich friendship both personal and professional.

Our time in Kyoto in 2012 was enriched by the community at the Kyoto International School (KIS) that embraced our family, and this project allowed me to return regularly to refuel the friendships made there. Thanks to the families of Sanae, Nobuko, Megumi, Vivi, Sachie, Kim, and Stella for their friendship and hospitality. Professionally, I am grateful to all of the tourism professionals who spoke with me, let me hang out in their spaces, and allowed me to join their tours—especially the Kyoto Tourism Association, Kyoto City Tourism Office, Kyo-Navi, and a host of tour guides and tourists. I was thrilled to be affiliated with Kansai Gaidai, where I first spent time in Japan. The Kyoto office of the Japan Foundation provided me with support throughout my fieldwork in 2012, and I am especially grateful to Fukuda Kazuhiro for his hospitality. Over the years, this research was funded by a range of grants, including the Japan Foundation Research Fellowship, Valparaiso University Research Professorship, North East Asia Council Summer Grants, Valparaiso University

Summer Research Grants, Valparaiso Alumni Association Faculty Research Grants, and the Christ College Alumni Fund.

While all the arguments, details, and errors are my own, I would like to thank the staff at the University of Hawaiʻi Press for seeing me smoothly through this process. I am grateful to Pamela Kelley, who published my first book and saw me through to a mostly completed manuscript; Stephanie Chun, who took over at the final stages; and Grace Wen, who saw it through the production stage. The reviewers provided thorough suggestions for revision, helping me solidify my argument, and I am grateful for that process and their generosity.

Last but never least, my family has sustained me throughout this project. My parents, Betty and Russ, have always encouraged my work, and this project is no exception. My sister, Kim Anness, used her geographer's talents to make the map for this book, and my brother-in-law Joel has been an astute sounding board for ideas along the way. Finally, Andy and Emmett, living in Kyoto with you, commuting to KIS, walking and running along the Horikawa, and exploring the city together was a highlight of my life. Andy, without your patience and encouragement, and ten years of conversations about tourism and Kyoto and word counts, this book would not have been possible. "Thank you" seems too trite; where to next, my love?

Conventions

Romanization follows the Hepburn system. When names have been standardized in English, as in "Tokyo" and "Kyoto," the "ō" has been removed. As Japanese businesses and government organizations create English versions of their websites, policies, and documents, they rarely use macrons. For consistency, I have used macrons except when quoting or referencing from a source that does not.

I have tried to make the text reader-friendly without losing the specificity of Japanese terms. The names of places have been transliterated in order to avoid cross-language redundancy as much as possible, such as "the Teradaya" instead of "Teradaya Inn." A few instances were easier to standardized with English, such as Kamo River, Kiyomizu Temple, and the Gion Festival. I chose to use the Golden Pavilion (Kikakuji) and the Silver Pavilion (Ginkakuji) rather than the Japanese because they are common in international tourism texts.

Personal names are given in the Japanese order: surname first, followed by the given name. In the case of authors, after the first mention they are referred to by their pen name (which is often the given name rather than the surname). Anonymous interview sources have been denoted as Ms. A—, Mr. B—, etc.

All translations are my own unless otherwise indicated.

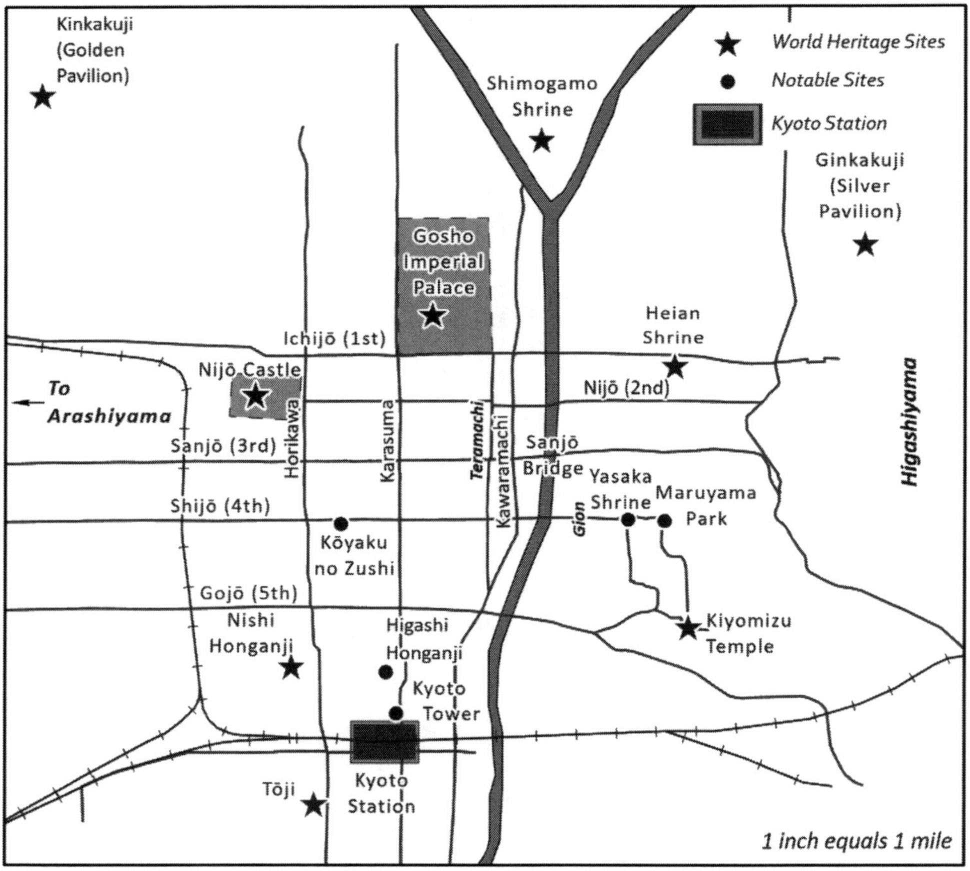

Points of interest in Kyoto. Cartography by Kimberly Anness.

Okoshiyasu (Welcome)

An Introduction

With over 1600 Buddhist temples, more than 400 Shintou [*sic*] shrines and 17 UNESCO World Heritage sites, Kyoto is one of the world's most culturally rich cities. These riches are the legacy of the 1000-plus years that Kyoto was the capital of Japan, the very stage on which Japanese history unfolded. And even though the capital has long since migrated to Tokyo, Kyoto remains the heart and soul of Japan, the place that modern Japanese visit to discover what it means to be Japanese.

—Chris Rowthorn, *Lonely Planet Kyoto*

Experience Kyoto—Making Kyoto the World's Hometown
Kyoto: The Experience Here Will Change you
Kyoto: This place will enrich your life

http://kyoto.travel/en[1]

The name "Kyoto" elicits a range of images: from World Heritage sites to Zen gardens; from the natural beauty of the autumn leaves and spring cherry blossoms to the tea ceremony and traditional Japanese arts; from the romanticized escapades of Genji in the Heian period to those of Sakamoto Ryōma in the late Edo period; from historic buildings to crowds of tourists trying to capture a hurrying geisha with cameras or phones. Indeed, the plethora of full-color photo books and social media posts—all of which highlight the city's historic charm and natural beauty—attest to its appeal as a destination, both in person or virtual. In popular conception, the city is shrouded by a romantic, nostalgic, Japanese mystique, not altogether unlike the artifice of golden clouds that long adorned images of the capital. At once historic capital, cultural center, and modern city, Kyoto has come to signify Japan writ small, a microcosm of Japanese history and culture.

The two epigraphs that open this book exemplify the ways that Kyoto is both promoted and treasured as a heritage city, as quintessentially Japanese, and as a tourist destination. The first epigraph typifies the tone of most writing about Kyoto, encapsulating the ways that the tourist industry markets its environs, as well as the sentiments of many tourists (both domestic and international) who visit the city to experience a taste of traditional Japanese culture. At the same time, the slogans in the second epigraph all appeared on the Kyoto City Official Travel Guide website over the past ten years. The bold catch phrases emphasize a personal engagement with Kyoto, as well as a kind of cosmopolitan comfort. The complex interplay between these two threads—the traditional and romantic sense of history and culture in the Kyoto tourist industry and the more recent focus on the personalized and participatory in tourism branding—comprises the warp and weft of this book.

Kyoto has long been an urban tourist destination—from visits to the capital's *meisho* (famous places) found in classical poetry; to trips along the Tōkaidō roadway in the Edo period; to countless pilgrims who have long flocked to its temples and shrines. Today, Kyoto is undeniably a modern metropolis with all the amenities of a contemporary city, exemplified by the postmodern atmosphere of Kyoto Station; but it is the charming old-world atmosphere of winding alleyways, gardens, and temples that are renowned. In the twenty-first century, in the wake of two decades of national recession (both economic and demographic), Kyoto's touristic promises have been rekindled. In response to the Tourism Nation Japan policies, which aim to cultivate Japanese cultural and historical assets into marketable shares of the global tourist economy, Kyoto embarked on an ambitious tourism promotion strategy. Initially targeting 50 million tourists by the year 2010, the ambitious goal was reached two years in advance. In 2014 over 55 million tourists visited Kyoto, 1.8 million of whom were international (Kyoto City Tourism Office 2002–2020). That is quite a feat: a city of nearly 1.5 million people with 55 million tourists. For those who live in the city center, the ebb and flow of tourists is unavoidable and often overwhelming. In the heritage districts in peak tourist seasons, one can barely make his or her way through the throngs of tourists. In the context of twenty-first-century recessionary and demographic challenges, Tourism Nation Japan policies, and the fast approaching Tokyo Olympics 2020/2021, I set out to revisit Kyoto, examining the ways that Japanese culture and history are represented, packaged, and consumed through tourist sites and experiences in the city today.[2]

Through a case study of Kyoto as a quintessential urban heritage tourism destination, the chapters in this book demonstrate the ways that heritage is complex—at once material and ethereal, nostalgic and personal, national and international. On the one hand, Kyoto is a palimpsest of Japanese history. Walking around Kyoto, one cannot help but encounter stone or wooden placards designed to commemorate events, historical figures, and literary references from the past twelve hundred years. Moreover, the city has long paid attention to urban planning in ways attentive to tradition, including constructing views of the surrounding hills and maintaining the narrow *roji* (alleyways) lined with *machiya* (townhouses). On the other hand, heritage in Kyoto is not mere preservation, cast in stone or protected from the elements of change, but rather renovation attentive to the past in ways that speak to the present. As seen throughout this book, heritage is a way interested parties—state and local, public and private, tourist and industry—tell stories about the past; it is a way that the past is commodified in an experience economy; and it is the way twenty-first-century tourists seek to engage with the past. Indeed, tourists, domestic and international alike, travel to Kyoto today to experience history, culture, and tradition in the context of a contemporary urban city. By examining how the Kyoto tourist industry dramatizes, packages, and sells these cultural touchstones, the chapters that follow reveal how the past is mobilized in constructing the identity of a place and the ways that meaning and a sense of a distinctive place have come to be valued in today's global and media-saturated world.

Beyond contemporary Kyoto or the Japanese brand, the issues at stake in heritage tourism promotion in Kyoto highlight one of the central tensions wrought by globalization: the push and pull of the local and the global. This juxtaposition is evident in the slogan quoted in the epigraph above: "Experience Kyoto—Making Kyoto the World's Hometown." While this slogan was on the Kyoto City

Official Travel Guide website only briefly, it captures something important. The idea of "hometown" conjures images of somewhere comfortable and familiar, somewhere one returns to again and again. Both of these registers fit a tourism campaign aiming at welcoming guests hospitably so that they will want to visit often. This is a prime aim for the Kyoto tourism endeavors. And yet, as noted above, the Kyoto brand markets Japanese heritage—that is, a particular history and culture. Throughout the chapters of this book we see examples of the cultivation of heritage spaces, narratives, events, and experiences that are infused with a sense of "Japaneseness." The tension inherent in this welcoming slogan situates this book within a broader touristic framework, one that draws out the ways that the local and the global are entangled in today's world.

This introductory chapter sets out the themes threaded throughout the ethnographic chapters that follow, situating tourism in contemporary Kyoto within the context of twenty-first-century Tourism Nation Japan policies as well as global heritage structures and tourism economics. Moreover, it puts the nucleus of this book in dialogue with academic conversations about tourism, heritage, and contemporary Japan. But first, it will orient the reader to the city of Kyoto.

Entering Kyoto (入洛 *nyūraku*): A Brief Historical Overview

The capital of Japan moved to current-day Kyoto in 794 CE, and it remained the capital until the late nineteenth century.[3] Known as Heian-kyō (平安京, capital of peace and tranquility), the new capital was modeled after the grid-shaped Tang dynasty capital of Chang'an (Xi'an today) with the palace in the north connected by a wide boulevard leading to the gate in the south. The imperial family and ranks of closely aligned courtiers remained in Kyoto for over one thousand years. In this way, Kyoto has always been urban: the city was built as an urban political and social center, constructed to support the demands, both cultural and economic, of the imperial system. Yet the location was originally considered auspicious because the city sits in a basin protected by hills to the west, north, and east. Even today, the urban landscape gives way to greenery as one looks down any of the major thoroughfares. Two rivers, the Kamo on the eastern side and the Katsura on the western side of the city, provided adequate water, and the waterway at the south allowed access to the Inland Sea via Osaka.[4] Finally, Kyoto sat near the crossing of the two main highways, the Tōkaidō and San'in.

The Heian period (794–1185), when political and cultural power was consolidated in Heian-kyō, is lauded as the Japanese renaissance. It is a time when the literary, artistic, cultural, and governmental forms adopted from China in the preceding two hundred years were indigenized to fit the local culture. Indeed, the legacy of Kyoto's having been the seat of aristocratic culture and power for centuries lingers in the prevalence of traditional arts and crafts found throughout the city still today: textiles, incense, fans, music, dance, flower arrangement, and tea ceremony. In the classical poetry and literature of the Heian period, Kyoto was the seat of all culture in Japan; the rest was all hinterlands. This is best illustrated through a small linguistic detail—the term used for going to Kyoto was *nobori* (to ascend), and the term used to go from Kyoto was *kudari* (to descend). That is, no matter in what ordinate one was heading, one went "up" to Kyoto (Nenzi 2008, 22–23). This sense of the centripetal force of Kyoto remained even after the seat of power shifted beginning in the Kamakura period (1185–1392).

The period between the end of the Heian period (1185) and the beginning of the Edo period (1603) was tumultuous as the medieval warrior culture came to dominate. Although some military rulers established their governments in other cities such as Kamakura (1185–1392) and Edo (1603–1867), Kyoto remained Japan's capital until the Meiji Restoration in 1868. That did not mean that the city was untouched by the political tectonics throughout these years. Kyoto suffered extensive destruction in the Ōnin War (1467–1477), which ushered in the Sengoku (Warring Factions) period, which lasted from 1467 to 1568. At this time, battles between samurai groups spilled into the streets and spread to the court nobility and religious factions as well. Nobles' mansions were transformed into fortresses, deep trenches were dug throughout the city for defense and as firebreaks, and numerous buildings burned. The city did not recover fully until the mid-sixteenth century (Stavros 2014, 133–150).

The Sengoku period ended with the unification of Japan through the political, social, and military prowess of the three great unifiers: Oda Nobunaga (1534–1582), Toyotomi Hideyoshi (1536–1598), and Tokugawa Ieyasu (1543–1616). Nobunaga returned military and political power to Kyoto in 1573. He also set about quelling rival factions throughout the land, including the great Buddhist monasteries in Kyoto, which had become political actors. In 1582, with about a third of the nation unified, Nobunaga was attacked and forced to commit seppuku at Honno Temple in Kyoto (Berry 1982, 41; Dougill 2006, 111). Quickly, his second in command, Hideyoshi, rode to Kyoto and set out to finish the process of unification that Nobunaga had started.

While Hideyoshi famously set up his castle in Osaka, he spent much of his time and efforts in Kyoto. In fact, as early as 1585, Hideyoshi set out to restructure the city, doubling the number of north-south streets in central Kyoto, creating rectangular blocks superseding the classical square blocks, and overseeing reconstruction of bridges and major temples. In addition, he moved a host of smaller temples to a road on the edge of the city to create a temple district known as Teramachi. Today, Teramachi is located in central Kyoto and is a bustling shopping area for locals and tourists alike, yet many temples are still peppered among restaurants and cafes, trendy boutiques, and souvenir shops (Berry 1982, 193–203; Stavros 2014, 162–165). Hideyoshi is also renowned for lavish parties through which the arts of the tea ceremony (*chanoyu*) and poetry were cultivated. The most famous of these was the Grand Kitano Tea Gathering, which was advertised on sign posts throughout the Kansai region as an open invitation to all tea masters; this ten-day event featured the construction of over fifteen hundred tea huts on the grounds of Kitano Tenmangu Shrine (Slusser 2003; Varley and Kumakura 1989). In this way, the contours of Hideyoshi's reconstruction can still be found in the city today. Hideyoshi died suddenly in 1598, leaving his legacy in the hands of his young son, Hideyori (1592–1615). By 1600 Tokugawa Ieyasu, one of five designated regents to Hideyori, gained control through the battle of Sekigahara. Tokugawa set up his capital in Tokyo, leaving Hideyori and his family to their castle in Osaka. In 1615 Tokugawa laid siege to Osaka castle, ending the Toyotomi line and securing the Tokugawa place in history.

The Tokugawa reign (Edo period) lasted until 1868 and is considered a time of peace as Japan was unified and closed to the world at large throughout the major years of European expansion. This period is known for a rigid class system and tight social controls, the isolationist policies that kept Japan largely free from outside influences, and the transformation of the samurai class from military to bureaucratic aesthetes. Over this long era, the city of Edo (Tokyo) grew in prominence and became renowned for the vibrant urban culture of the merchants and commoners that it cultivated. Even so, Kyoto remained home to the emperor, retaining its status as the capital. To emphasize his control, Tokugawa built Nijō Castle on the original site of the imperial palace in Kyoto. (The palace had been relocated to the east and north in the fourteenth century.) While Tokugawa Ieyasu marched into the city with an impressive military retinue in 1634, no shogun set foot in Kyoto again until the end of the era in the 1850s. Nijō Castle was manned by dignitaries who kept an eye on the city and the aristocracy, while the castle signified the shogun's presence in Kyoto through its material presence; today it is one of Kyoto's most popular tourist sites.

While tourists had long flocked to Kyoto when roads were safe, travel became increasingly easier in the Edo period through the development of a more structured road system—in particular the Tōkaidō roadway, which connected the new seat of power, Edo, with the capital, Kyoto, and the merchant hub of Osaka. As a means to keep the *daimyō* (feudal lords) in check, the Tokugawa shogunate required that they travel to Edo and live in residence every year or every other year. This travel policy helped codify the system of five roads (Gōkaidō), which were developed to accommodate such large and frequent travel groups. Kyoto's Sanjō-bashi (bridge over the Kamo River at Sanjō) was one terminus on the Tōkaidō, with Edo's Nihon-bashi at the opposite end. Throughout the Edo period, the economies of the three major cities—Kyoto, Osaka, and Edo—flourished through the infrastructure that connected the cities, enabling a flow of goods, services, and travelers.

The Edo period is certainly the era of Tokyo's ascendency, yet Kyoto became the site of political intrigue throughout the gradual demise of the Tokugawa reign in the late nineteenth century. Throughout the 1800s, there was growing discontent with the Tokugawa order. But it was the handling of Western encroachment, which began with US Commodore Perry's arrival in 1853, that largely precipitated the end of 250 years of Tokugawa reign. The fundamental threat posed by the arrival of American gunboats opened the door for growing dissatisfactions among low-ranking samurai. A critique of shogunal legitimacy raised the issue of a return to imperial rule. Accounts of this time depict Kyoto as virtually overflowing with samurai fighting for the future of their country, as Kyoto became the staging ground for the new nation (Jansen 1961, 100–102). The skirmishes between those calling for change and those loyal to the shogunate (including the infamous Shinsengumi),[5] made life in Kyoto tumultuous and often dangerous.

In January 1868 the Meiji emperor was restored to power, and in 1869 he moved to the nation's new capital, Tokyo.

The Meiji period (1868–1912) is typically characterized as one of the most significant turning points in Japanese history. During the European enlightenment, the birth of modern science, the industrial revolution, and the spread of democracy and colonialism, Japan was closed to the West except for a small contingency of Dutch traders who were allowed access at Nagasaki, where they shared knowledge and trade. The forced opening of Japan that began in 1853 was a crucible for Japan. Rather than suffer the fates of its Asian neighbors in this period of European and American expansion, Japan undertook a rapid process of modernization, crafting the modern Japanese nation-state as we know it today.

While accounts of this time often center on Tokyo, which was central culturally, socially, and politically, Kyoto was at a turning point for the first time in a millennium. Structurally the city was in ill repair after years of fighting. Perhaps more important, Kyoto was no longer the capital of Japan, a demotion that significantly weakened its economy. Indeed, it was unclear whether the city could thrive without the imperial household. Despite contemporary perceptions of Kyoto as a historic city, at the turn of the twentieth century, Kyoto embraced modernization to rebuild and revive. Major modern infrastructural projects included the 1890 construction of Lake Biwa Canal, which brought water from Lake Biwa to the city through a series of aqueducts, considered a major engineering feat of the time (Tseng 2018; Breen, Maruyama, and Takagi 2020). In addition to the new Kyoto station, which was added for the railway line from Tokyo, several major streets were widened to accommodate changes in travel, and trolleys and electric lights were introduced. Throughout the decades leading up to World War II, Kyoto continued to undertake major city planning projects, from parks to museums and libraries, shrines, zoos, and convention halls. As architectural historian Alice Tseng demonstrates, these modern projects were a part of commemorations for important imperial ceremonies and events replete with pageantry that bespoke the city's identity as the hometown of the imperial family (Tseng 2018). On the eve of World War II, in 1932, the population of the city exceeded one million.

At the end of World War II, the US military considered Kyoto a top target for an atomic bomb because of its national stature, as well as its topological location in a basin. In the end, the city was removed from the list of targets by US secretary of war Henry Stimson and replaced by Nagasaki. Historians speculate that this was in part because of Stimson's experience of the beauty and grandeur of Kyoto during his honeymoon there in the 1920s and also because he felt it would be a permanently devastating blow to Japanese culture and pride and might make American relations with the country harder after the war (Burr 2005). Furthermore, throughout the war, the city was largely spared from conventional bombing, although small-scale air raids did result in casualties. As a result, Kyoto is one of the few major Japanese cities that still has an abundance of prewar buildings. This is a part of its marketing and appeal as a tourist destination.

Today, Kyoto is undeniably a modern metropolis with all the amenities of a contemporary city. It is the eighth largest city in Japan, with 1.47 million people. As a contemporary city, Kyoto prides itself as "a city of universities," drawing students from all over Japan. As the epigraph that starts this chapter broadcasts, Kyoto is home to thousands of Buddhist temples and Shinto shrines, both large and small. In fact, many of the major Buddhist sects have their headquarters in Kyoto. Moreover, religious institutions comprise a significant portion of the tourist sites throughout Kyoto, including most of the popular venues like the Kiyomizu Temple, the Golden Pavilion, Fushimi Inari—the famous path of orange *torii* gates[6]—and numerous Zen temples throughout the city. So, too, Kyoto remains home to major schools of traditional crafts, including *ikebana* (flower arranging) and *chanoyu* (tea ceremony); but it is also the home of notable contemporary industries like Nintendo and Kyoto Animation, and it is an incubator for high-tech companies from semiconductors to robotics to data analysis development. Thus, while Kyoto's old-world charm is world renowned, much of daily life in Kyoto is no different from that in any other Japanese city, especially outside of the main tourist paths. Kyoto station provides a vibrant shopping and eating district as the central transportation hub; neighborhood *shotengai* (shopping areas, often covered streets for a few blocks), lined with restaurants, bars, small coffee shops, and shops for the necessities of daily life, pepper the city; department stores and malls are filled with the same brands one can find anywhere in Japan; and every corner has a *conbini* (convenience store) or two. On the streets, bicyclists whiz by pedestrians on the sidewalk, dinging their bells while balancing umbrellas and shopping or school bags, and gaggles of elementary school kids can be found commuting by bus and train.

Life in Kyoto is like life anywhere in Japan, although in the nooks and crannies of daily life, Kyoto foods, traditional crafts, a *machiya*-style house or store, or a temple or shrine can be found. Indeed, walking around Kyoto, one cannot help but encounter the ancient capital (*miyako*) in the grid of streets from Kujō (Ninth Street) up to Nijō (Second Street), all leading to the imperial palace. Drawing on this historical legacy, much of Kyoto's urban planning throughout the late twentieth and early twenty-first centuries has been driven by a combination of landscape and tourism policies that place emphasis on maintaining the city's rich cultural heritage. While Kyoto has long been a tourist destination, in the twenty-first century tourism has taken on a renewed focus at the local, national, and global levels. Tourism, too, is a part of the city's historical and contemporary imaginings.

Tourism Nation Japan: Cool Japan and Twenty-First-Century Tourism

Tourism seems frivolous—a leisure activity, hardly serious business. And yet it seems all too serious as we think of the environmental and social costs of a large influx of travelers that disrupts local life, flora, and fauna. Tourism is one of the ways that people relax on vacation, experience the world, and learn about other cultures and places; and tourism is a part of the way we are globally connected today. Indeed, according to the UN World Tourism Organization (UNWTO), in 2017, 55 percent of international travel was for "leisure, recreation, or holidays," and another 27 percent was for "visiting family or relatives, health, religion, or other" (World Tourism Organization 2018b, 3). While we love to travel, we hate (being) tourists. Either way, today tourism is an economic, political, and cultural force to be reckoned with.

According to the UNWTO, approximately one in ten jobs globally is related to travel, and hospitality and tourism comprise about 10 percent of the global GDP (World Tourism Organization 2018b, 3).[7] Moreover, the growth of tourism has been at an unprecedented high for the decade preceding covid. For eight consecutive years tourism growth averaged 4 percent, and in 2017 the number of international tourists grew by 7 percent (86 million) to reach 1,326 million globally. In addition, international tourism receipts increased an average of 5 percent to $1,340 billion in 2017 (World Tourism Organization 2018b, 2). Perhaps it is not surprising that the fastest growing region for tourism in the past five years (both inbound and outbound) is Asia-Pacific. As of 2017, Asia comprised 24 percent of the market share of tourism arrivals, coupled with the strongest growth rate, averaging 6.4 percent over the past three years (World Tourism Organization 2018b, 5).

In Japan, tourism comprised 7.4 percent of the GDP as of 2017, up 3.6 percent since 2016 (World Travel and Tourism Council 2019). In 2017, 28.7 million international tourists traveled to Japan, representing an increase of 19.3 percent that year. The UNWTO numbers indicate that Japan has been one of the fastest-growing tourism destinations, as inbound tourists have risen an average of 16.4 percent a year since 2010 (excluding 2011, the year of the Great Eastern Japan Earthquake and Tsunami) (JTB Tourism Research & Consulting 2019). According to the Japan Tourism Association's (JTA) "White Paper on Tourism in Japan," Japan was ranked sixteenth worldwide and fifth in Asia for international tourist arrivals in 2016 (Japan Tourism Agency 2017c). In 2017, for the first time, Japan made it to the top ten tourism countries, a category determined by tourist spending, "after six straight years of double digit growth" (World Tourism Organization 2018b, 8). This increase in tourism to Japan in the twenty-first century is significant. While Japan has long been seen as an exotic location and it has been an advanced industrial nation throughout the twentieth century, it has always lagged behind other advanced nations in the number of both inbound and outbound tourists. The perception of significant cultural and linguistic differences has shaped Japanese tourism patterns and policies for the past 150 years, making it more of a niche market than a primary tourism location. At the same time, Japan has had a thriving domestic tourism culture for centuries (see chapter 1). Even so, in the twenty-first century, tourism has become a central part of Japanese economic strategy.[8]

At the turn of the new millennium, in the face of over a decade of recession, the Japanese government reshaped economic policies to emphasize "soft power"—the marketing of cultural and intellectual products—rather than hardware, like the cars and consumer electronics of the 1980s. The 1990s are often referred to as the "lost decade," which became "the lost decades," or the Heisei Recession, as economic growth remained slow throughout the first decades of the new millennium. The twenty-first century economic policies turned to marketing Japanese cultural products as an area of growth for economic recovery in two main ways: through capitalizing on the global recognition of Japanese popular culture and through aiming to make Japan a tourism nation.

The first strategy, known now as the "Cool Japan Initiative," began in 2002 as the Intellectual Property Promotion Strategy (*chitekizaisan suishin keikaku*).[9] Its core aims were to actively promote the Japanese contents (*contentsu*) industry—products like anime, manga, music, and video games. It also sought to develop other forms of intellectual and creative content for a new global economy (Daliot-Bul 2009). The policy is reviewed and modified each year, and in 2010 a new Cool Japan Division was added in the Ministry of Economy, Trade, and Industry (METI) (Choo 2013). These new policies aim at both economic recovery and cultural diplomacy. Yet the government was a bit late to the game. In 2002 Japanese popular culture had amassed fans throughout the world, and these new policies sought to merely capitalize on the groundswell of popularity, further cultivating markets and capturing proceeds. In the ongoing iterations of this policy, cultural products such as sushi, kimono, and regional foods and goods have been added to the strategy to market Japanese intellectual and cultural products abroad (METI 2019). As Michal Daloit-Bul (2009, 261) sums up, "Through selective appropriation, promotion and combination of cultural products, this strategy aims to construct politically meaningful images of Japan for domestic and international audiences." By connecting Cool Japan content with Japanese culture, the Japanese government seeks to craft a new Japan brand in the face of increased regional and global competition (Choo 2013; Daliot-Bul 2009; Iwabuchi 2015). Thus, Cool Japan aims to sell more creative (cultural and intellectual) products globally but also to sell the idea of Japanese culture more broadly. Beyond just export revenue and global cache, this form of cultural diplomacy also serves to attract tourists to Japan.

The second prong of this soft power economic strategy is the Tourism Nation Japan policies. In 2003, just a year after the first Cool Japan plan, Prime Minister Koizumi Junichiro (2001–2006) proclaimed the start of the "inbound tourism initiative of Japan," setting the goal of doubling the number of inbound tourists to ten million by 2010. That same year, the large-scale "Yokoso! Japan" or "Welcome! Japan" campaign (referred to in government documents as the Visit Japan Campaign, VJC) was launched by the Japan National Tourism Organization (JNTO). According to the press release for the first five years of this plan, "VJC is being targeted in five main markets considered the most prospective for inbound tourism to Japan. These include: The United States, Korea, China, Taiwan, and Hong Kong" (Japan National Tourism Organization). Signs with the slogan "Yokoso! Japan" could be seen all over Japan for the past two decades, replaced in March 2018 by the new campaign heading into the Olympics, "Enjoy *my* Japan."

In 2007, the Tourism Nation Promotion Basic Law was passed, replacing the Tourism Basic Act of 1963. Also in June 2007, the Tourism Nation Promotion Basic Plan was established, setting a target of ten million international tourists, twenty million Japanese traveling overseas, and increases in the spending per tourist in Japan. The overall goal was to position Japan as a competitive tourism nation to ensure sustainable economic recovery for the twenty-first century, embracing this global age in the face of the declining birthrate and aging population (Japan Tourism Agency 2016). In 2008, the JTA was formed by promoting the former department to an agency responsible for overseeing and coordinating the efforts toward making Japan a top tourism nation. That year 8.35 million international tourists visited Japan (Japan Tourism Agency 2009).

In 2012 a new Tourism Nation Promotion Basic Plan was approved, laying out the project goals; initial target numbers of twenty million tourists by 2020; and the structural mix of national government, local governments, private partners, and citizen initiatives. The JTA website summarizes the goal of the new plan as follows: "It is . . . important that we make effective use of our assets, such as human, technological, and tourism resources, to ensure a sustainable future. Therefore, building a tourism nation with its capacity to revitalize regional economies, create job opportunities, and increase bilateral international understanding is a key component of Japan in the 21st century and will only grow in importance as a national strategy" (Japan Tourism Agency 2017b). Thus the plan emphasizes building tourism into a key factor in the national economy, facilitating the revitalization of regional economies and promoting the advantages of cross-cultural exchanges that come with tourists. The plan sets the new target at attracting thirty million international tourists by the year 2020, a goal that was revised to forty million when the twenty million mark was reached in 2016 (Ministry of Land 2017, 141). In addition, according to the Ministry of Land 2017 report, Japan aims to have 50 percent of international tourists travel beyond "the Golden Route" of Tokyo, Hakone, Nara, Osaka, and Kyoto; it aims as well to increase the number of repeat visitors by 2020 (Japan Tourism Agency 2017a).

Finally, particular emphasis has been put on attracting Asian tourists. Along with growing affluence in the region, China is the fastest-growing tourist demographic. In the past decade, Chinese tourists have begun to travel in record numbers, and they also spend at record rates. According to the UNWTO, in 2017 Chinese tourists spent US $258 billion overseas; the next closest competitors were Americans, at $135 billion (World Tourism Organization 2018a). Several initiatives within the Tourism Nation Japan strategy have focused on attracting Asian tourists. First, in 2013, visa restrictions were relaxed for five key nations: China, the Philippines, Vietnam, India, and Russia; since 2015 visa requirements for China have been gradually relaxed. Second, there was an increase in the visibility and availability of duty-free shopping throughout major cities, lowering the limit to purchases over 5,000 yen (roughly $50). Accordingly, Chinese tourists to Japan increased from 1.4 million to 7.3 million (a fivefold increase) between 2010 and 2017 (JTB Tourism Research & Consulting 2019). These policies have been so successful that the newest tourism campaign, "Enjoy *my* Japan," is now expanding to North America, Europe, and Australia (Ministry of Land 2017, 148).

One important convergence of Japanese popular culture and tourism is the rise of contents tourism. "Contents tourism" is a broader version of media tourism, wherein places and scenes from television, film, anime, or video games induce tourism. Media tourism, from Jane Austen to *Lord of the Rings* to *Lucky Star,* is an emerging sector of the global tourist industry (Beeton 2016). The term "contents tourism" derives from the Japanese word *contentsu,* coined in reference to ways that media content crosses platforms in the media mix of Japanese popular culture (think Pokémon, wherein recurring characters can be found in movies, manga, anime, and various gaming platforms). Contents tourism is a burgeoning form of tourism in Japan for domestic and international tourists alike and is receiving a lot of attention as a potential for Tourism Nation Japan (Beeton, Yamamura, and Seaton 2013; Masabuchi 2010, 2018; Okamoto 2015, 2018a, 2018b; Seaton and Yamamura 2015; Seaton et al. 2017). Until recently, contents tourism was seen primarily as an odd fan behavior. Communities watched with bemusement when suddenly a location—perhaps just in the middle of town—started to attract groups of fans on what they call "sacred pilgrimages" (*seichi junrei*) to a location seen in a beloved anime or manga. This fan-based tourism has become a part of regional revitalization throughout the last decade. Indeed, in *Junrei bijinesu* (Pilgrimage Business), Okamoto Takeshi (2018a) argues that anime should now be seen as a tourist asset.

Both the Cool Japan strategies and the Tourism Nation strategies that have dominated national policy in the twenty-first century are attempts to promote economic recovery after two decades of recession, but they also respond to the pressures and structures of globalization. Together these two sets of policies seek to market Japanese culture globally by crafting a new Japan brand that will increase creative content exports to replace the declining automobile and electronics industries while capitalizing on the popularity of such content to attract tourists to Japan. Both sets of policies advocate a mix of national and local and public and private ventures indicative of contemporary neoliberal governance. Furthermore, both plans seek a new cultural diplomacy focusing on East Asia through shared popular culture and tourist attractions, hoping that it will indirectly mitigate, or perhaps replace, the legacy of Japanese imperialism.

As I turn to focus on tourism in contemporary Kyoto in the rest of this book, it is worth noting that Kyoto sits in an interesting spot in relation to the tourist policies outlined here. Kyoto has long been a prime tourist destination for both domestic and international tourists, and it has seen significant increases in tourism in the past decade. Yet Kyoto's main selling point is its rich cultural history. While there are a handful of small-scale contents tourism interests, like *The Tale of Genji,* the Ikedaya and Shinsengumi, and the Kyoto Manga Museum, contents tourism plays a minimal role in the overall tourist strategy in Kyoto. Additionally, Kyoto is not the target of more recent tourist policies that aim to expand the destinations tourists travel across Japan. Still, the ambitious Kyoto tourism promotion plans discussed in chapter 2 highlight the ways that Kyoto's tourist appeal makes it an important player in the new national economic policies. The 2010 tourism promotion plan "Future Kyoto Tourism Promotion Project 2010+5" states, "As our nation is using soft power based on intelligence and cultural power as a trump card for economic revitalization, Kyoto, as the origin of Japanese culture, has to play a large role in promoting and attracting foreign visitors to Japan" (Kyoto City 2010). The initiatives, events, challenges, and policies discussed throughout this book are all a part of Kyoto tourism policies replete with local needs and goals, but they also exist in direct relation to the Tourism Nation Japan strategy, which is a part and parcel of global entanglements today.

Tourism Experiences in Twenty-First Century Kyoto

"Kyoto: This place will change you," a caption from the top of the Kyoto City Official Travel Guide website, brings us to the search for personal experiences in twenty-first century Japan.[10] One term that keeps emerging in promotional materials, industry accounts and offerings, and tourists' own comments is "experience" (体験 *taiken*), and the emphasis is on an embodied experience. (For more on *taiken,* see chapter 5.) This sense is highlighted in the JNTO campaign—"Enjoy *my* Japan!" It is important that the "*my*" is in italics or a script font to highlight that it is yours, unique, and different through the way it stands out in the sentence. The website for the campaign proclaims: "You too can make Japan your dream destination. Whatever your interest—cuisine, culture, the great outdoors—we help deepen your knowledge and craft a journey to Japan made just for you."[11] This personalizing language is echoed in the Kyoto slogans that open this book, emphasizing personal experiences of Kyoto.

Japan is not alone in marketing a personal experience; this is the language of tourism today echoed by tourists, industry personnel and analysts, and tourism scholars alike. This focus on experience emerged in the twenty-first century amid conversations about the experience economy. Joseph Pine and James Gilmore (1998, 2011) coined this term to indicate the ways that companies that want to succeed in the new millennial economy need to think in terms of the overall experience they are providing to consumers. They outline the economic shifts from extracting commodities to creating goods to delivering services to staging experiences: "An experience occurs when a company intentionally uses services as the stage, and goods as props, to engage individual customers in a way that creates a memorable event. Commodities are fungible, goods tangible, services intangible, and experiences memorable" (Pine and Gilmore 1998, 98). No longer is it the case that customers are satisfied with good service at the point of purchase. In today's economy the way consumers experience brands is critical to success. We, the consumers, want both our stores and our tourist destinations to feel good, beyond their just being clean or easy to access. Pine and Gilmore explain: "While prior economic offerings—commodities, goods, and services—are external to the buyer, experiences are inherently personal, existing only in the mind of an individual who has been engaged on an emotional, physical, intellectual, or even spiritual level" (Pine and Gilmore 1998). This new economic evolution elevates the personal.

Apart from theories of how to successfully develop brand experiences, economists refer to the shift to peer-to-peer transactions via the web and smartphones as the sharing economy. This new economic trend, epitomized by companies like Airbnb, Uber and Lyft, Etsy, and TaskRabbit, emphasizes on-demand access to goods and services, putting control into the hands of consumers and at their fingertips. Still, the notion of being in control personally, cutting out the middleman or at least making him or her an app, dominates this new form of capitalism. It is a personalized economy of choice. And travel services are a big part of the sharing economy.

Even so, personal experience has always been a driving force behind tourism. A tourist is a person who travels not merely to arrive somewhere, but also to experience something different—be it in culture or natural habitat, change in climate, or pace of life (Urry and Larsen 2011). Thus "experience" is entailed in the very definition of a tourist. What is meant by "experience" or the kinds of experiences tourists seek changes over time, across groups, and between individuals. While today's tourists might balk at mass tourism—safely managed bus tours taking tourists from Nijō Castle to the Golden Pavilion (Kinkakuji) and then across town to the Silver Pavilion (Ginkakuji), all in a day—such tourists also wanted to *experience* these world heritage sites, even if their experience was primarily in "seeing."

Tourism scholar Dean MacCannell (1999) theorized this touristic desire for experience as early as the 1970s, when he argued that tourists want to see more than the staged "front of house" of tourism and instead seek to see the "back of house" or unscripted life as well. He defined the idea of "modern tourists" just when a shift was occurring from large-scale, mass tourism to individual travel. MacCannell's theory of the tourist in the modern world shaped the field by positing that the tourist was both a result of modernity and an apt metaphor for modern life. That is, tourists seek authentic experiences in history or another culture because that sense of authenticity is missing from modern life, characterized by routinization, institutionalism, and commodification. At the same time, this way of skating through life, seeking new experiences, is what modern subjects are like, MacCannell posited. Quickly, other scholars took issue with MacCannell's semiotic and structural approach, arguing that tourists were not so monolithic; they travel for various and often multiple reasons, they are often savvy about artifice, and they affect the sites they visit in a variety of ways (Bruner 1994, 1995; Cohen 1985; Graburn 1983; Valene Smith 1989; Urry 1990). In particular, in the 1990s, the "performance turn" in tourism studies placed emphasis on tourists' actual experiences in the here and now (Bærenholdt et al. 2004; Coleman and Crang 2002; Haldrup and Larsen 2010; Rickly-Boyd et al. 2014). Michael Haldrup and Jonas Larsen write, "Although tourism performances are surely influenced by guidebooks, concrete guidance, promotional information and existing place myths, the performance turn argues that tourists are not just written upon, they also enact and inscribe places with their own stories and follow their own paths" (2010, 5). While approaches to tourism have changed with broader theoretical shifts, the notion that tourism is both reflective and constitutive of modern life has remained a central claim in the field of tourism studies.

As to the the ways people travel, throughout the twentieth century tourists have sought different kinds of experiences, from seeing famous places to staying in traditional forms of lodging and eating different foods to attending cultural performances or historical reenactments.[12] The growth of "off-the-beaten-path" tourism in the 1980s was a new turn in the way people sought authentic experiences; in particular this form of individual travel sought unique or "non-touristy" experiences (Cohen 1988). Rather than the bus tours or large-scale guided tours of earlier eras, these tourists wanted to find their own way, to explore and see a place differently. This turn to planning one's own trip added to the ways that travel was experienced, customizable, and personalized. It also provides more opportunities to see local life and encounter locals at home, something that is at once desirable and disruptive.

This shift in touristic desires over the past thirty years is one of personalization, from mass tourism to individual travel to personal encounters—from seeing (*miru*) to encountering (*fureau*) to a personal or embodied experience (*taiken*). In addition to heading off the beaten path and in so doing interacting with the locals, in recent years there has been a further push toward more hands-on or even embodied experiences—experiencing a place "like the locals." The sharing economy is one way that this kind of tourism is enabled by the new media landscape within which travel plans and conversations are conducted. Today one can stay with locals and be guided by a college student, housewife, or retiree who loves the city and enjoys meeting new people, rather than relying on professionals in the hospitality industry. This notion of experience, seen in Kyoto today, is in line with the performative turn in tourism studies in its emphasis on the embodied and emotive experiences of a particular place. However, while it has an affective and embodied component, tourism is not to be understood as entirely phenomenological; rather tourist experiences today are crafted through the production (material) and construction (conceptual or ideological) of tourist sites themselves. As demonstrated in the examples throughout this book, tourism is always about places and policies, travelers and locals, goods and services.

As the Kyoto examples in this book attest, today both tourists and industry providers seek more personalized and hands-on experiences. Certainly this trend of experiencing "*my* Kyoto" fits with wider global and national tourist trends, yet the examples in this book all aim for tourists to think about what it means to experience Kyoto (culturally, historically, aesthetically) in the twenty-first century. The chapters that follow provide analyses of different ways to experience Kyoto, paying attention to the material landscape of the city itself, the heritage atmosphere created for tourism, and the embodied practices created for and by contemporary tourists.

World Heritage, Kyoto Heritage

In tourism, the prominence of heritage, whether natural or cultural, ethnographic or experiential, is ubiquitous. Beyond the official UNESCO World Heritage List and Intangible Heritage List, across the globe museums have increased exponentially, as has the adaptive reuse of abandoned industrial sites in city centers and small towns alike in the last twenty years. Perhaps because heritage is omnipresent today, it is hard to discretely define. This section outlines with broad strokes the emergence of the notion of heritage with explicit reference to Japan's role in such global conversations.[13] At the most basic, "heritage" refers to any public reference to, preservation of, or commemoration of the past. With its roots in "inheritance," heritage assumes that something of importance to a common identity is passed on, be it material or immaterial. Heritage scholar Rodney Harrison begins with this working definition: "the formally staged experience of encountering the physical traces of the past in the present" (2013, 1). This definition highlights the public role of heritage, as well as the ways we experience it, both of which are important to this book. Thus heritage is always at some level about the past, but it is not itself history; rather heritage is always a retelling, reenvisioning, or reimagining of the past for the present. Moreover, heritage is not reducible to the material remnants of the past—historic monuments, national museums, or stone ruins; nor is it reducible to the customs, practices, and traditions that are disappearing in our modern world. In this way, heritage is not a passive handing down of things tangible and intangible, but rather an active process that (re)creates a sense of history in service of the present. Without a doubt, heritage is intricately connected to tourism. It is experienced, practiced, and performed at national and international sites from museums to religious sites to historic residences to parks by a wide range of staff, researchers, and tourists. Thus heritage is not simply a public value, a form of national or international memory; it is a commodity indexed through the currencies of the United Nations, national policies, and tourist desires.

UNESCO World Heritage

No conversation about heritage is complete without a discussion of the role of the United Nations Educational, Scientific and Cultural Organization (UNESCO) in solidifying the global discourse and practices of heritage making. While a range of nations, including Japan, already had national registers for historic sites, landscapes, and monuments, the shape of heritage conversations shifted significantly with the creation of the UNESCO World Heritage List in 1972. The underlying logic of the "Convention Concerning the Protection of the World Cultural and Natural Heritage" (World Heritage Convention) is that both cultural and natural heritage are of universal value to humanity and as such should be protected and conserved; furthermore, according to the logic of the World Heritage Convention, these valuable properties are under threat not only from the effects of time, but also from changing social, economic, and political conditions (UNESCO 1972). In the words of the World Heritage Convention preamble, "The existing international conventions, recommendations and resolutions concerning cultural and natural property demonstrate the importance, for all the peoples of the world, of safeguarding this unique and irreplaceable property" (UNESCO 1972, 1). What is most striking here is the notion that the heritage of a local people is of value to all of humanity and thus should be preserved. This sentiment is a homogenizing impulse—there is a universal value that can be determined and managed by UNESCO—but the value is found in the diversity of human creativity throughout history.[14]

The celebration of world diversity through the structures of World Heritage is, in the end, about sharing diversity with the world. Thus designation on the World Heritage List brings with it international prestige and promotion by UNESCO, but it also brings the requirement that the property be maintained as an accessible tourist site. Signage (in the local language and English), accessibility, and even availability of public restrooms are all a part of the structure of World Heritage created by UNESCO (Di Giovine 2009, 70–115). The designation also includes access to the World Heritage Fund to help offset the costs of such upkeep, and a site can be removed if it is not properly maintained. Thus World Heritage is about preserving historical and cultural diversity for us all to see and experience.

Each year twenty-one representatives, elected by the UN General Assembly, meet to determine which new site applications should be accepted. The first twelve properties were inscribed on the list in 1978 (UNESCO 2020b). In 1993 the first Japanese sites were added to the UNESCO World Heritage List: Shirakami-Sanchi and Yakushima natural sites, Himeji Castle, and Buddhist monuments in the Hōryūji area of Nara (UNESCO 2020b). Kyoto's cluster of seventeen sites, entitled "Historic Monuments of Ancient Kyoto (Kyoto, Uji and Otsu Cities)," were the fourth of Japan's listed properties, inscribed in 1994. In 2020, there were 1,121 properties on the Worlds Heritage List, and Japan had 23 sets of sites inscribed.

Originally the World Heritage List attempted to preserve or conserve historical buildings, monuments, and landscapes that had already largely survived centuries, whether through national protection of happenstance. Yet by the 1980s, there was growing critique of the Euro-centricity of the list, as well as the underlying assumptions behind the definition of what counted as heritage. In particular, the emphasis on stone remains privileged certain kinds of building materials and processes over others. Put simply, stone remains are the easiest to document—or authenticate, to use UNESCO's language—and the original list leaned toward the canonization of stone cathedrals or marble monuments or remains. This led to a list that largely inscribed sites in Europe. Beginning in the 1990s, definitions of what counted as heritage began to shift. Harrison summarizes the report from the World Heritage Committee meeting in Thailand in November 1994: "The group recommended the development of a global strategy to increase the number of types, regions and periods represented on the World Heritage List, but also pointed to the need to take into account 'the new concepts of the idea of cultural heritage that had been developed over the past twenty years'" (2013, 129). This led to several shifts in the conversations about what counted as heritage, what needed to be preserved, and the importance of "intangible heritage," like oral and performance traditions.

Japan played a critical role in this redefinition process. In 1994 the Japanese Ministry of Cultural Affairs and Nara Prefecture hosted a meeting of representatives from UNESCO and the International Council on Monuments and Sites (ICOMOS). The resulting "Nara Document on Authenticity" was ratified by the World Heritage Committee General Assembly in 1999, although it was in use throughout the 1990s (Lemaire and Stovel 1994; Stovel 2008, 15). The meeting in Nara and the resultant document aimed at expanding the definition of what counted as heritage through a consideration of diverse ways to define authenticity. As Japan's first heritage site designated in the Meiji period, Nara was an apt location for such discussions (Ishimori 1995). Additionally, Horyūji in Nara was a part of Japan's first World Heritage sites inscribed on the list a year earlier. According to Herb Stovel, the head of ICOMOS who spearheaded this process, "The Nara Document at a more profound level also created the conceptual conditions to legitimize Japanese (and many other culturally imbedded) conservation practices" (2008, 9). Quite simply, when the historic materials are paper and wood, structures do not last as long because fire and other forms of natural degradation are par for the course. Furthermore, in Japan there has long been a tradition of rebuilding temples and shrines periodically. Rather than original structures or remains, the markers of authenticity are in original building form/layout, type of materials used, and traditional building techniques. The most famous example is the Ise Grand Shrine. This important Shinto shrine, dedicated to the Sun Goddess Amaterasu, is rebuilt every twenty years using specific cypress wood and exacting building practices. Similarly, shrines and temples in Kyoto are likewise routinely renewed, not simply when there is enough visible destruction or damage to a building, but also on a set schedule. For example, in 2013, Higashi Honganji, a large Buddhist temple just north of Kyoto station, underwent its every hundred-year renovation. This notion of heritage renewal through attention to process and function is part of the way that Japanese heritage practices have broadened discussions of "authenticity" in heritage conversations more generally.

The Nara Document did not simply add traditional Japanese notions of authenticity to the definition but rather argued that there is a range of ways to understand authenticity and any definition must be in dialogue with the local understanding of tradition and authenticity. As Christina Cameron, a former chair of the World Heritage Committee and representative from Canada, recounts: "The Nara Document on Authenticity expanded the list of attributes for authenticity to include dynamic and intangible ones like tradition, function, spirit, and feeling. It acknowledged the importance of cultural diversity and promoted conservation approaches appropriate to specific cultural contexts" (Cameron and Inaba 2015, 36). This notion of what is authentic heritage pushed at the original definitions in two ways: it opened the definition of monuments, sites, materials, and forms to better represent traditions outside of Europe, and it also opened the door for conversations about intangible cultural heritage.

It would take nearly a decade for this notion of intangible cultural heritage to be codified, but in 2003 the Convention for the Safeguarding of the Intangible Cultural Heritage was established. The first properties were inscribed on the Representative List of the Intangible Cultural Heritage of Humanity in 2008 (UNESCO 2020a). Inverse of the original World Heritage List in its early years, the Intangible Cultural Heritage List reflects greater geographical diversity (Harrison 2013, 150). As of 2020, Japan had 21 properties on the list of 549, including the much-lauded addition of *washoku* (Japanese cuisine) in 2014. The only property listed from Kyoto is the "Yamahoko, the float ceremony of the Kyoto Gion festival," inscribed in 2009 and revised in 2016 as a part of the larger "Yama, Hoko, Yatai, float festivals in Japan" category. As of this writing, the mayor of Kyoto is part of a group trying to get the kimono added to the list (UNESCO 2020a). What is important for the purposes of this book is the global structure and international promotion of World Cultural

Heritage and the ways that Japanese notions of heritage have shaped that conversation.

Heritage in Contemporary Kyoto

Heritage is multifaceted, at once material and ethereal, nostalgic and national, international and personal. All of these layers can be found in Kyoto. At the most formal level, Kyoto is home to seventeen UNESCO world heritage sites, scattered throughout the city. All of these sites were national heritage sites before they were added to the World Heritage List, and many are places that tourists cite as the top reasons to visit Kyoto are on the list—Kiyomizu Temple, the Golden Pavilion, the Silver Pavilion, and Nijō Castle. That is, these sites have long had cultural significance, and they have come to have global cultural significance through their UNESCO World Heritage status.

While the UNESCO World Heritage sites loom large in the marketing of Kyoto tourism, a sense of heritage in Kyoto is hardly limited to these blockbusters. There are countless other gardens, temples, shrines, museums, subsidiary palaces, and the like to visit in Kyoto. Furthermore, over the past eighty years the city has designated historic preservation areas in which all new construction must follow guidelines for size, height, materials, and color; as of 2004, there are strict guidelines for advertisements and signs on the sides of buildings, specifying height, placement, and color scheme and expressly banning neon, especially in and around the historic districts. This sense of preserving and recreating a heritage atmosphere has been a part of the city development plans for almost a century, albeit not without controversy over what is appropriate for Kyoto (see chapter 2).

Japan has long taken heritage seriously, but what defines national and cultural heritage is more flexible than has been traditional in the West. Anthropologist Christoph Brumann's (2009, 2012) ethnographic work on heritage and urban planning in Kyoto in the 1990s highlights the many ways that heritage is understood by citizens and urban planners alike. Brumann argues that in Kyoto heritage is understood as living rather than petrified or encased. Parallel to the discussion of intangible heritage above, rather than merely preserving heritage in Kyoto, the approach is to cultivate heritage for today (Brumann 2009). Indeed, there are very few places in Kyoto that tout the preservation of heritage in the most stringent material sense wherein nothing can be repaired or added. This is, in part, due to the role that wood construction played in the Japanese architecture and the volatile geography of Japan; over the course of Japanese history, no temple, shrine, palace, or castle was saved from the periodic catastrophe of fire. Thus the assumptions of what it means for a site to be "authentic" in Japan are in keeping with a more dynamic notion of heritage. In his analysis of the *Kyō-machiya* (Kyoto-style townhouses) boom and the floats of the Gion Festival in Kyoto, Brumann (2009) argues that Kyoto's more flexible approach to heritage is in part because it is an urban heritage site. Brumann's insights are persuasive, demonstrated through careful documentation of citizens' concerns and mobilizations for the preservation of the ways of life in traditional Kyoto neighborhoods. The examples in this book all confirm the ways that Kyoto's urban heritage is critical to the unique manifestation of heritage throughout the city. But missing from Brumann's analysis is the way that tourism is also a critical part of this calculus in Kyoto. Most heritage materials, exhibits, and sites are curated and cultivated both as a way to commemorate events and to tell the stories of the past, but every story needs an audience, and for heritage, whether at temples, shrines, villas, or museums, the audience often includes tourists.

A Heritage Experience

Discussions about heritage, as well as tourist experiences, are always, at some level, about authenticity. This fraught, and often overwrought, notion has been a central theme in both tourism research and in tourists' own desires. The notion of authenticity has been an important part of tourism research since the founding of the field in the 1970s; despite or perhaps because of its centrality, much ink has been spilled clarifying the term, as well as both decrying and celebrating its role in the tourism industry. In his early work on modern tourism, MacCannell (1999) argued that tourists desire to see something authentic, something beyond the "front" or staged performances of culture, and the notion led to the creation of "staged authenticity" for tourists. The notion of "authenticity" that MacCannell introduced likewise permeates discussions of tourism as scholars have honed the multiple kinds of authenticity tourists seek. In general, the term is used to reference something "real"—true to history, unscripted, natural—and its opposites are considered "fake" or "touristy" in this context. Originally, claims of authenticity tended to focus on either the location of events—the "actual place" where an event took place—or artifacts—the remains of history and culture—from an event, time, or place. As discussed above, the notion of intangible cultural heritage was added to account for performances and rituals like *matsuri* (festivals) as the "stuff" of culture. So, too, experiences are thought of as needing to be "authentic" to the tradition, culture, or locale. Indeed, industry personnel, tourists, and scholars apply the notion of authenticity in a variety of ways: industry personnel might clarify what happened where or why a site is important for historical or cultural events in order to claim authenticity; tourists often want authentic experiences rather than ones sanitized or scripted; and scholars debate about what makes a practice, event, or site authentic. Chapters 2, 3, and 4 examine instances where differing notions of authenticity are being mobilized in Kyoto tourism through a heritage neighborhood renewal, the new creation of a traditional celebration of the seasons, and the commemoration of an early modern hero, Sakamoto Ryōma, respectively.

The issue that most requires attention for our thinking about authenticity, heritage, and tourism in Kyoto is the notion of invented traditions. Eric Hobsbawm and Terence Ranger coined the term "invented tradition" in their 1983 book, and the ensuing decades saw a spate of scholarship cataloguing and debating the multiplicity of invented traditions. Hobsbawm and Ranger argued that many phenomena of the modern world that are considered "traditional" are actually relatively new inventions, constructed by nation-states in order to solidify their national stories, political structures, and social orders. In Japanese studies this notion was powerful, especially given the way that Japan modernized so quickly and consciously created a new nation-state in the Meiji period. Scholars from history to literature to anthropology all found examples of traditions that were invented in early twentieth-century Japan, from sumo to *ryokan* (Japanese inns) to the adoption of Shinto as the national religion (Fujitani 1996; Gluck 1985; Ivy 1988, 1995; Morris-Suzuki 1997; Vlastos 1998). Critical to the issues discussed throughout this book, much of what is now considered Japanese cultural heritage was chosen, conserved, or created as such in the Meiji period as a means to solidify the new nation-state (Aso 2014; Ishimori 1995; Tseng 2018). As early as 1871, the first law protecting important cultural objects held by temples and shrines was enacted. At the time, important temples that held cultural artifacts were embraced as a part of this statecraft to be exhibited at world's fairs and at national expos to showcase the richness of Japanese heritage (Ishimori 1995, 19).

While scholars of all ilks identified and analyzed invented traditions from around the world following Hobsbawm and Ranger's theory, at the heart of the matter were assumptions about authenticity, change, and commodification. Many agreed that invented traditions were misleading at best and ideological at worst. In this line of thinking, because they are newly created yet claim authentic links to the past, such places or practices are deceptive. A wealth of work on heritage tourism, especially in Britain, takes this approach, decrying the historical inaccuracy of heritage sites and narratives (Lowenthal 1985, 1998; Wright and Krauze 2009). Yet implicit in this critique is the notion that authentic traditions or practices are relatively unchanging. That is, it is the newness, recent creation, evolution, or enhancement of traditions that make historical claims that are the problem because they entail falsification of historical facts and details. In contrast, other scholars argue that traditions are always changing, so pinpointing which moment represents the "authentic practice" is difficult at best (Bruner 1994; Cohen 1988; Urry 1990). In particular, anthropologists have long argued that like culture, traditions are constructed, actively created, and always evolving. In this line of thinking the notion that invented traditions are constructed or created anew is less at issue than what they are constructed for and how they affect the participants (Brumann and Cox 2010; Bruner 1994; Cohen 1988; Dallen and Boyd 2003; Silverman 2015; Wang 1999).

Finally, one of the prime concerns about authenticity and tourism in general is about the commodification of history, culture, and experiences. There is no doubt that heritage tourism commodifies places, history, culture, and experiences. What is lost or objectified in the process is at the heart of concerns about authenticity in the tourist industry. "Authenticity" is, after all, what makes tourism big business today. And all of these issues—of authenticity and experience from the perspective of the tourist industry, promotion, and tourists' own imaginaries—can be found in contemporary Kyoto.

By the Numbers: Kyoto Tourism Today

Following the Tourism Nation Japan policies, Kyoto has seen a dramatic increase in tourists in the twenty-first century. This section provides a snapshot of tourism in Kyoto in the past two decades. As noted above, in recent years Kyoto has had over 50 million tourists

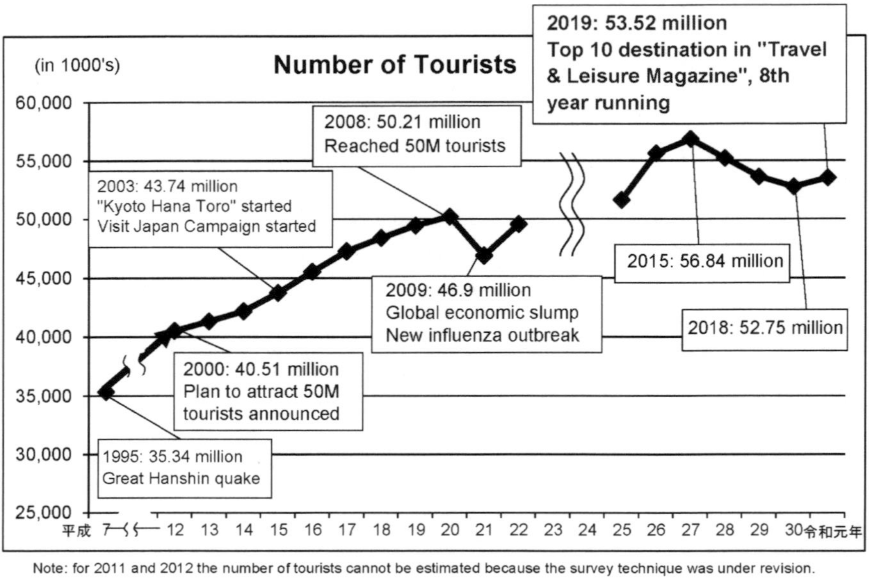

Figure I.1. Number of tourists to Kyoto. (Translation by the author.) Published with permission of the Kyoto City Industry and Tourism Bureau, Tourism and MICE Promotion Office.

a year, while throughout much of the postwar period, it had closer to 40 million.[15] In 2001 the goal was set to reach 50 million by 2020, a benchmark that was reached well ahead of schedule in 2008. Figure I.1 shows tourist growth across the past twenty-five years, indicating national disasters and local cultural events that effected increases and decreases.[16] As seen in the figure, in 2015 the number of tourists to Kyoto topped 55 million, and it has remained above 50 million for several years. To put this into perspective, New York City first reached the 50 million mark in 2011 and had 55 million in 2014, and in 2016, 60.5 million tourists visited "the big apple" (NYC & Company 2017). Kyoto hit 56.8 in 2014, just 2 million fewer than New York. And yet Kyoto is a city of 1.47 million people, compared to New York's 8.3 million.

When we think of tourists, more often than not we think of international tourists; yet, as indicated above, Japan lags behind other nations in attracting inbound tourists. This does not correspond, however, to a dearth of tourists overall. In fact, a large share of the

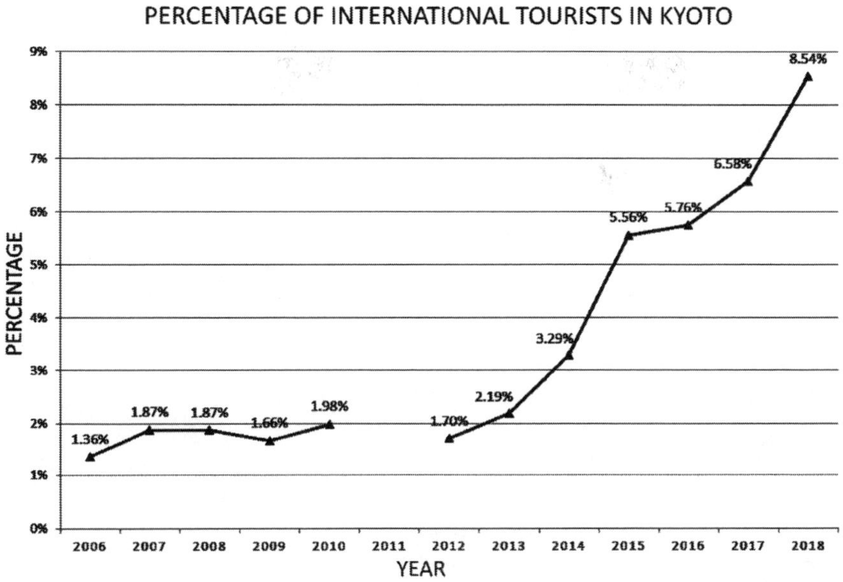

Figure I.2. Percentages of international tourists to Kyoto, 2006–2019. (Numbers for 2011, the year of the Great Eastern Japan Earthquake and Tsunami, were never released.) Kyoto City Tourism Office, 2007–2020.

thriving tourist industry in Japan is domestic. This is especially true for Kyoto, which attracts an average of only 12 percent of all international tourists to Japan (JTB Tourism Research & Consulting 2019; Kyoto City Tourism Office 2002–2019). When I started this research in 2012, international tourists to Kyoto comprised only 1.7 percent (844,800) of all tourists in in the city. As seen in figure I.2, over the past decade the number of international tourists visiting Kyoto has increased sixfold, from nearly 657,000 in 2006 to 4,503,000 (or 8.5 percent) in 2018 (Kyoto City Tourism Office 2019, 69).[17]

The increase in the international numbers has come predominantly from Asian tourists, reflecting the growth in outbound tourism trends in China, as well as the Tourist Nation Japan policies.[18] In particular, as noted above, Japan has changed visa restrictions for East Asian tourists (Henderson 2017). Yet the figures for East Asian tourism in Kyoto diverge from wider national trends, and they were a topic of discussion throughout my research. While Chinese tourists to Japan were on the rise in 2012, industry personnel in Kyoto all said that Chinese tourists were not interested in Kyoto. As Mr. K— put it, "In China they have beautiful nature and temples, so Kyoto is less interesting to Chinese tourists; they tend to prefer shopping in Osaka and Tokyo" (Mr. K— 2012). Since 2012 Chinese outbound tourism has soared. By 2017, after Japan's visa policy changes and marketing campaigns, Chinese tourists to Japan increased from 1.4 million (2010) to 7.3 million (a fivefold increase), while Chinese tourists to Kyoto over that same period rose from 79, 800 to 944, 500 (an elevenfold increase). I want to highlight two points here: first, tourism, and international tourism in particular, has been increasing in Kyoto throughout the last decade due to a confluence of national policies, along with Kyoto's ambitious tourism promotion plans; second, even at its peak, international tourism comprised only 8.4 percent of tourists to Kyoto; thus the remaining over 90 percent were domestic visitors (Kyoto City Tourism Office 2019).

Thus far, discussions of tourism in this chapter have focused largely on international tourists. Indeed, most of the major tourism organizations discussed here were created during attempts to increase inbound tourism to Japan—the JTB in 1912, the JNTO in 1964, and the JTA in 2008. In his discussion of the development of tourism policy in Japan, David Leheny (2003, 58–59) argues that the structures created for foreign tourists were often later promoted for domestic tourists as well. In significant ways, domestic tourism trends are different—domestic tourists do not require a system of translators (linguistic or cultural), and the natural beauty and historical and cultural significance of Kyoto are taught almost through osmosis from a young age in any class on history, literature, art, or politics. In fact, most Japanese go to Kyoto for the first time on official school trips, known as *shūgaku ryokō* (school excursions).

According to Kyoto's city tourism statistics, domestic tourists accounted for 98.3 percent of all tourists in 2012 and 91 percent in 2018. Most domestic tourists to Kyoto are excursionists from the Kansai region. Excursionists tend to visit frequently and return home the same day. On average 61 percent of domestic tourists to Kyoto have visited over ten times or more, and 81 percent have been there five times or more. Over the past decade an average of 64 percent of the domestic tourists were female and 36 percent were male. Moreover, an average of 70 percent of these domestic tourists are over the age of fifty, with the sixty-plus demographic at the highest levels in recent years (Kyoto City Tourism Office 2013–2019). Yet anyone who has been to Kyoto recently will have in mind the flocks of Japanese schoolchildren there on official school trips. These school excursions were established early in the Meiji period as a part of educational restructuring, and the first such trips were to Kyoto and Nara (Ishimori 1995, 19; Oedewald 2009, 116–118). Today each child takes a trip somewhere in elementary, middle, and high school respectively. While student visitors make up only about 2 percent of the tourists to Kyoto, during their peak seasons popular spots like Nijō Castle, the Golden Pavilion, and Kiyomizu Temple are a sea of yellow hats (elementary-school children) and school uniforms (middle-school students) (Kyoto City Tourism Office 2013–2019).

All this is to say that the bulk of visitors to Kyoto are domestic tourists who tend to come in just for the day and who have visited many times over their lifetimes. In addition, in the early part of this research the tourism promotion initiatives were successful in attracting domestic tourists as well as increasing the number of international tourists. However, as the number of international tourists has escalated the overall numbers for domestic tourists have declined. In 2017, for the first time in over a decade, domestic tourist numbers dropped (Kyoto City Tourism Office 2019). The volume of tourism promotion, in a city that was already a tourist destination, fuels the maintenance of heritage districts even as it puts strains on everyday city life. All of this has a bearing on city-level tourism initiatives and tourism industry changes, as well as on tourists' own desires. The charms and challenges of being a tourist city are addressed across the chapters of this book.

Situating This Project: Research on Tourism, Writing about Kyoto

Like tourism itself—at once pleasure, education, and unforeseen challenges—this book is based on twelve months of ethnographic fieldwork in Kyoto, focused on the production and consumption of Kyoto as a heritage tourist destination.[19] This project was started in earnest almost a year after the fateful earthquake, tsunami, and nuclear disaster of March 2011, known as the Great Eastern Japan Earthquake and Tsunami (colloquially, 3/11).[20] While Kyoto was not directly affected by the natural and human-made disasters, the whole country reeled from the loss and controversy over nuclear power safety and management. For most of my primary fieldwork, only one of the nation's fifty nuclear power plants was up and running, the others having been shut down due to post-Fukushima fears and public outrage over the low levels of regulatory oversight at nuclear facilities in the earthquake-prone nation. In the summer of 2012, across Japan there were mandatory energy cuts of 10–15 percent. In Kyoto during the summer of 2012, there were daily power alerts, low-usage days for businesses, and the threat of rolling blackouts. While ongoing concerns and social movements against nuclear energy in Japan received scant international attention, after the triple disaster of 2011 tourism was down significantly and was just starting to recover in 2012. This state of affairs tinged all of my conversations about tourism in Kyoto. Just a year after my initial fieldwork, in September 2013, it was announced that the 2020 Olympics would be in Tokyo. This announcement was seen as heralding the potential for both economic and spiritual recovery after the recent disasters and years of recession, despite the difficulties that hosting the Olympics brings. Between then and now Tokyo has been in the throes of preparing for this global event, and the rest of the nation, including Kyoto, has been preparing for the surge of tourists that such events bring. However, as I was making my final revisions in the spring of 2020, the world was "sheltering in place" in response to the global threat of COVID-19. The tourism industry was one of the first to be affected by this global pandemic, with travel bans and cruise ship contagions. In Kyoto, in February 2020 international tourism was down 53.4 percent, a trend that escalated throughout the year (Kyoto City Tourism Association 2020). In March Japan announced that the 2020 Olympics would be moved forward a year, to July 2021. Thus the exponential tourism growth in Kyoto that sets the context for this book is sandwiched by two catastrophes, circumstances that mirror a precarity that has come to characterize life in the twenty-first century.

Throughout this book I aim for a holistic approach to studying tourism in Kyoto, attending to tourists, industry personnel, and other local interlocutors alike. Since I am an anthropologist, it was relatively easy to start research on tourism. It was not hard to find field sites—popular tourist destinations—nor was it hard to locate tourist information centers or industry hubs like the Kyoto Tourist Association (KTA), the Kyoto City Tourism Office, the Convention and Visitors' Bureau, and the Tourist Information Center (Kyo-Navi; short for Kyoto Navigation) in Kyoto Station.[21] After all, a significant portion of Kyoto's economy is related to tourism—hotels, restaurants in tourist districts, tour companies and guides, museums, shops, and tourist sites. The wide variety of citizens who work in the tourist industry was also a part of this research, both formally and informally. And tourists themselves are unavoidable in Kyoto. At times, even the daily commute to take my son to school was fieldwork, as the bus from our house to his school was also the bus heading to the ubiquitously popular Golden Pavilion. Finally, in the course of daily life I spoke with friends and neighbors, hotel and temple staff, and shopkeepers and tour guides about my research, getting their opinions and experiences about things that I was discovering and noticing and often their overview of what it was like living in a city with so many tourists.

At the same time, tourism research is surprisingly elusive. While I spoke with a wide range of tourists (in the two languages I know, English and Japanese),[22] throughout the eight months of initial fieldwork and four follow-up summer trips, it was hard to move conversations with tourists past the stage of initial impressions—the beauty of Kyoto, its historical grandeur, its humidity and crowds. The deeper relationships and experiences that come with traditional anthropological fieldwork are elusive in tourist interactions, which are fleeting. This is at once an admission of why an analysis of tourists' comments may feel thin to the anthropologically minded and an accurate reflection of engagement at tourist sites and tourists themselves. The issue here is twofold: first, it was often hard to get past the thin veneer of comments about history and culture, even though people have thick experiences when they travel. Second, tourists travel, especially to significant destinations like Kyoto, for multiple reasons. While this means that different people travel for different reasons, it also means that one person will likely travel for multiple reasons. In Kyoto, a tourist may be interested in temples and shrines, geisha or traditional crafts, hiking in the hills, *The Tale of Genji,* the events of the Meiji Restoration and/or popular culture that retells these tales and events, or all or none of these.

In addition, as an anthropologist I embarked on this project thinking about connecting with people, asking myself, "With whom should I talk in order to get various perspectives on history and tourism in Kyoto?" And I certainly did that. But one of the biggest innovations in tourism discourse in the twenty-first century is the internet and especially social media (Urry and Larsen 2011); even in the ten years I worked on this book the use of social media in Kyoto tourism evolved exponentially. At the most basic level, many of the people with whom I spoke in Kyoto pointed me to their web pages for additional data. For example, the Kyoto City Tourism Office makes its "Kyoto Tourism Survey Report" available yearly on its website (Kyoto City Tourism Office 2002–2020). So, too, the city's tourism promotion plans are all available through the city's website (in Japanese). These kinds of resources are increasingly accessible to scholars; in fact, increasing governmental regulations on regular reporting are a boon to academics.

More ethereal, social media are part of the way that tourists learn about locations and share their tourism encounters; they have also become a way the tourist industry attempts to reach and engage its markets. This kind of mediated connectivity is one of the fundamental ways that tourism connections (to use Jennie Germann Molz's [2012] term), are changing in the twenty-first century. At the end of several of my interviews, guides and industry personnel asked me to review their tours online, "like" their Facebook page, or "follow" them on Instagram or Twitter. Both the KTA and Kyoto City have a Facebook page titled "Like! Kyoto." Similarly, one of the companies that runs weekly tours of Kyoto posts pictures on Facebook of each tour with an accounting of how many visitors were there and from where; and each of the kimono rental locations discussed in chapter 5 posts daily photos of guests on Facebook and Instagram. In the spring of 2019, the KTA sponsored a #kyotogenic campaign on Instagram with prizes for the winning photos. Even though the contest is over, #kyotogenic seems to have become a mainstay. These are just a few of the myriad ways that tourists and the tourist industry are integrating social media into their practices (Elliott and Urry 2010; Germann Molz 2012). All of this is tourism data as it is a part of the broader tourism strategies, conversations, and culture. But just as tourism itself is filled with brief encounters, social media are structured by short interactions. As a part of this research on tourism, I make use of social media data where appropriate, not to replace conversations and interviews but to add to them, enabling me to sample a broader swath of tourist perspectives, engaging with tourists "where they are." Thus despite Kyoto's traditional reputation, this research on heritage tourism draws on the mobilities turn in tourism research, in which the movement of people and the availability of connections shape the global and the local in our media-saturated world.

Kyoto is not an understudied place. In fact, there has been a renewed academic interest in the city in recent years (Brumann 2012; Dougill 2006; Stavros 2014; Tseng 2018; Breen, Maruyama, and Takagi 2020). Yet tourism in Kyoto is often treated, by tourists and scholars alike, as an unfortunate consequence of the city's charm. This book adds to this vital body of literature, taking heritage and modernity, history and culture, in Kyoto seriously, through the lens of contemporary tourism. So, too, tourism studies is a growing field that is taking on new prominence as tourism itself becomes central to the global economy. Indeed, Kyoto is mentioned in almost every book on contemporary tourism, cited in awe or dismissed as a city that has become a museum to itself. In answer, this book provides an in-depth analysis of Kyoto as a heritage tourist site attendant to the ways that contemporary trends of experiential tourism are imbricated in Kyoto today.

In Japanese studies, much of the research on Japanese tourism has focused on the ways *rural* communities have participated in the development of heritage projects aimed at recapturing what has been lost in the process of modernization—the mystical and communal aspects of premodern life (Creighton 1997; Guichard-Anguis and Moon 2009; Ivy 1995; Martinez 1990, 2004). This argument is critical to our understanding of modern and contemporary Japan as it highlights the ways that a sense of "Japaneseness" is crafted in the face of international and now global pressures—a balance we see again in the Cool Japan and Tourism Nation Japan policies and discourses. In contrast, the chapters in this book draw attention to the ways that tourism in *urban* Kyoto cultivates a contemporary sense of the past by intertwining nostalgia and tradition with the amenities of modern urban life. In dialogue with recent scholarship on heritage construction discussed above, I begin with the premise that Kyoto's rich sense of history and culture is invented, through packaging and promotion in the tourist industry, but it is not "inauthentic." In fact, Kyoto houses 20 percent of artifacts and buildings designated as national treasures in Japan. Thus my focus is not on what is being manipulated but on the ways that heritage, history, and culture are invested in the spaces of Kyoto through the tourist industry, local histories, and the people involved in cultivating particular places. Contemporary tourism in Kyoto consciously mobilizes the echoes of the past and the amenities of the present, presenting Kyoto as a living city with a past, present, and future. Focusing on the city of Kyoto as a tourist site, this book theorizes the ways that history and culture are deployed today in an urban setting for a variety of cultural agendas, social purposes, and economic strategies.

Finally, it is frequent in academic literature on tourism to list Kyoto as the epitome of manufactured heritage or as an urban heritage museum, in an offhand fashion. Part of my project in this book is to complicate this view of Kyoto as the epitome of postmodern heritage tourism while interrogating the use of history in Kyoto tourism branding. To be sure, Kyoto is not a historical fantasy park; there are notorious urban blights and modern marvels as well. Kyoto Station itself is either adored or abhorred for its postmodern styling in the historic capital, and the quintessentially 1960s Kyoto Tower, located just outside the central exit to the station, is often referred to as a modern architectural blunder. The electric power lines that hang low in some of the historic districts like Gion lead tourists to mumble, "Such a shame," and there are traffic jams getting to and from the most popular tourist locations during the peak tourist seasons. In recent years, discussions of overtourism have come to dominate news stories about Kyoto, always featuring the crush of people and the bad behaviors of international tourists. Last but not least, the same hills that bring bright green light into the urban center hold moisture in the city basin, making the winters damp and cold and the summers unbearably humid and hot. Yet all of these factors—romance and charm; city-, town-, and nature-scapes; tourist seasons; tourism management; and tourist desires—are key to the chapters in this book.

Kyoto Imaginings: Writing about "The Heart and Soul of Japan"

It is no small task to write a book about Kyoto, so large is its imprint on Japanese history, culture, and imagination. Tourism in Kyoto encompasses such a wide range of topics that it would be impossible for anyone to master them. In a way, to write about history and culture in Kyoto tourism, one needs to become fluent in much of Japanese history and literature, tackling topics as disparate as *The Tale of Genji* and the *bakumatsu* period (the end of Tokugawa rule that ushered in the start of modern Japan in the late nineteenth century); the tea ceremony and the traditional arts; geisha; and contemporary economics; thus this project took me into the heart of Japanese studies across a wide range of disciplines. But it is important for readers to keep in mind that this book is about the role of history and culture in Kyoto tourism today. Where a broader knowledge of topics (such as Nishijin textiles or Japanese gardens) was required, I relied on a combination of my fieldwork and interlocutors' views, along with the secondary scholarship in these areas. My goal here is not to make significant contributions to our understanding of Genji, Japanese religion, or the *bakumatsu* era; rather, I have made use of the wealth of expertise in the field of Japanese studies to provide the reader with a broader context with which to think about the tourist industry in Kyoto today. My own scholarly contributions are in the analysis of personal experiences of urban heritage in Kyoto. Nevertheless, readers familiar with Kyoto will undoubtedly encounter things they wish I had covered, so large is the topic at hand, and I beg their generosity if their own delights or horrors, quandaries or bemusements, are not addressed in this book.

A final note: throughout the text I have tried to impart a sense of the exuberant and romantic ways that this city is imagined, written about, promoted, and experienced without romanticizing it myself. This is a tricky proposition because there *is* something charming about Kyoto; the city is surrounded on three sides by hills that cast the urban center in green light; the centrally located Kamo River provides public spaces to stroll, run, read, or cool off; around almost every corner one can find a small temple, shrine, or historic site; and the city landscape policies have paid attention to views from within the city. When I discuss my research, even scholars of Japan often launch into stories of their own favorite (or least favorite) things about Kyoto. The draw of Kyoto is foundational for this book (it has, after all, been a significant tourist destination for thousands of years), and yet it haunted me in the writing process: how can I write a book that thinks critically about the construction of heritage with this romance lurking in the background? I mark this romance, the charm—to use the phrase the city endorses—up front to highlight the ways in which, in tourism and in Kyoto, the construction of heritage is affective—at once grounded and ethereal, constructed and experiential.

An Itinerary: The Chapters that Follow

Each of the chapters in this book seeks to examine one aspect of the making and marketing of heritage experiences in contemporary Kyoto. Starting with an overview of travel patterns and practices in Japan, chapter 1, "The Essence of Travel," lays the groundwork for the ethnographic chapters that follow. Since its inception as

Heian-kyō, the capital, Kyoto has been an urban destination for travelers. Moving historically, this chapter discusses several features of travel culture in Japan that shape the contours of tourism in Kyoto today. The first half focuses on premodern travel through the role of poetry and place, the evolution of infrastructure, and social patterns that shape the way people traveled and travel in Japan. The second half outlines the advent of modern mass tourism in the high-growth years through the stories of several veteran tour guides in Kyoto, charting the ways that travel shifted from "seeing" to "encountering" to "experiencing." It ends with a discussion of the challenges of a tourist city today. Grounded in the cityscape itself, this chapter highlights the material ways that Kyoto has been shaped over the years by tourism culture and practice.

Chapters 2 and 3 elucidate the ways that heritage atmosphere is constructed in contemporary Kyoto through an analysis of a neighborhood renovation project and the creation of a new seasonal festival. Framed by the notion of "the Kyoto brand," chapter 2, "A Brand of History," seeks to understand how the city of Kyoto crafts heritage conceptually and materially. I begin with an analysis of the two most recent tourism promotion plans (2010 and 2015), drawing out the ways that these plans mobilize heritage and hospitality to enhance tourist experiences. The second half of the chapter focuses on a neighborhood revitalization project undertaken in 2012 and is attentive to the heritage atmosphere and experiencing Kyoto today. The chapter ends with a discussion of tourist etiquette and the challenges to hospitality that masses of tourists bring. Chapter 3, "Seasonal Travel," turns its attention to the ways that the Kyoto tourism industry markets itself through the traditional aesthetics of nature. The heart of the chapter analyzes yearly seasonal events in which natural beauty is at the fore, focusing on two new events created to attract tourists in the off-season and off-hours—Hanatōro (Flower and Lantern Pathways) and Kyō no Tanabata (Star Festival in Kyoto). A close reading of recently created tourist events through the lens of prior narratives and aesthetics of the nature in the city allows us to think about the ways that Kyoto promotes tourist experiences in relation to its long past. With the creation of events that affectively integrate nature and traditional aesthetics into the contemporary cityscape, visitors feel like they experience Kyoto as both new and old. These chapters demonstrate the ways that the Kyoto brand crafts Japanese heritage for the present and future.

Stepping away from the large-scale tourism promotion campaigns and projects, chapters 4 and 5 analyze the cultivation of tourists' personal encounters with heritage in Kyoto. Chapter 4, "*Bakumatsu* Vacation," focuses on heritage contents tourist sites that commemorate the *bakumatsu* period through a case study of sites commemorating Sakamoto Ryōma. This chapter focuses on how these small-scale local sites recreate historical stories for a contemporary audience in ways that keep the past alive and bring it into the present. In keeping with this more ground-up approach to history and tourism, each of these sites curates exhibits, stages events, and encourages personal connections with the characters in these historical stories. The face-to-face history that is being both cultivated and sought out in these sites commemorates an important national moment, one that combines the bravado of samurai culture—of nobility, honor, and swords—with the import of modern ideals—of democracy, love, and guns. I argue that these small-scale, hidden-in-plain-view sites cultivate a nostalgia for the role of youth in the birth of modern Japan in the midst of twenty-first-century precarity. Moving away from the small scale, chapter 5, "Kimono Crowds," returns to the busiest tourist district in Kyoto to examine the trendiest tourist experience today: kimono rental. The boom for seeing Kyoto while wearing kimono is one of the most visible changes in Kyoto tourism over the past decade. This chapter investigates the ways that tourists seek to experience heritage in the increasingly crowded tourist corridor, drawing together the "Walking City Kyoto" projects, tourists' own desires for heritage experiences, and the embodied experience (*taiken*) of walking in Kyoto in kimono. Through comparing tourist kimono rental to other forms of embodied tourism from historical reenactment to cosplay, I emphasize the ways that somatic—sensing and feeling—experiences of a heritage atmosphere shape travel in Kyoto today. Building on the affect of the seasons and personal encounters with history discussed in prior chapters, the somatic experiences of walking through the heritage district in kimono provide new ways to experience Kyoto, drawing on identifiable Japanese traditions, those not experienced in daily life in modern Japan.

The epilogue, "Experience Kyoto—Making Kyoto the World's Hometown," gathers together the threads that emerge across the ethnographic chapters and returns to national and global trends in tourism, framed by the Olympic Games in Tokyo in 2021. Last held in Tokyo in 1964, the Summer Olympics were an important way for

Japan to showcase its economic and cultural recovery after World War II, and Kyoto was seen as an important part of this message. The first bullet train (Shinkansen), itself symbolic of Japan's economic and technical rise, debuted just months before the Olympics to bring tourists from Tokyo to Kyoto. With the return of the Olympics on the horizon, I conclude by looking at the ways Kyoto has prepared for the onslaught of tourists, suggesting how Japanese culture may be differently presented and experienced after three decades of economic stagnation and social precarity. This framing brings together the threads of a romance with Japanese history, experiential tourism, and the mingling of tourist imaginaries in contemporary Kyoto. In the end we see that Kyoto is marketed as both comfortably familiar to global travelers and quintessentially Japanese in ways that reveal the entanglements of the global and the local today.

Ж Ж Ж

At its core, this book sets out to examine the way that Japanese culture and history are represented, packaged, and consumed as a means of asserting culture and tradition in today's globalized and commercialized context. Each of the following chapters analyzes the ways that particular moments in history are mobilized to construct cultural tourist sites and visitor experiences and how those representations in turn shape the image and cultural meanings of a particular place—contemporary Kyoto. In what follows, we will revisit Kyoto not as a repository of the past or an antiquated remnant of Japanese culture, but as an important site for thinking about the desires of twenty-first-century tourists and opening a window on crucial cultural and social issues facing both individuals and modern mass society.

Chapter 1

"The Essence of Travel"

The Social and Material Traces of Travel in Kyoto

Do you know why Kyoto is called "raku"?
Long ago, following the model of the capital of China, the eastern half of Heian-kyō was called 洛陽 (Rakuyō), while the western half was called 長安 (Chōan). Since the Rakuyō side prospered more, the character 洛 "raku" became the pronoun for Kyoto. *Rakutabi* combines this "raku" (洛) with "*tabi*," journey (旅). Yet you can use "fun" 楽 (*raku*) or "repeat visits" 度 (*tabi*) or even "tabi socks" (足袋) to make up *rakutabi*. After all, walking in Kyoto can be as smooth as gliding along in socks.

—Rakutabi Kyoto guidebook series, inside flap

I hope to make Kyoto one of the best cities in the world for encountering people, culture, history, and even yourself in a way that touches the heart, enabling you to enjoy the "essence of travel" to the fullest.

—Mayor Kadokawa,
Future Kyoto Tourism Promotion Project 2010+5

The two epigraphs that open this chapter emphasize the notion of personal experiences in Kyoto. I start with these two quotes because together they not only highlight experience, but they also speak to different audiences—tourists and the tourism industry—both of which are critical to tourism in Kyoto. Rakutabi is a Kyoto-based publisher that specializes in pocket-sized, themed Kyoto guidebooks (in Japanese). This guidebook series targets repeat visitors to Kyoto who want to focus their experiences by exploring a particular facet of the city's offerings, such as *bakumatsu* history, world heritage sites, *matcha* (powdered green tea) cafes, Buddhist sites, or Kyoto at night. As the epigraph above highlights, the series specializes in unique ways to learn about and explore Kyoto today. So, too, the excerpt of Mayor Kadokawa's opening remarks in the tourism promotion plan released in 2010 emphasizes experience through the notion of "the essence of travel," highlighting personal encounters with culture, people, history, and even self-discovery in Kyoto. The Rakutabi series addresses travelers while the city's tourism promotion plan outlines city-level projects, yet both speak of a contemporary journey that connects the past and present, history and culture, with personal encounters. Indeed, because of the city's stature as the ancient capital, history and culture have always been the main attractions; yet the turn to personal experience is relatively recent, in flux, and part of current trends in tourism. In Kyoto, many tourists today seek a more hands-on engagement with Japanese culture and history through experiences such as staying in a *ryokan;* watching geisha perform; seeing how traditional handicrafts or foods like fans, kimono, woodblock prints, and tofu are made; and perhaps even trying their hand at making such items themselves.

Exploring the turn toward experiential travel, this chapter lays the groundwork for the chapters that follow by tracing the social and material effects of tourism in Japan. The first part of this chapter outlines prewar patterns of travel, with a focus on the role of poetry, the development of infrastructure, and Japanese travel practices. Rather than giving an overview of travel in Japan, these three snapshots highlight prior practices that linger in contemporary tourism today. The next section of the chapter identifies some of the ways that Kyoto tourism spaces have shifted to accommodate changing travel patterns in the postwar period through the experiences of long-time tour guides. In tracing the move from mass tourism to individualized and even personalized travel, I argue that we can observe a shift from "seeing" (*miru*) to "encountering" (*fureau*) to "experiencing" (*taiken*), as noted in the introduction. The final section introduces some of the challenges that tourism (whether mass or individualized) brings to the city, with an eye toward the problems of overtourism in recent years. Thus this chapter provides an overview of travel practices in

Japan past and present by tracing the social and material effects of tourism on the contours of Kyoto.

Tourism in Japan: Historical Traces

In Japanese four terms roughly translate to mean "travel" and "tourism." *Tabi* (旅) is the oldest word, and it means "journey" or "trip." Today *tabi* harbors aesthetic connotations, eliciting notions of poetic journeys, the romance and hardships of traveling by foot, and the awe of seeing famous sites. *Ryokō* (旅行) became common in the early Meiji period and is the most versatile word for travel, whether for work or fun or both. *Kankō* (観光) is closer to the notion of sightseeing and is used in the title of many tourist associations, making it feel a bit more institutional. Finally, *tsūrizumu* (ツーリズム) is a more recent addition, from the English word "tourism." All of these terms can be found ubiquitously and often interchangeably in tourism discourses in Japan today.

People have long traveled for multiple reasons, whether political, economic, religious, health, cultural, or even out of curiosity. Generally speaking, the roots of tourism are usually traced to travel for religious reasons, open largely to the wealthy or upper classes; tourism expanded to a wider array of people and purposes through the process of industrialization. Within this broader trend, scholars have noted that domestically Japan had a robust travel culture long before the introduction of Western notions of tourism (Funck and Cooper 2015; Graburn 1983, 2009; Guichard-Anguis and Moon 2009; Ishimori 1989; Vaporis 1995).[1] While most of this chapter will focus on shifts in travel culture during the postwar years, I begin by sketching three aspects of travel in prewar Japan that are critical to understanding tourism in Kyoto today: poetry, infrastructure, and travel practices. Each of these topics addresses a different moment in Japanese travel history; each is important to Kyoto tourism; and together they speak to the ideational, material, and social aspects that shape the contours of the culture of travel in Japan highlighted throughout this book.

Poetic Places: Literature, Allusion, and the Making of Destinations

Meisho (名所) might be the most important concept in Japanese tourism. While it simply means "famous places," it refers to specific places that have been renowned for much of Japanese history and that have accumulated a sediment of cultural meanings and associations for centuries even as their number has evolved throughout the ages. Imperial travel to famous places (*meisho*), summer palaces, and shrines in the mountains near Nara comprises some of the earliest accounts of tourism, dating back to 794 CE. In the Heian period, when the court reigned from Kyoto, emperors, court nobles, and family members would travel for periods of time to shrines and other locations in the hills of Kyoto and the surrounding region (Ishimori 1989). Escaping the heat (whether meteorological or political) was common and appears in court records, travel journals, and novels from this time. In the late Heian period travel to religious sites in and around Kyoto grew more common.

One of the unique features of Japanese travel is the connection between poetry and places. The most influential literary texts of the Nara (710–794) and early Heian periods were both anthologies of poetry—the *Man'yōshū* (Collection of Ten Thousand Leaves, 759) and *Kokinshū* (Collection of Japanese Poems Old and New, 905).[2] According to Haruo Shirane (2012, 27–32), the *Kokinshū* was the main source of poetic reference throughout the Heian period, and by the thirteenth century it had become the most influential classical text. Both of these poetry anthologies feature themes of nature, but they also include poems about travel (Traganou 2004, 69). The poems in these collections were not only memorized and recited, but they were also referenced in other poems, literature, and even card games like *sugoroku*. Many poems honored particular places for their natural or seasonal beauty. Arashiyama, in western Kyoto, is famous for its brilliant autumn leaves. Yoshino (in nearby Nara Prefecture), known for its lush cherry blossoms, became synonymous with melancholy through the association of the spectacularly short-lived blooms and the Buddhist aesthetic of impermanence. Place names referenced in such poems were known as *utamakura;* literally the term means "pillow words," but literarily its meaning is closer to "poetic places" (Nenzi 2008, 37). Through their use in poems linking an emotion, a place, and a natural image, *utamakura* became imbued with certain feelings from classical poetry. In turn, the places referred to in *utamakura* were made famous for the particular season, sentiment, or aesthetic associated with them from literary allusion. Nenzi recounts the poet Shōtetsu's emphatic sense of the conceptual quality of *meisho*: "If someone were to ask me what province Mount

Yoshino is in, I would answer that when it comes to cherry blossoms I think of Mount Yoshino, when it comes to bright autumn leaves, I think of Mount Tatsuta. I would write my poems accordingly, *not caring whether these places are in Iga or Hyūga Provinces.* It is of no practical value to remember which provinces these places are in" (2004, 36; emphasis in the original). In this account, knowing where places are, presumably so one could travel there, is secondary to the poetics they impart. Thus this notion of famous places so familiar from tourism marketing today, has a deeper resonance in Japan through association with poetry, seasons, and affect (see Chapter 3).

Yet *meisho* were not only referenced in poems, but they also served as a kind of aesthetic guide to planning one's travels. Readers could travel vicariously, not only through travel journals, novels, and poetry, but also through art and games. Accounts of travel from the melancholy to the hilarious are celebrated in some of the most famous works in the Japanese literary canon, including the following: Matsuo Bashō's (1644–1694) mix of prose and haiku, like *The Records of a Travel-Worn Satchel;* earthy novels about the joys and hardships of travel, like those by Ihara Saikaku (1642–1693) and Jippensha Ikku's (1765–1831) Tōkaidō adventure *Shank's Mare.* Just as literature and poetry served to cultivate a culture of travel, the popularity of travel in the mid- to late-Edo period is documented by a wealth of print materials (Vaporis 1989, 462). The *Miyako meisho zue* (Famous Places in the Capital Illustrated Book) was the first of these illustrated guides to famous places; published in 1780, it focused on sites in and around Kyoto. Filled with woodblock print illustrations, over four thousand copies of the book were made in the first edition; it sold out the first year it was published and went through multiple reprints (Ishimori 1989, 189). Illustrated guidebooks like these index the thriving print culture that developed in the Edo period—despite rigid travel restrictions—as well as the popularity of travel, whether in practice or imagination. Moreover, scholars of Japanese travel note that even in the premodern period travel writing was often focused on personal experiences or the personal changes that came with traveling, presaging contemporary travel themes (Nenzi 2008).

As more and more people started to travel in the Edo period, *meisho* served as popular travel stops because they were already familiar from poems, novels, and stories. Travelers often report adding an excursion to a famous destination to their official travel plans

(Ishimori 1995, 13). Kyoto, famous as a literary and political capital, was one such important place. In the medieval and early premodern periods, western Japan—Ise-Kyoto-Osaka—was the center of gravity for sacred travels, and most *meisho* were in this region as well. In the Edo period, the increase in sightseeing, whether for pilgrimage or domain retinue, helped both reinvigorate and add to the list of famous places (Guichard-Anguis 2009a, 9–10). *Meisho,* both older and newly created, remain a significant part of tourism in Japan today, in tourist imaginaries and tourism promotions alike.

Tōkaidō Travel: Roads, Accommodations, and the Making of Travel

In contrast to the poetics of *meisho,* the material infrastructure built up in the Edo period shaped travel in ways that are still visible today. After the unification of Japan in 1603, travel gradually became easier through the development of a more structured road system, including the iconic Tōkaidō, which connected the new seat of power, Edo, with the capital, Kyoto. It was the new political structure instituted by the Tokugawa shogunate that instigated the development of travel infrastructure in this period, including checkpoints and way stations for travelers. As noted in the introduction, the system of *sankin kotai* (alternate attendance) required feudal lords (*daimyō*) to travel to Edo and live in residence every year or every other year, and their primary wives and children were required to stay in Edo. As the *daimyō* traveled back and forth between their domains and Edo, along increasingly managed roads, they displayed their power and prestige by traveling with retinues in the thousands. Politically this served to keep them under watch in Edo, and organizing the elaborate processions drained their coffers. But the alternate attendance system also codified the system of five roads (Gōkaidō)—Tōkaidō, Nakasendō, Nikkō kaidō, Ōshū kaidō, and Kōshū kaidō—that was developed to accommodate such large and frequent travel groups.

In service of travel, the infrastructure of the Gōkaidō was developed through the widening and straightening of roads; the addition of bridges, ferries, and tunnels; and the establishment of post stations along the way (Ishimori 1989, 184). The fifty-three stations along the Tōkaidō, famously depicted in Hiroshige's woodblock prints, were checkpoints along the road, spaced about a day's walk from each other. More than two hundred of these post stations peppered the five roads, serving not only as government checkpoints, but also as places where travelers could find lodging, a meal, a porter system, and entertainment (Vaporis 1995, 26). The structure of travel, required for samurai and allowed for pilgrims, facilitated the development of what could be considered tourist towns. At the outskirts of station stops, famous temples and shrines; domain strongholds; and a host of inns, restaurants, and entertainment industries developed throughout the Edo period.

While the notion of tourism, or travel for leisure, was not an officially recognized category of the Tokugawa government, the appeal of travel to see famous places was the veritable leitmotif of the mid- to late-Edo period. By the 1700s travel became more common for those outside the ranks of samurai. While permits were monitored and checkpoints manned with varying degrees of strictness throughout the era, permission to travel on pilgrimage or to healing hot springs was obtained by a wide range of people. Constantine Vaporis documents the travel culture among commoners that emerged during the Edo period. In his translation of an early guidebook, *Precautions for Travelers* (*Ryokō yōjinshū;* published by Yasumi Roan in 1810), Vaporis writes: "After they have visited Ise, travelers from the eastern provinces like to sightsee and make pilgrimages to scenic spots, places of historical interest, temples, and shrines in Yamato province, Kyoto, Osaka, Shikoku and even Kyushu. Those from the western provinces, similarly, after Ise journey to Edo, Kashima, Katori, Nikkō, Matsushima in Ōshū, Kisagata, and even go as far as Zenkōji in Shinanno to pray" (1989, 469). Thus with pilgrimages for the spirit or health as the excuse, travel boomed in the middle of the Tokugawa period. These travelers knew where to go because the important destinations, cultural and religious sites, were all well known from the literature and poems discussed above. Indeed, the period from the late 1700s through the mid-1800s is considered to be the first travel boom in Japan (Ishimori 1989, 1995; Nenzi 2008; Traganou 2004; Vaporis 1989, 1995).

As the number of travelers increased, facilities at the post stations along the highways did as well. A range of inns added meal services, which made travel significantly easier as food supplies did not need to be packed and carried (Ishimori 1989, 184). So, too, other amenities proliferated, including baggage delivery services; shops; and peddlers selling travel necessities like straw sandals, fans, guidebooks, and travel and health talismen, as well as a host of local goods, both perishable and nonperishable (Vaporis 1995, 35). By the 1800s, the post stations had expanded enough to almost run together, especially along the less mountainous parts of the Tōkaidō and close to either end (Traganou 2004, 17). Similarly, a host of small towns grew up around the entrances to significant pilgrimage sites, providing travelers with food, shelter, theaters, brothels, and souvenirs (Funck and Cooper 2015, 14; Ishimori 1989, 185). Originally lodging was provided by temples and shrines to support pilgrimages, and from these accommodations small towns known as *monzen machi* (temple towns) developed much like post stations (Traganou 2004, 75). In fact, temples or shrines even sent traveling representatives out to offer travel packages to ensure smoother travel for groups going on pilgrimage—a precursor to the group travel discussed below (Vaporis 1995, 36). By the middle of the Edo period, the areas around Ise, and later around the famous Buddhist temples Kōfukuji and Tōdaiji in Nara, were burgeoning tourist towns (Ishimori 1989, 185). Here, too, travelers could not only stay the night, but could also dine, bathe, and be entertained. Many of the features of travel in this era set the stage for patterns of travel in the modern period.

Domestic travel took a modern turn in the Meiji period with the inception of the railway system. In 1868, the Edo period, characterized by strict isolationist policies, ended, and Western modernity flooded in as Japan refashioned itself as a nation-state complete with a new parliamentary government, modern military, standardized education system, and industrial railways. As a symbol of the restoration of the emperor, in whose name the shogunate had been overthrown, in 1869 the imperial family moved out of Kyoto for the first time in over a millennium to Edo, newly renamed Tokyo. The Edo class system was abolished, and travel was democratized. Built along already established travel roots, a new railway system made it easier to travel and would become one of the important features of life in Japan (Traganou 2004). The first eighteen miles of track from Tokyo's Shimbashi to Yokohama opened in 1872; in 1877 a second line from Kyoto to Kobe was opened. By 1890, a line was completed from Tokyo to Kobe, and in 1895 it was officially named the Tōkaidō line (Freedman 2011, 5; Tseng 2018, 167). The only deviations from the original road were areas where the terrain made it difficult to lay track (Traganou 2004, 21–22).

Building on the travel routes of the premodern era, the new railways transported goods and the military and also conveyed tourists to their favorite spots. Ishimori notes the prominent role tourism played in railway development: "The railway network had to be designed to accommodate tourists travelling to hot springs, temples, and shrines located in various parts of Japan. For example, the Sangū Railway Company was established in 1889 for the purpose of transporting visitors and pilgrims to the Ise Shrine" (1995, 19). The new railways shaped the space of travel in similar ways as the old roads preceding them had done. That is, towns surrounding stations along the railway boomed while those off track diminished. Following the Edo travel routes, modern travelers set out in two different directions. On the one hand, many went to see the *meisho* of old in Ise, Kyoto, and Nara, all of which were newly integrated as important cultural heritage properties for the modern nation (Aso 2014, 89–93).[3] On the other hand, many traveled to Tokyo, to see the wonders of modernity (Traganou 2004, 83). This stereotypical juxtaposition lingers in tourism in Japan today.

Likewise, traditional lodging was gradually supplemented and eventually surpassed by Western-style hotels clustered just outside of major stations, a modern incarnation of the temple towns of the Edo period. Many of today's tourist hot spots, like Mt. Fuji, hot spring resorts, and famous temples or shrines, are a modern continuation of this development (Guichard-Anguis 2009a, 9). The area lining the road to Kiyomizu Temple in eastern Kyoto, discussed in chapter 5, is an almost quintessential example, featuring chock-a-block restaurants and snack shops, and stores selling Kyoto's *meibutsu* (famous local goods and foods marketed and packaged for souvenirs), some recent additions, and others dating back eight hundred years. Here we see the ways that places, including urban Kyoto, are shaped by the structure of travel as it evolves over time.

Finally, while it is clear that a culture of travel, and travel for leisure, existed in Edo Japan, it was in the Meiji period that the tourism industry was established. The JTB opened in 1912 to both promote and package the wonders of Japan for international tourists who clamored to see the once closed country (Leheny 2003, 59–61).[4] Japanese aesthetics and culture were all the rage in Europe and North America at the turn of the twentieth century, influencing everything from impressionism to literature to architecture and the decorative arts. The early years of the twentieth century witnessed open exchanges between Japan and the West as Japan fashioned itself into a modern nation-state. So, too, in the salons and parlors of the West, things Japanese excited connoisseurs, from woodblock prints to china, fans, dolls, and lacquerware (Napier 2007). With new technology, photographers in Japan, like Felice Beato and Kusakabe Kimbei, responded by meeting the demand for romantic souvenir photographs, which were widely circulated throughout the West (Wakita 2009). The fashion for all things eastern encouraged the development of Western tourism in Japan, which boomed until the rise of militaristic nationalism in the early 1930s (Funck and Cooper 2015, 13), While Kyoto was always on the list of destinations for international tourists, the city came late to promoting tourism, relying on its reputation as the capital. It was not until 1930 that Kyoto City opened its first tourism office, followed a year later by the first Tourist Information Center (Kyoto City 2010, 2015). Thus by the start of World War II, the infrastructure of modern tourism, from railways to lodging, souvenirs, famous foods, and promotional offices, was established in much of Japan, including Kyoto.

Pilgrimage Patterns and Souvenir Sociality: Group Travel and the Making of Tourism

Most accounts of the origins of tourism note the connection between tourism and pilgrimage, and Japan is no exception (Funck and Cooper 2015; Graburn 1983; Guichard-Anguis and Moon 2009; Ishimori 1989, 1995; MacCannell 1999; Nenzi 2008; Seaton et al. 2017; Traganou 2004; Turner and Turner 1978; Vaporis 1995). While scholars of tourism in the West often take great care to parse out the difference between religious and secular tourism, the distinct dichotomy between the sacred and the secular is not indigenous in Japan. Even in the more restrictive Edo social system, travel for pilgrimage was rarely a purely religious affair (Graburn 1983; Ishimori 1995, 58; Nenzi 2008; Traganou 2004; Vaporis 1995). Travel journals from this time include itineraries that stop at seasonal, cultural, or historical sites before and/or after the main religious pilgrimage site(s). Today, tourism scholars have sought parallels between pilgrimage to religious sites and what might be called "new sacred spaces." One of the newest incarnations of the connection between tourism and pilgrimage is the contents tourism boom, in which fans of anime have adopted the term "pilgrimage to sacred sites" (*seichi junrei*) to refer to their travels to locations depicted in contemporary popular culture (Okamoto 2018a, 2018b; Seaton et al. 2017; Sugawa-Shimada 2015; Yamamura 2009). As demonstrated throughout this book, cultural heritage sites can be treated with the same reverence allotted religious sites, especially in a place like Kyoto. So, too, religious sites often bear the same markers of commercialization as the most secular of sites.

There are several significant religious pilgrimage routes in Japan today, one of which traverses Kyoto (the Saigoku Kannon pilgrimage), where pilgrims in their white garb can be seen from time to time.[5] Several times during my research I encountered a group of two or three women who traveled together several times a year to gradually visit all one hundred of the Kannon temples. However, rather than discussing pilgrimage routes in contemporary Kyoto, my focus in this section is on the social organization of travel, emphasizing the ways that travel practices are shaped by social relations. While much has changed in modern tourism in Japan, several of the earlier social patterns remain imprinted in contemporary practices.

Travel to important religious sites, renowned Shinto shrines, and Buddhist temples to pray for crops, good fortune, health, or a cure for ailments dictated much of the nonmilitary/nonpolitical travel until the modern period in the late 1900s (Vaporis 1995). In the Edo period, it was said that everyone should make the pilgrimage to Ise once in their lives. Even so, travel was still quite expensive. From the middle of the Edo period on, religious communities, called *kō*, developed to provide a way for villages to pool their resources and send a delegation on pilgrimage for the benefit of the whole community. As a trip approached, there was a gathering to wish the travelers well. At the sending-off event, gifts for travel (often monetary), called *senbetsu,* were given to the travelers by members of the community. The pilgrims were aware of the weight of their responsibility since they traveled to represent the group. At the destination temples or shrines, souvenirs symbolic of the location, called *omiyage,* were purchased to give to those back home (Graburn 1983, 44; Traganou 2004, 76; Vaporis 1995, 30).

Evidence of souvenirs as mementos and presents for loved ones appear in poems dating back to the *Man'yōshū*. Yet most *meibutsu* evolved from the commercialization of Edo-period temple towns. Nenzi writes, "Temples, shrines, and circuits first created the commercialized souvenir by putting a price tag on their amulets. The secular versions did not wait too long to enter the scene. Early world traveler, Engelbert Kaempfer, describes children selling keepsakes along the streets of Kyoto in the 1690s and adds, 'One thing is certain: nobody travels through the city without buying some goods made in

Miyako to take home for himself and others' " (2008, 149). This is still true today as souvenirs specially packaged to take home to family and friends can be found in the endless shops and stalls outside any major tourist destination.

While the formal system of sending representatives to travel is, of course, gone today, as is the practice of travel gifts, *omiyage* (bringing home souvenirs for friends and family) is alive and well. It is well known that Japan is a gift-giving culture. In anthropological terms, gift exchange networks function as extra-economic practices that uphold and signal not only hierarchy, wealth, and indebtedness, but also interconnected social relations (Hendry 1987; Mauss 1967). This is certainly true in Japan, where ritualized exchanges of gifts or cards at the new year and again in midsummer at Obon remained common well into the late twentieth century. While these practices are less common outside of older or more traditional circles today, department stores still stock beautifully wrapped prepackaged goods that can be sent directly to important relations, colleagues, and friends. Similarly, the practice of bringing *omiyage* home to friends and family shapes the kinds of souvenirs available in tourist locations. In particular, each region or city in Japan features local foods specially wrapped in packages made to travel well and look beautiful so that they can be taken home as gifts (Graburn 1987). No doubt souvenirs signify the duality of tourism—at once integral parts of travel experiences and memories and key examples of the crass commercialization of culture and history. Shopping for souvenirs for oneself or loved ones is an important part of touristic desires and the tourism economy, and souvenir shops all over Kyoto feature a wide range of goods from handcrafted items to the kitschiest commercial goods. Yet there is a sociality involved in souvenir culture, and the role souvenirs play in Japanese concepts of travel connects past and present practices.

Perhaps the best example of the ways that earlier travel patterns continue today is through school excursions (*shūgaku ryokō*). These school trips were established early in the Meiji period as a part and parcel of educational restructuring, taking groups of schoolchildren to sites of historical and cultural importance as a part of their education (Ishimori 1995, 19; Oedewald 2009, 116–118; Traganou 2004, 83). The most common destinations are places of historic and national significance—Kyoto, Nara, Tokyo, Hiroshima, Nagasaki, Hokkaido and Okinawa—although in recent years the destinations have diversified to include international sites. Today every child goes to Kyoto at some point in his or her time in school.[6] While school excursion visitors make up only about 2 percent of tourists to Kyoto, in October, late May, and June, Kyoto is overflowing with students—sometimes in large groups but more frequently in groups of three to five—escorted by a guide, often a cab driver hired for the day (Mr. K— 2012).[7] Near the throngs of kids outside of popular spots one can overhear plans to get a sweet or what souvenirs to take home: famous *yatsuhashi* sweets, Yojiya cosmetics, or tea from Uji—all famous Kyoto goods. It is hard to overstate the role such trips play in the national imaginary; nearly everyone has been to Kyoto and Tokyo at some point through one of these educational excursions.

I have concluded this section on prewar travel patterns in Japan with the example of school excursions because it is a ubiquitous feature of modern tourism in Japan. It is also an experience intended to introduce students to international tourists from abroad. Students traveling in uniform often practice their English by asking foreign tourists assigned questions are a nearly universal experience of Westerners in Japan. The features of group travel identified here in school excursions are exemplary of travel in Japan. Groups traveling to famous sites, eating local delicacies, and purchasing souvenirs for those back home all harken back to earlier patterns of travel from pilgrimages to early modern nation building through the transformation of *meisho* into heritage sites today.

Navigating the City: Shifts in Kyoto Tourism in the Postwar Period

The previous section charted how poetics, infrastructure, and the social practices of group travel have shaped the ways that people travel in Japan today. In this section, I return to the city of Kyoto itself, highlighting its tourist places and the material effects of recent trends in tourism on the city. Regarding tourism in Kyoto in the postwar period, several significant features stand out: the effect of global expos and events, group tours and mass tourism, and the turn to individualized and then personalized travel. More than historical details, each of these features can be felt through material remnants left in the city today. This shift to more recent events allows for an anthropological approach to the ways people travel today through the voices of tourism industry professionals. In order to examine the mass tourism of the high-growth years and the marketing of tourism in the recessionary years, this section emphasizes the people and places of Kyoto tourism in the late twentieth and early twenty-first centuries.

The life experiences of guides who have worked in Kyoto for over fifty years made not only for engaging conversations, but they also revealed some of the ways that tourism trends have changed over the years. Through my interviews with several of these guides, I learned how trends in tourism were influenced, in part, by national and international events, such as the 1964 Olympics. They also clarified the shift from scripted private and group tours to mass tourism to today's individualized and mediated approach. Scholarship on tour guides emphasizes the ways they shape tourists' experiences through their role as cultural mediators (Cohen 1985; Salazar 2005, 2010). The guides who told me their life histories were thinking about the ways that they presented Japanese culture, and Kyoto in particular, to international tourists. They were also attentive to the ways that the experiences they provided changed over the years, tailored to tourist interests alongside shifts in the structural features of tourism.

Almost all of my conversations with industry personnel, whether formal or informal, employee or volunteer, included a brief description of the ways that things had changed in tourism since the age of mass tourism. Such discussions almost always started with the Tokyo Olympics of 1964. The Olympics not only brought droves of international tourists to Tokyo, but also, in anticipation of their arrival, the first bullet train line was established along the old Tōkaidō road. To highlight the rich culture and economic recovery of Japan it was thought appropriate that the Olympic tourists be given a chance to see Kyoto and Osaka and that they could travel there in the world's first high-speed train. The economic and technological recovery that the bullet train symbolized also marks the birth of modern mass tourism in Japan. The promotional success of the Olympics was followed by the 1970 Osaka Banpaku, or Expo '70, the world's fair held in Osaka. Both events brought international tourists to Japan, but, more important, they initiated a domestic tourism boom that capped the start of the high-growth years and lasted well into the succeeding decades (Wilson 2012, 161). These events, as well as the tourist booms they prompted, brought with them a host of structural changes in transportation, traffic, accommodations, and city centers, at least throughout central Japan.

The peak of the growth years, the 1980s, witnessed a significant increase in the number of Japanese traveling overseas, paired with domestic tourism campaigns such as "Discover Japan" and then "Exotic Japan," which aimed at promoting tourism within Japan as a way to discover what had been lost in the process of high-growth modernization (Creighton 1997, 2009; Ivy 1988, 1995). While such campaigns set out to promote travel by rail, they also fueled individual travel with the rise of cars, a trend that the city of Kyoto is still battling today. As early as the 1980s there was a turn toward more individual travel, especially among younger generations (Ivy 1988; Moeran 1983). And yet group travel remained important, both overseas and domestically, for Japanese tourists into the 1990s, and bus tours are still available today. While European and North American tourists were much more interested in finding their own paths in the late twentieth century, group tours lingered as options for international tourists in Japan, due to language and culture barriers, both real and perceived, on the part of the tourists and the Japanese travel industry alike (Leheny 2003; Malcolm, Jankowska, and Eades 2007).

The economic downturn, which began in earnest in the early 1990s, slowly shifted the pace of life in Japan and has continued to do so for thirty years now. This shift dovetails with the turn to individualized tourism, which began in the 1980s and came to dominate travel for both domestic and international tourists in the following decade. As the guides' narratives below attest, in the 1990s there was a shift toward more individualized travel, with travelers finding their own way using guidebooks. This era also saw the rapid rise of the internet, bringing with it access to information online and an increasing ability to make reservations online and in a variety of languages; today, social media put sites and tourists in dialogue, allowing travelers to share information, plans, and experiences. Thus the life stories of guides in Kyoto index fundamental structural shifts in how people travel and show the ways that these shifts roughly follow the economic trends. And in the twenty-first century, tourism again became a hope for the economy through the Tourism Nation Japan policies discussed in the introduction.

Mass Tourism and Packaged Places

Over tea in their apartment in Kyoto, Johnnie Hillwalker (Hirōka Hajime) and his wife Shihoko talked to me about their years of giving tours in Kyoto.[8] Their life stories outlined many of the changes in Kyoto tourism over the past fifty years. "It was around 1962 when I took the tour guide licensing test, which is offered once a year," Johnnie started.[9] When he passed the test, Hirōka was hired by the JTB, the main national tourism company. "At the time" he said, "I lived in Osaka with my mother, but the JTB didn't need tour guides in Osaka because no foreigners went there, so I was assigned to Kyoto. Every day I traveled from [Osaka's] Umeda Station to Kyoto, but it was harder to get around in Kyoto back then. I had to take busses from the station all the way up to the Miyako Hotel, which is where all foreigners stayed. I met them there every day at 9:00 a.m. and returned them every night. It was the JTB's set plan" (Hirōka and Hirōka 2012).

According to Hirōka, at this time the JTB had the corner on the international visitor market in Japan. Most of the tourists were wealthy Americans, and all the guests traveled on all-inclusive tours set up by travel agents in their home communities who then contacted the JTB to organize the day-to-day schedule. When a travel agency contacted the JTB, it would find out where the visitors wanted to go (mostly Tokyo, Kyoto, Hiroshima, and Nagasaki) and for how long, and then the JTB would provide a set plan. "Back then, nothing was tailored for tourist preferences," Hirōka continued, "so we guides clearly knew what to expect and exactly what to do. When guests arrived at the hotel, they would get a schedule, very nicely printed on a small piece of paper, that would provide the next day's itinerary. At the end of the day they would get the schedule for the next day. It was all very organized, and people always commented on how efficient, easy, and organized it all was" (Hirōka and Hirōka 2012). When the guide arrived at the hotel in the morning, there was a hired car waiting for the guests for the day. The itinerary would state, "Meet your guide in the hotel lobby at 9:00 a.m., and you will go to Heian Shrine, the Golden Pavilion, and Nijō Castle in the morning and then head back to the hotel for lunch." Because of the differences in food and the expectations for comfort and Western amenities, Hirōka explained, "There were no suitable restaurants in town for these guests at all, so we always went back to the hotel to eat." At 1:30 p.m. the same car and guide would pick up guests and take them to Sanjusangendo (a Buddhist temple famous for its 1,001 statues of Kannon, the goddess of Mercy) and then a few shops for souvenirs. This, too, was set up by the JTB, and there were only four or five shops to which the guides were allowed to take tourists. According to Hirōka, visitors were taken to two or three different shops so that they would have some choices. The shops sold traditional items like fans and woodblock prints. After shopping, the visitors would go back to the hotel for the evening (Hirōka and Hirōka 2012). As can be seen here, over the course of our conversation about Hirōka's career as a tour guide, we incidentally discussed some of the most significant changes in tourism over the years.

Shihoko is also a tour guide. She moved to the Kyoto/Osaka area for Expo '70. She also worked for the JTB, and in the years following the expo she often worked with the larger bus tours, which were the main way for both Japanese and foreigners to travel in the 1970s and 1980s. The JTB launched Sunrise Tours in 1964. These prominently featured bus tours can still be found, although they have dwindled over time as the ways that people travel have shifted. The Sunrise Tour kiosk in Kyoto sits just outside the north entrance of the train station, by the city busses, although these days there is never a line.

According to the guides, there was a predictable pattern of places to visit and narration to accompany the ride. In what another interviewee referred to as the "bus tour days," tourists, both domestic and international, would get on a tour bus just outside of Kyoto Station; as they drove from site to site, a guide would tell them about the sites visible from their windows and those they were heading to visit. Shihoko said that she stood facing the visitors, her back to the upcoming sites, and it became so routine that she didn't even need to look out the window to see where in the city they were. Tours were often themed: gardens, World Heritage sites, and the like. It is easy to see why such tours would be popular in Kyoto in particular. For one thing, it would make getting to these sites much easier. The most popular sites are not right next to each other but tend to be scattered around the eastern or western hills, making it difficult for individuals to manage on their own and expensive if they do so by taxi. Just going to the top five tourist sites (Kiyomizu Temple, the Golden Pavilion, Nijō Castle, the Silver Pavilion, and Arashiyama), as one might do on a typical one- or two-day trip, still requires a handful of busses and quite a bit of walking (see map). Managing the distances between popular sites is something with which the city tourism industry still struggles, but in the 1970s and 1980s busses were the solution of choice.

This organizational structure of mass tourism in the 1970s and 1980s shaped the contours of the tourist industry through the

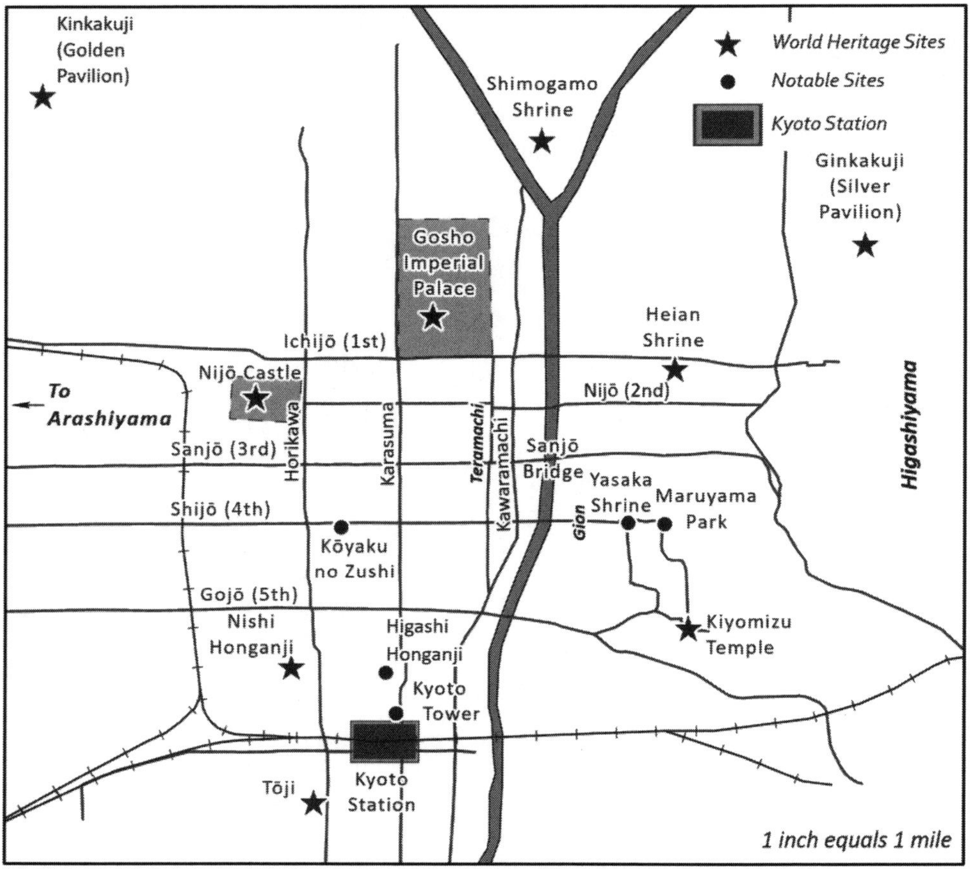

Points of interest in Kyoto. Cartography by Kimberly Anness.

increase and development of tour agencies and guides to accommodate such group bus tours. This structure also influenced the growth and location of hotels and other tourist venues. This was highlighted in my interview with Mr. B—, a manager from the Westin Miyako Hotel, the second oldest hotel in Kyoto, built in 1890 (where Mr. Hirōka used to pick up guests).[10] As Mr. B— walked me through the meandering hallways of the hotel, he explained the ways that the building itself has morphed over its 120-year life to suit the needs of new tourist trends. One particularly apt example was a long hallway with dated orange carpeting from the 1970s. This area, he explained, was built in 1970 for Expo '70 and was connected to the main building only in the 1980s or early 1990s. "This eastern wing of the hotel is comprised of four floors, each with forty identical rooms plus two smaller rooms, and a bus holds exactly forty passengers and two drivers. So, basically, you can see in the structure of the building a section for four busloads of Expo '70 goers," he explained. The expo aside, bus tours continued to be popular even as individual travel was increasing. This is a tangible example of the ways traces of mass tourism can be seen throughout the city. The school excursions, discussed above, are another example of the material effects of mass travel. Many mid-size Japanese hotels are built to accommodate not only individual travelers, but also busloads of students during their yearly trips to Kyoto. There are several other remnants of mass tourism in Kyoto today, such as the Nishijin Textile Center and Gion Corner, both of which aim to explain traditional arts to international tourists, and the Kyoto Handicraft Center, which in its heyday provided a one-stop souvenir shop for busloads of tourists. While all of the mass tourism institutions discussed here are still in use, they feel a bit outdated and underutilized today; in the turn to individual travel tourists seek less structured and sterilized experiences.

Individual Travel and the Diversification of Tourism

Two threads about the way people travel today can be seen in Hirōka's life story: individualization and experience. These trends speak beyond Kyoto tourism, dovetailing with current tourism scholarship, which focuses on performance and mobility. Theories of tourism that focus on performance are attentive to the ways that tour industry personnel create experiences for tourists and sometimes literally perform for them, as well as to the ways that tourists themselves shape sites through their usage, ways of participating, or engagement (Bærenholdt et al. 2004; Coleman and Crang 2002; Haldrup and Larsen 2010; Rickly-Boyd et al. 2014; Urry and Larsen 2011). So, too, there is increasing attention to the multiplicity of reasons why tourists may visit a site and to the understandings they come away with (Bærenholdt et al. 2004; Light 2015). Outside of this body of scholarship the guides and industry personnel with whom I spoke all indicated an increase in the twenty-first century in tourists seeking more personal experiences beyond just seeing the World Heritage sites. The shift here is to more individualized travel, both less scripted and structured or in smaller groups.

From the 1990s on there has been a steady shift to travel in smaller groups of family or friends (Oedewald 2009, 114). According to the Kyoto City Tourism Survey reports, in 2003 10 percent of tourists traveled in groups; in 2011 it was 4.5 percent, and by 2017 that figure was down to 2 percent, almost half of which were school excursions (Kyoto City Tourism Office 2012, 2018). In the past decade over 40 percent of tourists to Kyoto traveled in pairs, and over 25 percent traveled alone, a significant shift from the heyday of bus tours (Kyoto City Tourism Office 2012, 2018). Many of the veteran tour guides, industry personnel, and local shopkeepers with whom I spoke consistently mentioned the *Lonely Planet Kyoto* guidebooks as a part of the changes in the tourism industry. Mr. I—, from the Kyoto Tourism Association, was bemused by some of the obscure temples and shrines that appeared in *Lonely Planet Kyoto*. "Suddenly" he explained, "there were foreigners wandering around a neighborhood way out west or up north, where tourists never go. When locals asked them if they were lost, they held up the *Lonely Planet Kyoto* guidebook and said they were looking for a small neighborhood shrine or something. It was so surprising" (Mr. I— 2012). While neither the *Lonely Planet Kyoto* guidebooks nor their authors are actually responsible for these shifts, the focus on traveling cheaply, exploring on one's own, and finding unusual places emphasized by the Lonely Planet franchise are a part of this shifting tourism terrain. This notion of finding one's own way using guidebooks or advice from tourist information centers and wandering around out of the "tourist bubble" has come to characterize tourism today, although there are certainly still plenty of tourists who are interested in ease of travel and seeing the famous sites. It is important to note that when tourists wander off the beaten path through local neighborhoods, it can be disruptive, especially when numbers swell, a point to which I will return (Germann Molz 2014).

This sense of a turn to individualized travel came up as the final phase of the Hirōkas' careers. Both Hirōkas, like all employees for large companies in Japan, had to retire when they turned sixty-five. While many continued to freelance for the JTB, Mr. Hirōka was eager to create his own tour: "I always had ideas for how they could make their tours better," he recounted. "Too many unique ideas for the JTB," Mrs. Hirōka chimed in laughing. Mr. Hirōka continued:

> I asked the JTB how many tourists they take care of a year. They said about 30,000. Back then we all knew that Kyoto had 300,000

> tourists a year, so I wondered what happens to the other 270,000? At that point, in the 1990s, there were still a lot of bus tours, but it was starting to change. More and more people were reading *Lonely Planet,* and people could find their own way to Kyoto; there were increasingly okay hotels and restaurants for foreigners. So there were many more options for finding and connecting to tourists who weren't contracted exclusively with the JTB. Back then, there was a big JTNO office just across from the station, and everyone would arrive at the station and then cross the street to the JTNO; it was a madhouse. Foreigners would arrive at the JNTO and say, "Where can I stay, and what can I see?" There weren't internet booking options like today, and if they didn't speak Japanese, which most didn't, they needed this kind of service (Hirōka and Hirōka 2012).

In this context, Hirōka set out to craft a tour that could cater to these new travelers. Pragmatically, hiring and organizing a bus for a reasonable price would be difficult for an individual, so Hirōka hit on the idea of creating a walking tour that would start right at the station, where everyone entered the city. He started his tour in 1996 and named it "Walk in Kyoto, Talk in English—Johnnie Hillwalker's Kyoto Tour." As he talked about how he created this tour, I noted that what made it stand out was that it wandered around in the back streets so that one got a glimpse of places that were off the beaten path and not on the typical list of famous must-see sites. Mr. Hirōka laughed and said, "I didn't plan it that way. I needed places we could walk to from the station to make it easy, and to keep it cheap I needed those places to be free" (Hirōka and Hirōka 2012). According to Mr. Hirōka, this style of tour just happened to dovetail with tourist trends that had shifted around that time toward a desire for unique, behind the scenes or "authentic" (*honmono*) views of Kyoto, so over the years his five-hour walking tour evolved.

Today the tour still first visits Higashi Honganji and ends near the hill leading up to Kiyomizu Temple, the area known for pottery craftsmanship.[11] Along the way tourists see small fan and lantern workshops, a Shinto shrine, Buddhist alter and prayer bead craftsmen, the original Nintendo office building, one of the smaller geisha districts, and a community center dedicated to urban planning (*machizukuri*), and there is a small break for tea and a traditional sweet along the way. In 2010, Hirōka asked WaRaiDo Guides, a private tour company, to take over the walking tour, although for a few years he continued to run it occasionally. WaRaiDo markets the "Walk in Kyoto, Talk in English" tour as follows: "No touristy spots; look inside the real Japan" (WaRaiDo Guides 2017).

Another Kyoto tour guide known as Samurai Joe (Okada Joe) has been running a series of experiential walking tours for several decades. I met him as he was stocking brochures for his newest tour, "Cool Walking Tour Japan," in the Kyoto Tourist Information Center in June 2012. Like Hirōka, Okada worked for the JTB and specialized in entertaining and educating large bus tour groups throughout the early postwar years. His latest tour takes visitors on a five-hour walk north of Hirōka's tour, and it discusses traditional crafts, Buddhism, the city's history, and postwar changes along the way. Like Hirōka, Okada sought out places he could take guests for free and built up relationships with local businesses along the way. When I attended one of his tours in 2012, it ended at a typical *shotengai* (shopping arcade) out of the main tourist route, a small covered street lined with small shops and restaurants—the kind of place where locals do their daily shopping. There, guests were given small samples of fried chicken and fresh tofu, foods that the average person out running errands might pick up. With its 1970s feel, the shopping arcade embodies the character of daily life in Japan, a far cry from the tourist bubble of the historic preservation districts of Kyoto. The experiences of Hirōka and Okada exemplify changes in tourism globally and in Kyoto specifically. The turn away from going to famous places to seeking off-the-beaten-path or non-touristy spots is evidenced in the creation of these two five-hour walking tours. At the same time, there has been a shift from large group tours and even smaller scripted, managed tours toward finding one's own way out of the crowds.

This form of individual travel is further structured through the Kyoto Tourist Information Center (Kyo-Navi; short for Kyoto Navigation) in Kyoto Station. Until 2010, there were two tourist centers in Kyoto Station: one, located centrally on the second floor, served Japanese tourists; the other, for foreigners, was located decidedly out of the way on the ninth floor. The international center was hard to find but it was larger, less crowded, and it offered more resources because it supported foreign tourists and residents alike. The perception at the time was that Japanese tourists and international tourists had different interests and needs. However, in March 2010 the two offices were combined. The explanation for this change is telling and reveals the increase of Kyoto's national and international appeal. As

Mr. Y—, a staff member at the Kyo-Navi, recounted, "We found that Japanese tourists and foreign tourists were primarily interested in the same things: tours to Kinkakuji, Kiyomizu Temple, Gion, and the like. So it made sense to centralize our operations" (Mr. Y— 2012). At a bright location on the main corridor of Kyoto station, the Kyo-Navi is a one-stop shop for all tourist information, from pamphlets on current museum and temple exhibits to updates on what flowers are blooming. There is a counter with six stations staffed by employees able to provide guidance and tour and hotel bookings in Japanese, English, Chinese, Korean, French, Spanish, German, and Thai. For ten days in June 2012, I conducted fieldwork in the Kyo-Navi, talking with employees and tourists alike. People came in for information about how to get where they wanted to go, how to use public transportation, and what to see and what to do. Some just browsed the wall of brochures highlighting current events and things to see and do in the city. Some used the one or two computers available for booking rooms while others headed right to the counter lines to ask specific questions and get help. This relatively new center serves the same purpose as the JNTO office that was across the street from the station until the late 1990s, but today, it is easier to find one's way. Fliers abound, but the best information, guidance, and maps are kept behind the desk. Here, too, we see a structural shift in both travel habits and industry technologies offering a range of ways to find information, whether general or specific for a visit to Kyoto.

This turn to individualized travel—from mass to micro—is accompanied by a shift to a potentially more engaged form of tourism. Finding one's own way and venturing out of the tourist bubble provide for more *in situ* forms of travel. The goal is to encounter rather than simply see the sights and sounds of a place. Inherent in this touristic desire is a notion of discovering the "real" or "authentic" Japan. To be sure, this notion has long been sought by tourists, as evidenced as early as 1881 in Isabella Bird's (1881, 1) account of her travels in Japan, *Unbeaten Tracks in Japan*. Still today, the desire to experience the "real" Japan includes getting out of Tokyo, perhaps even past the Golden Route (Tokyo, Mt. Fuji, Kyoto, Hiroshima); going to places off the beaten path; experiencing tradition by staying in a Zen temple, participating in a tea ceremony, staying in a *ryokan* or even a traditional-style rental through Airbnb with tatami and futons rather than Western-style beds; or walking around the tourist areas of Kyoto in kimono.

The turn to individualized travel in the 1980s and 1990s marks a turn in the ways that people travel from "seeing" (*miru*) to "interacting" (*fureau*). In the earlier model of mass tours, people traveled in large groups, often with a guide or two, visiting famous places. Marilyn Ivy sums up the importance of this kind of travel in the world of Japanese tourism: " 'Discover Japan' summed up the cultural nostalgia of an entire decade, the decade of the 1970s. The phrase took on a resonance that far exceeded its pragmatic function as a publicity slogan for the railways, as it came to symbolize a generation's desire to escape to its origins. Unlike conventional Japanese tourism—in which groups travel together to view and photograph famous sights such as Mt. Fuji or Kyoto—'Discover Japan' advocated a more solitary and small-scale form of travel" (1988, 21). The shift to smaller-scale travel allows for interaction in several different ways. As seen here, booking one's own trip allows a level of individualization but also requires more knowledge of a place, its sites, transportation, and accommodations. Further, moving away from the predetermined or scripted tour, off-the-beaten-path tourism brings tourists out of the tourist bubble. Although this kind of travel does not guarantee more encounters, it has the goal and the potential to do so. Changes in the Kyo-Navi, as well as in the two walking tours discussed here, exemplify this shift to interactive tourism, in terms of both tourists' desires and industry structures. In what follows, we shall see the ways that this individualization and desire for interaction have shifted again in the twenty-first century toward a further personalization of experience.

Experiencing Culture: Domestic Tourist Experiences in Kyoto

Building on the trends toward individual travel in recent years, the ante on personal experiences has been raised. Hirōka's account of his new tour speaks to this trend; his tour meanders just off the beaten path, highlighting local craftsmen and local life. Today, tourists—domestic and international—search for personal experiences of everyday Japan, and touristic desires have shifted again from "encountering" (*fureau*) to "experience" (*taiken*). This trend of "experiencing *my* Kyoto" fits global and national tourist trends and yet harkens back to the pull that drew Isabella Bird and countless others to Japan over the years. Yet even as trends change in the ways people travel and tourist destinations are structured, these various ways of traveling are not mutually exclusive. Just as large bus tours have continued to be offered even as more and more tourists have wanted to find their own way, so too not all tourists have the time or inclination to participate in a more embodied experience. Still, identifying the overall shift from "seeing" to "interacting" to "experiencing" highlights shifts in tourist patterns in Kyoto and beyond in ways that are ideational, material, and social.

While much of this discussion of tourist experiences has focused on international tourists, Japanese tourists comprise the largest demographic of tourists traveling to Kyoto by a significant margin, 93.5 percent (Kyoto City Tourism Office 2018). Moreover, domestic tourists also travel to Kyoto to experience tradition and culture, although, as Nelson Graburn (1995, 59) puts it, for Japanese travelers, the discovery is of "us," not "them." In part, this is an extension of ongoing tourism campaigns that aim to attract domestic tourists from the urban centers to more rural or peripheral locations so as to aid local development. In this regard, Kyoto sits in an interesting spot: it is never the target of national policies because it has always been a prime tourist location, and yet it benefits from any promotion of Japanese culture. To be sure, the emphasis on "experiencing Kyoto like a local" today is much more subtle for domestic tourists. Yet this is, to some extent, a matter of degree; tourism brochures and guidebooks in Japanese play up the difference in Kyoto etiquette and culture. The use of Kyoto words, like *ōkini* instead of *arigatō* (thank you), is encouraged and explained in Japanese tourism materials, playing up the distinctness or exoticism of Kyoto for a domestic audience.[12]

Certainly the ubiquitous school excursions are an important example of traveling to Kyoto to experience Japanese history and culture. The Kyoto City Tourism Office provides suggestions for planning school excursions through a website, as well as books and DVDs that include lists of "experiences" for which students can sign up. In recent years the number of and emphasis on craft or tea ceremony experiences has increased in promotional materials (Mr. I— 2012; Oedewald 2009, 70). Beyond educational school excursions, Kyoto markets Japanese culture and tradition to domestic tourists more broadly. One apt example is the "Kimono Passport." Each year a Kimono Passport is released offering small gifts or discounts to anyone wearing kimono around the city.[13] The discounts are offered at a wide range of local businesses, from temples and shrines, to public transportation, to restaurants and souvenir shops. Even before the kimono rental boom (discussed in chapter 5), it was more common to see people in Kyoto out and about in kimono, although it was still not a large percentage. The Kimono Passport can be used by international visitors, but all the information is in Japanese, signaling a primarily domestic audience. Moreover, as of 2019, it was not widely advertised at the many kimono rental shops.

Domestic tourists also participate in experiences like the tea ceremony, short versions of which are available at popular shrines like the Golden Pavilion and the Heian Shrine. Eating traditional Kyoto foods, especially *yūdofu* (boiled fresh tofu) or *shojin ryori* (plant-based Buddhist monk food), is also popular, as are demonstrations and hands-on experiences of making traditional Kyoto foods, especially *wagashi* (Japanese-style sweets). In fact, as of 2016, the Kyoto City Tourism Office (2016) added a question about cultural experiences (*bunka taiken*) to its domestic survey for the first time, a category that has been on the international survey since 2011. Even staying in a *ryokan* is a luxury that some associate with traveling in Kyoto. One middle-aged Japanese couple with whom I spoke in the Tourist Information Center said, "We don't have tatami in our apartment in Tokyo, so when we come to Kyoto each year, we always stay in a *ryokan* so that we can really experience the *wafu* [Japanese-style] life; it is Kyoto-esque." In this instance what is "different" is a sense of heritage or quintessential Japaneseness experienced in Kyoto by domestic tourists. As these examples attest, the language of "authentic" and Japanese experiences speak to both domestic and international tourists in Kyoto today, albeit in different ways.

New Frontiers, Old Challenges: Experiencing Twenty-First-Century Kyoto

In keeping with the focus on infrastructure in this chapter, the internet and new media provide new opportunities and challenges to the tourist industry today (Urry and Larsen 2011, 54–60). While the shift to personal tourist experiences is not exclusively driven by the advent and evolution of the internet, it certainly is a part of the turn. The internet affects tourism in two significant ways: it puts trip planning in the hands of individual travelers with greater ease, and social media add a new layer of crowd sourcing and peer-to-peer advertising (Seaton et al. 2017, 205–262). One way that the internet has shifted travel in Japan is in the ease of finding and booking one's own trip, from airfare to lodging to transportation (Urry and Larsen 2011, 57–58). In Hirōka's account, the earliest trips to Japan were all packages put together by a travel agency like the JTB. Due to differences in language and culture, international tourists needed guidance. Even in the early 1990s, when I first started traveling to Japan, hotel reservations were made by phone, and booking lodgings was one of the main features of a tourist information office. Yet both of these models involved deals between hotels and providers, as well as a sense that there were particular hotels that were good for international travelers. Today, one can book a hotel in Kyoto online in almost any language through a host of sites, and the selection is almost overwhelming.

Scholars writing on the sociology of tourism highlight the ways that infrastructure, in this case the internet, has shifted patterns of travel. Notably, Jennie Germann Molz's (2012) research on couch surfing and social media tours demonstrates the ways that traveling post-internet provides us with new ways to both connect and disconnect from each other as we travel. This is one aspect that has developed during the course of my research, as the Kyoto tourism industry—government offices and local businesses and organizations—has attempted to increase infrastructure for such networked travel within the city, as well as to enhance outreach on social media. As the popularity of online maps and guides increases, reliable access to the internet poses new infrastructure challenge for tourist locations. In Kyoto in 2012, "Wifi Kyoto" was newly online. In main tourist areas, like the long shopping arcade areas along the Shijō artery, between Karasuma and Kawaramachi roads, one could get free wifi on the street, although in 2012 the log-in process was so cumbersome that it was not worth the effort. In the intervening years wifi has been added at most bus stops, train stations, and select locations in the main part of the city, although it is still not completely user friendly (there is a registration process that must be repeated every thirty minutes). In addition, major convenience stores and many coffee shops and restaurant chains have free wifi hotspots (with registration). All of these options are well advertised throughout the city and at tourist information centers.

Finally, tourists use social media to plan their trips, checking sites, travel blogs, and vlogs, as well as Facebook and Instagram for travel advice and recommendations (Urry and Larsen 2011, 59–60). This is one of the significant ways that new media connect us as travelers in new ways (Germann Molz 2012). In recent years, Kyoto tour guide companies, associations, and the city offices have explored ways to promote the city through social media. Today, each major tourism organization has a Facebook, Instagram, and Twitter account, along with increasingly user-friendly travel navigation apps. In particular, the "Visit Kyoto," "*Kyototte ii ne!!*" or "Like! Kyoto" Facebook pages stand out as sites where events, photos, and videos are promoted, and tourists add in their own experiences and suggestions. Thus even in traditional Kyoto, mobile tourism and crowd sourcing has begun to shape the tourist landscape in both official and unofficial ways. Not unlike earlier patterns discussed here, new media shape tourism in Kyoto through the addition of wired and wireless infrastructure; they also shape the ways that the tourism industry reaches tourists; and they shape the ways that tourists seek information, personalize their experiences, and craft online connections, profiles, and stories about their travel.

The Challenge of Overtourism

Thus far, I have highlighted the prominence of famous places from history and literature, the evolving role of infrastructure, and the significance of earlier travel patterns in tourism today. Each of these plays a role in Kyoto today. Perhaps most notably, many of the *meisho* in Kyoto are still favorite tourist destinations. I have also discussed shifts in tourism patterns, through both material remains on tourist locations and changes in social practice—from "seeing" to "interacting" to "experiencing." Yet no discussion of travel would be complete without a discussion of the challenges and complaints that come with tourism, and here too we see that different styles of tourism bring different issues.

While Kyoto has always been a tourist destination, tourism has boomed in the twenty-first century through ambitious tourism promotion plans (discussed in chapter 2), as well as the wider Tourism Nation Japan policies. While tourism always brings complaints and challenges, in Kyoto two infrastructural constraints have come to the fore in recent years—namely, traffic and lodging. Part of the appeal of Kyoto is the way it is contained by mountains on three sides, making the core of the city relatively compact; however, the tourist locations are scattered throughout the city. The train lines are primarily at the outer edges of the city center, and the subway is relatively small, making busses or cabs the main form of transportation in the city. The north entrance to Kyoto Station is dominated by a large, open city bus center, where there are nearly always long lines for busses heading to the prime tourist spots. Enhancing the ease of use, especially for foreign tourists, has been a feature of all recent tourism plans. But it is the traffic that dominates complaints about the tourist industry in Kyoto. Many a tourist, cab driver, and tour guide has cited traffic jams heading out to Arashiyama in November as a prime example of what is now called "overtourism." As of 2012, the city started a "Walking City Kyoto" campaign to discourage the use of personal cars for tourism, and as of 2017 there has been a 20 percent decrease in car traffic (Kyoto City Tourism Office 2016). In addition, one main artery in the center of town, Shijō, gets backed up with both cars and pedestrians from Karasuma to the eastern hills. To be in keeping with a pedestrian-friendly city, in recent years the sidewalks have been widened and bus stops consolidated, making it easier to navigate while constraining car traffic. In the summer of 2019, city staff manned bus stops all along Shijō, helping travelers navigate the complicated bus system and keeping lines neat and tidy.

The other consistent infrastructural issue in Kyoto is lodging. Here too the peak seasons are illustrative. During the fall and spring, rooms throughout the city must be booked well in advance. The city is often booked at 80–90 percent as much as a year in advance at these times (Mrs. A— 2012). Kyoto is known for its small-scale traditional Japanese-style inns, or *ryokan*.[14] Smaller than hotels, *ryokan* provide tatami rooms with a small table and chairs; futons are put out for guests in the evening; often breakfast and sometimes dinner are included with the stay. The sleeping quarters are private, but the bath is traditionally shared. While Kyoto is full of *ryokan,* there is also a whole host of hotels throughout the city. In addition, during my fieldwork people in the tourist industry all mentioned the need for a five-star hotel in Kyoto. The 2015 tourism plan prioritized luxury tourists and included plans for several five-star hotels (Kyoto City 2015). As of the summer of 2019, several were being built near the station. In part, the issue is the same as in any other urban area where tourism has expanded: where can space be found for more hotels? In anticipation of the Olympic crowds, a new cluster of hotels has popped up throughout the city.

In the twenty-first century, the sharing economy has reached the hospitality industry through peer-to-peer lodging systems like Vacation Rental by Owner, Couchsurfing, and Airbnb. Each of these companies aims to make travel both cheaper and more personalized. They are all organized via apps on a mobile phone or a website.

Through these sites, one can arrange to stay in a home, with others or on one's own, and "live like the locals" rather than in a standardized hotel. During my research Airbnb entered the Japanese market, setting off a succession of new legislation. When I was conducting research in Kyoto in the spring of 2017, "the *minpaku* problem" was a topic of grave discussion among industry personnel, both official and volunteer. *Minpaku* (民泊) refers to short-term shared private lodging. According to those with whom I spoke, local residents were upset that their quiet neighborhoods were now being disrupted by tourists. As one tour guide explained it, "Suddenly in a quiet neighborhood without tourists, there appeared foreigners who rolled their suitcases down the street, *gatta gatta/gatta gatta/gatta gatta,* late at night; they talked and walked loudly when they came home and didn't know when to put the trash out or how to do it properly" (Mrs. M— 2017). These complaints are not particular to Japan; they fit with the issues that major tourist cities are facing; however, fastidious trash handling and neighborhood etiquette are a part of this discussion, especially in Kyoto.[15]

In July 2017, the Private Temporary Lodging Law (Jyūtaku Shukuhaku Jigyōhō or Minpaku Shinhō) was passed. Referred to as the "Minpaku Law," it made room rentals for short-term stays legal (before this time Airbnb was operating but technically was not legal), but there were restrictions on the size and type of room; it also put a cumbersome licensing process in place. When the law went into effect in June 2018, Japan and Airbnb were in the news as Airbnb revoked 80 percent of the listings in Japan, canceling countless reservations with them (Kawaguchi, Yusuke, and Natsuki 2018). Kyoto put even tighter restrictions into place, requiring that an owner live within eight hundred meters of a rented space (Eric Johnson 2018). These ordinances are controversial. Many feel that these laws protect their quiet neighborhoods, especially with the ramp up of tourism as the Olympics approach; yet others appreciate the flexibility that *minpaku* rentals provide for tourists to travel more economically and the cultural exchanges that can be rewarding through such arrangements. Yet for towns where it is difficult to attract tourists or get large hotels built, options like Airbnb have allowed for a kind of peer-to-peer tourism to emerge (Germann Molz 2014; Gibson and Molz 2007; Schreiber 2018). This is even the case in Kyoto, where lodging can be hard to find in peak tourist times. In all of these examples, we see the weaving together of marketing, structural and infrastructural management, and tourist demands, which come together in tourism. And these examples are all driven by touristic desires for more personalized experiences.

Finally, as tourist numbers have soared in the early twenty-first century through the Tourism Nation Japan policies and Kyoto's own ambitious tourism promotion plans, overtourism became the new catchphrase in conversations about Kyoto. Throughout Japan in 2018 and 2019 almost any news story about Kyoto decried in graphic detail the crowds and bad behaviors of tourists. Images of graffiti carved into the famous bamboo in Arashiyama and tourists harassing *maiko* (apprentice geisha) in Gion abounded. And the problems of overtourism dominated the most recent mayoral election in early 2020. To be sure, Kyoto has always been crowded with tourists and yet in the past decade the tourists have come to overwhelm the city. The following chapter takes a close look at Kyoto's tourism promotion plans and some of the problems wrought by overtourism through the lens of heritage and hospitality.

Ж Ж Ж

This chapter has provided a broader context for tourism in contemporary Kyoto through an outline of historic and contemporary travel routes and patterns, both material and conceptual famous places, reasons for travel, and seeking new experiences. The ways to travel, as discussed here, have changed over time—from an emphasis on *meisho* to large-scale bus tours, to seeking off-the-beaten-path tours, to small-group personal travel that encourages more interaction with locals, to the increase in hands-on or personal experiences in the city, the contours of which shape the cityscape as well. Thus tourist city Kyoto both creates and responds to the desires of tourists who arrive to experience its offerings. Ultimately, pilgrims, sightseers, mass tourists, off-the-beaten-path tourists, and travel-like-the-locals tourists all, in different ways, at different times, seek different experiences. What defines the sense of difference can be something out of the everyday—as in the case of excursionists from nearby Osaka who come to Kyoto to see the cherry blossoms—or it can be an exotic culture—as in the case of international tourists who come to Japan and stay in a *ryokan* to see a different way of living; or the sense of difference can be ways that "the past is a foreign country" (Lowenthal 1985)—as throngs of Japanese and international tourists alike travel to Kyoto to experience Japanese heritage. The chapters that follow address these very issues—heritage atmosphere and the Kyoto brand, the aesthetics of seasons in a new light-up event, small-scale tourist sites commemorating and celebrating Japan's modern heritage, and the crafting of Kyoto experiences exemplified by the Kimono rental boom—all examining ways of experiencing Japanese heritage in a global tourist city.

Chapter 2

A Brand of History

Heritage and Hospitality in Kyoto City Tourism

In the spring of 2012, a new venue opened that caused quite a stir—the Kyoto Aquarium (Kyoto Suizokukan). While the aquarium opened in March—just in time for spring break travelers—when my family arrived in January, the controversy was already stirring. The new aquarium was built just a mile west of Kyoto Station in Umekoji Park, a large public park that already housed a steam engine railway museum; a playground; and ample green space for sports, walking, and picnics. The controversy surrounding the new aquarium was essentially about the Kyoto brand. "Why an aquarium here?" seemed to be the main question—and all of the responses spoke to the identity of the city. Detractors argued that the venue did not fit Kyoto: the aquarium had no links to Kyoto's history; Kyoto was not even near an ocean, and nearby Osaka had a world-class aquarium on its bay; aquariums were not eco-friendly; and, worst of all, the development money was all from Tokyo. As one a cab driver remarked, "Kyoto shouldn't build large concrete buildings; those are for Tokyo." And one local business owner quipped, "It's just like the new station—doesn't fit Kyoto's image or style" (a reference to similar controversies over the building of the "new" station in 1997).[1] Proponents argued that the aquarium would be a great place for local families. Indeed, the families in my son's school were excited about having a new place to take young kids, although when the aquarium opened, it was more expensive than had been imagined. Finally, the main rationale that the city officials gave was that the aquarium would attract new tourists to

Kyoto, including families with young children, who are not among the traditional tourist demographics for Kyoto.[2]

This small controversy highlights several themes that I will draw out in this chapter, focusing on heritage and the Kyoto brand. Each of the issues examined in this chapter weaves together the broader sense of what is appropriate for Kyoto, its style, history, and character; the material effects on the townscape and city life;[3] and the ways that the economic prominence of the tourism industry shapes these conversations. In some ways, this debate is par for the course in the kinds of conversations cities have when they are building a new large venue, be it a museum, a stadium, or a park; and certainly the trend to renovate the urban core is a global one. Typically, these conversations lead to debates about economics, usage, and identity (Spirou 2011). But in Kyoto, at the forefront and in the background of all such conversations is the prominence of history and culture, shaped through the city's position as the ancient capital. It is this feature that draws millions of domestic and international tourists every year, and this economic sector shapes the city's contours today.

That Kyoto is a city where heritage tourism looms large is hardly a surprise; in discussions of heritage it is often listed as a city that has become a museum to itself; some of the city's own documents use this language. Yet there is no one simple "heritage" in Kyoto. Long before the first sites were inscribed on the UNESCO World Heritage List in 1994, Kyoto had landscape policies and heritage preservation ordinances in place to retain or restore a historic atmosphere. Moreover, history and heritage are never reducible to one particular moment in time. Heritage in Kyoto is layered—walking along the streets of the city center, one is likely to encounter a tall stone marker for a historic spot from the Heian period or the Edo period or the Meiji period; the marker may be for the aristocracy or commoners, for pro-*bakufu* or anti-*bakufu* heroes,[4] or for literary greats and their characters from across the ages. Next to that marker one may also find a newer wooden historical site sign marking the same event or a different one in the same location. (An example can be seen in figure 4.3 in chapter 4, showing the markers for the location of Sakamoto Ryōma's death.) In addition, the city is peppered with new buildings, hotels, cafes, and businesses with distinctly Kyoto-style facades. Walking around Kyoto, one may encounter a traditional-style townhouse sandwiched between concrete high-rises from the late twentieth century, all these around the corner from a street that bears the markings of the import of modern Western-style brick architecture as the city renovated in the early twentieth century; so too, one finds traditional cobblestone streets abutting aging asphalt. The layers of historical features indicate not just attention to but also the conscious crafting of a sense of heritage throughout the city. These features are part of what makes Kyoto appealing and what makes it feel historical to visitors, but they are also important sources of pride for citizens, a part of what makes the city a unique place to live. In all these complex ways, heritage is created, preserved, renovated, and marketed in Kyoto today. This chapter builds on the concepts of experiential tourism discussed in chapter 1 by laying out two fundamental trends in contemporary tourism in Kyoto: heritage and hospitality.

Emma Waterton and Steve Watson astutely point out that the authenticity people desire in heritage tourism today is rooted in experiences: "The coffee you sip in the Piazza San Marco in Venice is more than an infusion of the coffee bean; it is more than a complex product of the tourism industry; it is an experience writ large around you, keenly felt. And, if you have any doubts that it is more than a commodity, you will find the evidence in the bill" (2015, 8). What you purchase sipping coffee in Venice or *matcha* in Kyoto is at once a hot beverage, a break from walking and sightseeing, and heritage atmosphere. Of course, a tourist (or anyone for that matter) can "feel" an encounter with history or culture at a place that is nothing but artifice. And yet, as the examples in this chapter attest, there is something deeper going on in the ways that multiple actors care about a heritage atmosphere in Kyoto for tourism and for living. To understand the living heritage atmosphere of Kyoto, in what follows I will examine the crafting of the Kyoto brand through city tourism policies, an *in situ* example of heritage renovation, and the challenges to hospitality that masses of tourists bring. In Kyoto, the heritage atmosphere is bound up in history, experience, and hospitality.

The Kyoto Brand: Urban Cultural Heritage

When I arrived in Kyoto in the winter of 2012 to begin this research, I was first on the lookout for a logo or slogan for the Kyoto brand. We are, after all, in the era of branding, when companies, cities, and even nations pay millions for the creation of a unified vision complete with a logo, a slogan, a color scheme, fonts, and (in Japan) mascots. My initial conversations with city officials and industry personnel were rife with references to "the Kyoto brand," but there is no such identifiable branding in Kyoto. As one city employee quipped, "The Kyoto brand goes without saying." It is a palpable sense of history and culture that attracts most tourists to Kyoto, and it is this notion of heritage that most of the tourism industry personnel with whom I spoke meant when they referred to "the Kyoto brand." Romantically referred to as the "heart of Japan," Kyoto's thousand-year reign as the capital; its association with the Heian period's flourishing of art and literature; its traditional crafts like weaving, kimono, fans, and incense; and its myriad of temples, shrines, and gardens all make Kyoto a nexus of history/culture/nature that is embraced as quintessentially Japanese. This is how the city has long been portrayed, and it is this sense that the city markets as the "Kyoto brand."

Indeed, domestic tourists begin to learn the contours of the Kyoto brand in elementary school classes on literature, language, and history. The system of school excursions, discussed in chapter 1, ensures that one's first tour of Kyoto happens as a part of his or her compulsory education. For international tourists Kyoto is frequently a secondary destination, and only about 25 percent of international tourists go to Kyoto during their time in Japan (Japan Tourism Agency 2017c). Despite such differences in numbers and knowledge, there is a remarkable similarity among the top attractions for both domestic and international tourists. According to Kyoto City's tourism survey data, the top five places that Japanese tourists consistently say they visited as of 2015 were Kiyomizu Temple, Arashiyama, the Golden Pavilion, Nijō Castle, and the Silver Pavilion. For international tourists the top sites were Kiyomizu Temple, the Golden Pavilion, Nijō Castle, and the Silver Pavilion; recently Fushimi Inari and the Kyoto Station area have been added to the top grouping (Kyoto City Tourism Office 2008–2016).

In recent years, as the number of international visitors has tripled, there has been a shift in top sites for Japanese tourists. In 2016 and 2017 several new walking, shopping, and sightseeing clusters were added to the list. These included the Kyoto Station area, Kawaramachi, the Sanjō and Shijō area, and the *Kinukake no michi* (a walk in the western part of the city connecting three famous temples—the Golden Pavilion, Ryoanji, and Ninannji) (Kyoto City Tourism Office 2017, 2018). The city survey data also report that Japanese tourists "were most moved by" the famous places (*meisho*), temples and shrines, nature, museums, and the town's atmosphere.[5] For international tourists the top contenders were temples and shrines, nature, history and culture, the hospitality of the people, and the beauty of the city (Kyoto City Tourism Office 2015–2019). Landscape, cultural heritage, and temples and shrines are not surprising categories to have on a survey in Kyoto, but "the hospitality of the people" and "the town's atmosphere" reflect central features of the most recent tourism promotion plans. Thus while familiarity and an understanding of the city's history certainly vary between domestic and international tourists, the kinds of activities, attractions, and reasons for going are fairly consistent and revolve around a sense of experiencing Japanese history and culture.

Mayor Kadokawa's Kyoto Brand

Kadokawa Daisaku was first elected mayor of Kyoto in 2008, and he has been reelected three times, most recently in 2020. Mayor Kadokawa's focus has been on making Kyoto a top global tourist city, and indeed, the number of tourists to Kyoto soared in the past decade (see figures I.1 and I.2 above). The mayor himself embodies a particular vision of the Kyoto brand, always appearing in public in *hakama* and kimono, celebrating a Japanese aesthetic and local Kyoto craftsmanship.[6] Under his watch, the city has released a series of strategic plans for tourism promotion, city planning (*machizukuri*), and landscape policies that build on the city's reputation, customs, and traditions so as to craft a heritage city.[7] With this legacy at the forefront, the most recent election in 2020 was hotly contested as the negative effects of overtourism on the city took central stage.

Kadokawa's Kyoto brand is perhaps best exemplified through the language of the tourism promotion plans. Starting with a multipronged survey and analysis to assess the status of tourism in Kyoto—its strengths and weak points and how the city should move forward—the first plan, entitled the "Future Kyoto Tourism Promotion Project 2010+5: Toward the Essence of Tourism—7 Projects in Process" (in short, "Future Kyoto Plan 2010") was released in March 2010 (Mr. K— 2012).[8] This citywide tourism promotion plan opens with Mayor Kadokawa's aspirational words:

> "If I had returned home without knowing Kyoto, I might have misunderstood Japan"—[These are] the words of a European President.

> In Kyoto we live and breathe the scenic beauty, magnificent nature, and eternal transcendence of 1200 years of history, temples, shrines, tea ceremony, flower arranging, Noh, and Kyōgen. And these remain rooted in the unbroken flow of inherited wisdom, heart, and philosophy.
>
> In the uncertain times of today, the people of the world are looking for healing, hope, and spiritual satisfaction. Kyoto, which is the origin of Japanese culture, can bring the "effects of the heart" to people. As such, Kyoto has an increasing role to play as Japan implements the national strategy of becoming a tourist nation. This is an extremely important responsibility.
>
> The aim of Kyoto tourism was to become a "fifty million tourists city." Since we have reached that goal, the next stage will be to meet the challenges it brings.
>
> About eighty years ago, during the Showa Depression [the Great Depression], the Tourism Promotion Section opened in the Kyoto City Tourism Office, and the Tourist Information Center was set up. Today, we, the citizens of Kyoto, have decided again to build Kyoto tourism for the future of Kyoto and to use this plan, "Future—Kyoto Tourism Promotion Plan 2010+5," as a compass.
>
> We hope to make Kyoto one of the best cities in the world for meeting people, culture, history, and oneself in a way that touches the heart and enables one to enjoy the "essence of travel" to the fullest.
>
> Everyone who loves Kyoto, including the citizens, tourism-related industries, government, and tourists will unite with one heart to work on these seven projects, which can only be done in Kyoto, and pursue the essence of travel (quoted in Kyoto City 2010, 2).

In this opening salvo, all the threads that this book addresses come to the fore: national- or governmental-level tourism strategies; why people today desire travel; how to manage so many tourists; experiential travel; and the history, culture, and environs of Kyoto. What stands out in this plan for the purposes of this analysis is threefold. On the local level, the plan seeks to implement a strategy to make this lofty goal sustainable by evaluating how to meet the needs of both citizens and tourists. On the national level, the plan posits Kyoto tourism as a solution to Japan's continued financial and social woes. And on the global level the plan positions Kyoto heritage as a potential solution to what people seek worldwide in today's uncertain times.

Future Kyoto Plan 2010 outlines seven projects for both city planners and tourists:

1. Travel as though you live here (暮らすように旅する)
2. Walk to understand Kyoto (歩いてこそ京都)
3. Let citizens rediscover Kyoto (市民の京都再発見)
4. See Kyoto with your heart (心で "見る" 京都)
5. Reduce tourist dissatisfaction to zero (観光客の不満をゼロに)
6. Acquire new fans for Kyoto (新たな京都ファン嚶得)
7. Convey the charms of Kyoto (京都の魅力うまく伝える)

Across these projects there is an emphasis on ways to experience Kyoto more fully in keeping with the turn to "experience" in tourism. In "Travel as though you live here," "Walk to understand Kyoto," and "See Kyoto with your heart," we see different ways for tourists to experience the city beyond just seeing the famous sites. Moreover, these projects also seek to integrate citizens into the mix through projects like "Let citizens rediscover Kyoto" and "Convey the charms of Kyoto." In "Travel as though you live here" and "Walk to understand Kyoto," there is a sense of encouraging citizens to interact with tourists as guides to the city, marketing its rich cultural history and charm.

Just five years after the Future Kyoto Plan 2010 was released, a new tourism promotion strategy, "For the World to Yearn for Kyoto Tourism—Kyoto Tourism Strategy Plan 2020" (in short, Yearning for Kyoto Plan 2015), was released, with the 2020 Olympics in mind.[9]

While the prior plan was centered on seven projects to enhance tourist experiences, this plan emphasizes the "quality" of those experiences. The language of "a city the world yearns for" and traditions of hospitality threaded throughout the plan make it clear that the focus is to spread the word of Kyoto's charms internationally and affectively. Again, the mayor's opening remarks set the stage:

> In recent years, the world has become more interested in various facets of Japanese culture—history, tradition, food, arts, crafts—and

> matters of the spirit, heart, character, etc. In addition, in 2020 the Olympics and Paralympics will be held in Tokyo, bringing even more attention to Japan. As home to so much of Japan's rich culture, Kyoto has the opportunity to help advance the goals of "Tourism Nation Japan."...
>
> On the occasion of the Olympic and Paralympic invitation we [Japan] popularized the word "*omotenashi*" [hospitality] broadly to all the world. The core of "*omotenashi*" is compassion for the people and things around you. Kyoto is the home of "*omotenashi*"; as the capital of Japan for over a thousand years, it has cherished hospitality at its heart, refined its diverse culture, and welcomed many visitors. I am confident that taking advantage of the strengths unique to Kyoto in this fashion will lead to the development of a city many people will "yearn" for.
>
> This tourism policy is a collaboration across all sectors. A city that will attract the hearts of diverse tourists is a city that makes its citizens happy to live there. Eliminating the gap [between government and the private sector], we will do our best to build an attractive city that brings a high level of satisfaction to its many citizens, to everyone related to it, and to people who visit the city (quoted in Kyoto City 2015, 2).

As seen in these excerpts, set within the context of the Tourism Nation Japan strategy, there is a sense that the 2020 Olympics offer Japan a new opportunity to showcase its culture and to offer something to the world at large—namely, heritage and hospitality, both of which are exemplified in Kyoto.

Through its focus on "quality" over "quantity," the Yearning for Kyoto Plan 2015 is more visionary than it is pragmatic, focusing on what cultural resources Kyoto can and should draw on to create a sustainably livable tourism city. The plan emphasizes the following:

> A tourist city the world yearns for
>
> In Kyoto, manufacturing (material culture) and storytelling (spiritual culture) mutually stimulate and enhance each other. Through an integration and deepening of this inherited sensibility, craftsmanship, and spirit, we have continued town development for over a thousand years. It is the source of the vitality and the way of life that Kyoto has valued, and it is what people "yearn" for when they come to Kyoto.

> Many people from around the world come to Kyoto in search of the high-quality culture and depth that is embodied in the unparalleled spirit of Japan.
>
> By making this deep charm the essence of Kyoto forever, protecting, polishing, nurturing, and utilizing it and announcing it to the world, Kyoto will not be just "the jewel of Japan" but "the jewel of the world"; and we aim make Kyoto a city that is desired as an authentic tourist city (Kyoto City 2015, 24).

In this language we see a connection among craftsmanship, storytelling, aesthetic sensibilities, and spirituality as a part of what Kyoto has inherited and nurtured. Time and again the plan points out that living in Kyoto means a daily communion with what is inherited from the past (scenery and nature, cultural arts, traditional industry, cultural heritage), and this essence of Japanese culture is what Kyoto can share with the world. The plan sees Kyoto as critical to Japan's national efforts: "Kyoto is the center of cultural expression in Japan, and while Japan's population declines and economic power is feared to fall, the role required for tourism in Kyoto is expanding as a city that stewards the history, traditions, culture, and mind of Japan today" (Kyoto City 2015, 3). Keeping this inheritance alive while exhibiting Kyoto as a global tourist city is envisioned as a part of this stewardship.

Like the Future Kyoto Plan 2010, the Yearning for Kyoto Plan 2015 calls for the work to be shared by many sectors, including citizens, so that together they create a hospitable city in which to live, work, and play. Certainly there are stresses on any city with a large influx of tourists, and the ratio of 55 million tourists to 1.47 million citizens in Kyoto is extreme. The tension for citizens living with so many tourists would be high anywhere. Indeed, my commute to take my son to school on the city bus was, at times, nearly impossible due to the sardine-packed busses on their way to the Golden Pavilion. Like anywhere, locals—at least those who are not themselves in the tourist industry—assiduously avoid the tourist areas, especially at peak times. Still, in both the 2010 and 2015 tourism strategies, there are projects that aim to make Kyoto a desirable city in which to live. For example, there is a plan to make commuting routes easier to use through an increase in communication about changes to public transportation routes during peak tourist seasons (Kyoto City 2010). However, there is something further in these plans: a call for citizens to embrace "tourist city Kyoto" and actively participate in welcoming tourists.

Hospitality as Citizen Engagement

About 10 percent of Kyoto residents are employed in a sector related to tourism (restaurants, hotels, tour guiding, shops, and the like), and the figure is increasing (Kyoto City 2015, 5). In fact, several of the tour guides with whom I spoke had recently moved to Kyoto because it is a thriving and beautiful city and because the tourist industry is in need of people as the number of tourists increases. While some work in salaried positions for hotels, shops, or small tour companies that cater to international tourists, others work in the gig economy, finding work where available through connections with a hotel or shop. In fact, only a few of the people with whom I spoke who were working in hotels and as tour guides had grown up in Kyoto, although most were from the Kansai region. Yet beyond the tourist industry itself, the tourism promotion plans analyzed here hope that citizens will become welcoming hosts to visiting guests. The Future Kyoto Plan 2010 emphasizes this hope through the "Let Citizens Rediscover Kyoto" project. The aim of this project, as described in the plan, is to "make Kyotoites fans of Kyoto by making them experts." The first paragraph of this project makes the goal clear:

> In order to create a vibrant spirit of hospitality for tourists, we must start by getting close to the tourists' hearts. To do that, first of all, citizens themselves should enjoy, know, learn, and have fun with the globally famous properties of Kyoto; it is important that "Kyotoites be Kyoto's number one fans." This kind of rediscovery involves more than people taking pride in Kyoto or getting a taste of how wonderful it is. Rather, we seek to polish the etiquette of the citizens of Kyoto. For this rediscovery of Kyoto to take effect, Kyotoites need to become experts, welcoming tourists sincerely and demonstrating a vital presence. This will make Kyoto a great tourism city (Kyoto City 2010, 22).

This goal is striking as it actively seeks to make all Kyoto citizens potential tour guides or at least hospitable and knowledgeable citizens who will promote the city's rich history and culture to tourists they encounter.

It is not surprising that the first prong of this project aimed to make Kyoto's children into "fans of Kyoto" by providing opportunities for elementary and middle school students to learn about Kyoto history and culture through special events promoting the historic spots and national treasures of the city. This educational aspect of the plan is particularly important to Mayor Kadokawa, who served as superintendent of the Kyoto City School Board before becoming mayor. In fact, Mayor Kadokawa helped produce a Kyoto tourism supplementary reader especially for elementary-aged children (Kyoto City 2010, 22). The *Junior Japanese Culture Official Textbook: Historical City, Learning from Kyoto* (Kadokawa and Takakuwa 2010) is an odd mixture of a history of the city and a tourism promotion text. The book, which was readily available at local bookstores in 2012, reads like a historical guide to Kyoto, with breakout boxes about local sites today. This guide teaches young Kyotoites about their city in ways directly connected to things they can experience themselves, and in so doing, it gives children a touristic sense of the city's history. Moreover, according to the Future Kyoto Plan 2010, because children must shoulder the responsibilities of the next generation, this text was developed to deepen grade school children's understanding of the city's tourism promotion goals as well (Kyoto City 2010, 22). In a sense, the book teaches them how to put Kyoto hospitality into practice and about the important work that supports tourism. Thus Kyoto's city heritage and tourism promotion are a part of public education in Kyoto.

For adults living in Kyoto, the final goal under the "Let Citizens Rediscover Kyoto" project is to create "Kyoto tourism supporters" by working with tourism organizations, traditional industry organizations, and volunteer groups. Casting this wide net, the plan aims at creating a network for exchange among Kyoto citizens, students at the city's numerous colleges, and international tourists. The plan encourages Systematized Goodwill Guide Groups (SGG), registered with the JNTO to provide local tours on a volunteer basis. Several such groups already existed in 2012. One group, whose meetings I attended several times, the Kyoto Tour Guide Association, held monthly gatherings where the soon-to-be guides met at a temple, shrine, or museum and learned about the place, its history, and ideas for a tour there.[10] The 15–30 attendees at each meeting ranged in age from college students to retirees; most were interested in becoming Kyoto tour guides as either volunteers or professionals. The participants all had international tourists in mind, so gaining an English vocabulary and ways of explaining religious and cultural ideas to international tourists were a part of the experience.

In this effort to engage citizens in the project of making Kyoto a global tourist city, the notion of *omotenashi,* or hospitality, comes up over and over again. No doubt hospitality is an important part of tourism, but *omotenashi* signals a particularly Japanese form of hospitality. Moreover, this term has become a central feature of the 2020 Olympics promotions, starting with the official launch in 2013 (Pellicano 2019). Through this emphasis on hospitality, the Kyoto tourism plans aim at developing intimate connections between host and guest and creating hospitable spaces. The Yearning for Kyoto Plan 2015 expressly aims for "a city of hospitality where citizens warmly welcome all tourists." It states: "The Kyoto City Citizen Charter, enacted in Showa 31 [1956], first called for us to warmly welcome travelers and build a beautiful city of 'hospitality.' Reaffirming the charms of Kyoto and taking pride in our town, through customs like 'stoop sweeping,' rooted in the Kyoto lifestyle, citizens and businesses together can implement 'The world's Kyoto • Town beautification citizen mobilization' efforts and warmly welcome all travelers with hospitality unique to Kyoto" (Kyoto City 2015, 25). "Stoop sweeping" (*mon haki;* literally "gate sweeping") refers to a Kyoto tradition that involves sweeping the entranceway to one's house, as well as the sidewalk or street in front of one's house, in order to keep the neighborhood tidy. While keeping the street or walkway clean in front of one's business or house is a custom everywhere in Japan, it is one that is emphasized in Kyoto, where the houses traditionally abut the street. Here we see the custom of keeping neighborhoods clean as a form of hospitality, a way of creating or maintaining welcoming spaces for citizens and tourists alike.

There is no doubt that the language of the 2010 and 2015 strategic plans exemplifies the careful crafting of a lofty vision. The details of the individual projects and goals are both pragmatic—outlining infrastructural projects like roads and internet access—and idealistic—making every citizen a tour guide or salesperson for the city. Like all strategic plans, the vision and mission are grand and romantic, yet this notion of being a steward of the cultural gifts of Japan can be seen in the ways that heritage is crafted—polished and developed, felt and experienced—throughout the city today. These plans capture both the pride many feel living in Kyoto and the tensions that come with being a global tourist city.

The Stuff of Heritage in Contemporary Kyoto

I discussed the notion of heritage in the introduction, suggesting that it is the commemoration and often commercialization of history and culture. What exactly that means and whether it is bad or good has been hotly debated for more than two decades (Harrison 2013; Kirshenblatt-Gimblett 1995, 1998; Lowenthal 1998; Waterton and Watson 2015; Wright and Krauze 2009); and debates about heritage are also always about authenticity. The fundamental problem arises when it is assumed, whether on the part of curators, industry personnel, or tourists, that heritage is an uninterpreted or "authentic" remnant of the past—that is, when heritage is construed as history. In this regard, I find Barbara Kirshenblatt-Gimblett's definition of heritage as "cultural production for the present with recourse to the past" to be helpful for thinking about heritage because it places emphasis on the present use rather than a sense of preserving the past (1998, 149–150). Building on this, through the example of Kyoto, I argue that "heritage" is at once a way interested parties—state and local, public and private, tourist and industry—tell stories about the past; it is a way that the past is commodified in an experience economy; and it is the way twenty-first-century tourists seek to engage with the past. All of these aspects are woven into the crafting of the Kyoto brand discussed above, and they are all entangled in the ways that a heritage atmosphere is constructed in Kyoto today.

While the seventeen UNESCO World Heritage sites in Kyoto are the gateway to Kyoto heritage, featured prominently in promotional materials because they provide a global status, heritage in Kyoto is hardly limited to these blockbuster sites. There are thousands of other temples and shrines throughout the city, as well as a host of historical residences, museums, parks, and gardens. Furthermore, over the past century the city has gradually defined historic preservation areas in which all new construction must follow guidelines for size, height, materials, and color. The first City Planning Act was promulgated in 1919 to designate building zones. In 1930, Kitayama, Higashiyama, and Kamogawa were designated scenic zones, the first historic preservation areas in Kyoto (Kyoto City Landscape Division 2014, 28; Yamajō 2007, 162–186; Breen, Maruyama, and Takagi 2020). The most recent landscape policy was enacted in 2007, with revisions almost every year since. The New Landscape Policy (Shin Keikan Seisaku) was framed around the idea of creating vistas.

This was done by lowering building height restrictions in historic city areas and residential areas near the foothills, reviewing materials used in historic and town center areas to create urban landscape districts, moving power lines underground in historic districts, and increasing rules against blocking *shakkei,* or "borrowed scenery" (Kyoto City Landscape Division 2014, 83).[11] Stricter rules for outdoor advertising were initiated, limiting the size, location, and even color of signs in the city center and historic districts. In 2014 the city publicly released a booklet explaining the history and goals of the Kyoto City landscape policies in both Japanese and English, making these policies a part of the public narrative about Kyoto (Kyoto City Landscape Division 2014).

One of the most innovative features of the New Landscape Policy was a focus on promoting, preserving, and renovating the Kyoto townscape through the creative reuse and preservation of *machiya*. *Machiya* translates to "town house" and is the general term for an urban merchant and/or craftsman's house made of traditional materials and using traditional building styles. The term is usually reserved for prewar wood construction, although new *machiya* using the same materials and styles have become popular in recent years in Kyoto. Such townhouses are not exclusive to Kyoto; they can be found all over Japan, although there are regional and local differences in style. In Kyoto, they are sometimes called *Kyō-machiya* to designate the specific Kyoto features. Because taxes were levied originally based on street frontage, *Kyō-machiya* fit the long and thin plots in the grid of streets in central Kyoto, giving them the nickname "bedchamber of eels" (*unagi no nedoko*). Traditionally, these one-to-three-story townhouses were comprised of a small shop or business at the front and living space behind and above (Stavros 2014, 55–61). Of course, there is a range of styles, depending on the wealth and rank of the family and the location in Kyoto; some include larger compounds and others are smaller long, thin townhouses, but all are embedded along the backstreet living spaces of central Kyoto.[12]

Kyō-machiya sit nearly flush with the small streets and thus incorporate a range of features to ensure privacy and air flow. No matter the size or grandeur, these include traditional features like dark, unpainted wood beams and lattice windows (*kōshi* or *degōshi*); mud walls (*tsuchikabe*); floors of wood or tatami; and rooms divided by *shōji* sliding doors. Front windows are faced with latticework to keep out a bit of street noise and prying eyes. Some other distinctly Kyoto features include straight roof tiles (*ichimonji-gawara*); "insect box" windows (*mushiko*), in which the mud wall texture covers the window slats on the second floor; latticework windows and doors are patterned depending on the craft, trade, or goods sold; and "dog fenders" (*inu yarai*), which are curved bamboo facades to keep the front of the house clean (Kyoto Center for Community Collaboration 2009, 28–29). Depending on the size, these townhouses feature one or more gardens, including a pocket garden (*tsuboniwa*), a small garden that helps bring light and air into the closely packed townhouses, incorporating nature into city living (Kyoto Center for Community Collaboration 2009, 11, 14). Figure 2.1 shows a typical small *machiya* in central Kyoto, featuring the straight roof tiles, "insect box" window (on the top right), and latticework window on the bottom left. Many of these features originated as innovations to provide a bit of privacy for compounds that fronted major streets, but they also work together to make houses more comfortable in the bone-chilling and damp cold of the winter and the sweltering humidity of the summer (Kyoto Center for Community Collaboration 2009, 12–13).

Figure 2.1. Typical small *machiya* in central Kyoto. Photo by author, 2019.

Concentrated in the city center, primarily between Horikawa and Kawaramachi to the west and east and Ichijō to Shichijō to the north and south, *machiya* have become a vital symbol of the Kyoto townscape. Beginning in the mid-1990s, a citizen's movement was started to preserve and maintain these important buildings, which shape the atmosphere and pace of life for locals in Kyoto. According to anthropologist Christoph Brumann, "Between 1983 and 1993 alone, the percentage of pre-war architecture in Kyoto's four central wards fell from 48.1 per cent to 25.4 percent. There are still around 25,000 *machiya* today, but there were many times more fifty years ago" (2009, 112).[13] According to the Kyoto Center for Community Collaboration (KCCC; 2009, 43), between 1996 and 2003, 13 percent of the remaining townhouses disappeared.[14] Yet by the time Brumann started his fieldwork in 1998, Kyoto was in the throes of a *machiya* boom which still continues today. As Brumann (2009, 2010) illustrates, the townhouses are preserved in a variety of ways, from a restoration of the building to its original state at a particular time to the use of traditional materials and building techniques to, restore, maintain, or even update the building. One of the ways that *machiya* affect the cityscape of Kyoto today is through the reuse of their distinctive architectural features, especially the latticework windows, the "insect box" windows, and the "dog fenders" in the newer, even decidedly nontraditional, buildings. For example, a style of latticework was developed recently during restoration to hide air conditioning units; this is an example of renovation for living today as opposed to an attention to restoration for historical tours (Kyoto Center for Community Collaboration 2009, 66). All the architectural features discussed here are historical features put to new use in the city today to create a heritage atmosphere.

Beyond the most prominent manifestations of "heritage" in Kyoto—UNESCO World Heritage sites and Kyoto-style townhouses—heritage resides in Kyoto through the continued existence of countless craft workshops found in the mesh of small streets and alleyways among the bustling avenues of Kyoto. Specializing in lanterns, fans, kimono weaving and dyeing, Buddhist prayer beads and altars, and gravestones and incense, the craftspeople supply goods for local and national festivals, temples, businesses, and the like. On a larger scale most of the famous flower arranging schools, pottery schools, and tea schools have their headquarters in Kyoto. So, too, the geisha districts, for which Kyoto is famous, visibly uphold a sense of Japanese tradition and culture through the promotion of traditional music, dance, and hospitality.[15] Pride in these traditional crafts and the continuation of small-scale crafts workshops can be seen in souvenir guidebooks and promotions, as well as in the increasing availability of hands-on crafts tours and experiences endorsed on the city's tourism website and seen in the offerings of the Convention Bureau, tour companies, and local businesses. Souvenir shops, which line the tourist areas, are overflowing with traditional craft goods (alongside cheaper, mass-produced Kyoto- and Japan-themed trinkets). Moreover, heritage even appears on menus as a part of the cultivation of traditional Kyoto foods, especially heritage vegetables (de St. Maurice 2016; Rath 2014). Kyoto foods and cooking styles infuse tourist events, activities, and restaurants throughout the main tourist districts.[16]

As I have tried to outline here, heritage, both material and intangible, is a part of life in Kyoto. Christoph Brumann's (2009, 2012) work on the Kyoto townscape and citizens' movements demonstrates the ways that heritage in Kyoto is understood not as a thing to be preserved in a glass case or as a petrification of the past, but rather that heritage in Kyoto is alive and well. For example, Brumann writes: "A central motive uniting a large number of otherwise diverse people was seeing these traditions and one's own involvement with them as part of an ongoing series of transmissions emanating from the past and projecting onwards into the future, rather than as belonging to an essentially closed historical period. . . . Both with regard to the *machiya* and Gion Festival, informants used the metaphor of a relay race through time in which one has been passed the baton to carry, until the next generation takes over" (2012, 238–239). This sense of a living heritage became apparent throughout my research as well and is demonstrated in each of the ethnographic examples in this book.

While Brumann's work emphasizes the perspectives of individual community members involved in keeping local traditions alive, the landscape and tourism policies discussed here are likewise illustrative of the ways that heritage in Kyoto is more than just a preservation of the past. The focus on tourists experiencing Japanese culture today throughout these plans is another way that the baton of tradition is passed in Kyoto heritage. The "See Kyoto with your heart" project in the Future Kyoto Plan 2010 is an apt example. This project emphasizes “authentic encounter tourism” (*fureau kankō*). A vivid depiction of ways of seeing sets the stage for this project: “In Kyoto, the flip side of the things you can see with your eyes are the charms you can't see just with your eyes. . . . When we close our eyes and feel the flow of time and the Japanese spirit, we sense the spiritual culture of a city of religion, tea ceremony, flower arranging, incense, Noh, Kyogen, Kyoto cooking, the craftsman trades, even the knowledge of college students and citizens who live here; we want to move from ‘seeing tourism’ to ‘encountering tourism.’ This is the mystery of travel in Kyoto” (Kyoto City 2010, 24). *Fureau,* “to be in touch or in contact with,” elicits both an emotive and a tactile sense. Perhaps “affective tourism” is an apt translation, wherein one is moved by the experience. Thus this project aims at a more affective and experiential tourism. One prong of this project includes developing more ways of seeing Kyoto culture through experiences. An example is the creation of new evening events to draw tourists at off-peak times and provide something to do in the evening; the Hanatōro and Kyō no Tanabata analyzed in chapter 3 are two such events. A second prong of this project is to promote experiences of everyday life in Kyoto. This includes highlighting the charms of Kyoto in the early morning by suggesting jogging, cycling, and local breakfast opportunities. Likewise, the project encourages visitors to opt for more Kyoto-style lodging to get a feeling of and appreciation for traditional Kyoto living; it suggests renting or staying in a *machiya* or a newer hotel with a Kyoto aesthetic.

Thus these strategic plans for tourism in Kyoto draw on new experiential trends in tourism, the language of Tourism Nation Japan, and notions of living heritage in contemporary Kyoto. The goals encompass all levels of tourist promotion, from construction ordinances and the development of historic preservation/renovation centers, to increasing the quantity and visibility of World Heritage sites, to encouraging Kyoto hospitality and the wearing of kimono around town. The project descriptions in the Future Kyoto Plan 2010 conclude as follows: “Of course citizens, but also tourists and everyone, can enjoy traditional industry goods and Kyoto foods, all of us watching our manners so as to have a good time, not just protecting the charm of Kyoto, but also increasing it” (Kyoto City 2010, 26). It is this sense of experiencing heritage and hospitality in Kyoto that looms large in tourist promotion and in many tourists' own articulations of why they come to the city.

Crafting Heritage: City Planning, Hospitality, and the Kyoto Brand

Despite the fact that the main entrance to this historic city is dominated by a contemporary cityscape through the postmodern architecture of Kyoto Station, the 1960s stylings of Kyoto Tower, a sprawling bus center, and the sleek offices of major semiconductor companies, it is still heritage that brings most tourists, domestic and foreign, young and old, to Kyoto. To weave together the threads that I have been teasing out of the city's strategic plans, as well as the material and conceptual ways that heritage is embodied by the city today, I turn to an analysis of one instance of atmospheric urban renovation that exemplifies the confluence of heritage and hospitality in Kyoto city planning. The Kōyaku no Zushi street renewal was an event for which I serendipitously had a front row seat.

In 2012 we rented a *machiya* in the central part of town where the festivities for the Gion Festival are located. The Gion Festival is one of three traditional festivals that are celebrated each year in Kyoto; for the first half of July, its preparations dominate the center of the city. The festival culminates in a parade of floats and is a major tourism event in Kyoto. In the weeks leading up to July 17, the whole area is vibrant as all the local neighborhood blocks assemble their elaborate wooden floats (*yamahoko*), which sit two stories high on tall wheels.[17] The sounds of traditional Gion Festival music waft through the streets as each neighborhood group practices in preparation for the parade. As the parade day gets closer, the central area of Kyoto is filled with locals out working on floats and selling charms and souvenirs of their floats. The neighborhood in which we lived was on one of the small *roji* (alleyways) that zigzag through the city in between the major avenues. The street is known locally as Kōyaku no Zushi, although signs marking it as such have appeared recently.[18] This area is not a historic preservation district, nor is it on the main tourist pathways except for the weeks surrounding the Gion Festival. Yet the area is infused with historic stores and buildings beyond the major thoroughfares of Sanjō, Shijō, Gojō, Karasuma, and Ōmiya.

Despite the quaint old buildings, the street itself was old asphalt, patched here and there and uneven, as seen in figure 2.2. In late April, we got a notice that the street was going to be repaved, with an apology for the inconvenience. Admittedly, my first response was, "Great; our quiet street will be noisy"; other than that, I went about my everyday business of fieldwork. As the renovation progressed, workers replaced the traditional stone gutters with nicer gravel and evened out and paved the street with blacktop; it looked like new. Just when we thought they were done, another sign went up on the notice board in the front of the street announcing that phase two of the road reconstruction was starting. One morning my husband and I watched as they proceeded to mix a watery concrete and spray it on the blacktop so that it had a thin layer of stony gray that resembled granite. It looked better, cleaner, and older. Now I was curious and started doing some research. Several stories about the street renovation in local newspapers declared that this new technique had been used only one other time in a neighborhood in Tokyo. Kōyaku no Zushi was the test case for this new process in Kyoto. Then a sign went up explaining the next step: creating tiles. The workmen spent two days methodically marking off a clear grid of rectangles and then spent four days meticulously cutting it into "tiles." Finally, they rewashed the grid with the watery concrete and sanded it down. Voilà! The street looked quite like the cobblestone tiles seen in some of the historic areas. The city, neighborhood, and Kyoto University part-

Figure 2.2. Part of Kōyaku no Zushi before and after the street renovation. Photos by author, 2012 and 2019.

nered on this project to maintain the atmosphere of this older area in a traditional Kyoto style.

One of the most innovative things about this street renewal was that it aimed at both aesthetic and pragmatic environmental renewal. The gray stony concrete was carefully cut to resemble cobblestones. This (re)creates a heritage atmosphere at a much lower cost than if genuine cobblestones were used; furthermore, the gray stony material retains water, keeping the street cooler in the heat of the summer. According to the city White Paper, the new technique uses water-retentive pavement, which is layered to suppress the rise in road surface temperatures by utilizing a cooling effect that comes with the evaporation of moisture stored in the pavement on top of older asphalt. "For regular asphalt pavement, the temperature rises to nearly 60 degrees Celsius in summer, but this cobblestone water-retentive pavement reduces that to about 45 degrees" (Kyoto City 2012). As the report sums up,

> Pavement that takes the landscape into consideration (cobblestone-style asphalt pavement) has a beautiful look like granulated granite, is lower in construction costs than conventional cobblestone pavement, and is easier to maintain. In Kyoto City, we have developed a new pavement with a water-retentivity function to suppress the rise in road surface temperature on pavement . . . that also takes into consideration the landscape. We conducted test construction of the newly developed pavement on the street known as Kōyaku no Zushi. Kyoto's long-established culture of "water sprinkling" [*uchimizu*] inspired this cobblestone water-retentive pavement, which will sustain even further benefits as residents experience the new "coolness" with "water sprinkling" (Kyoto City 2012).[19]

The notion of "water sprinkling" is a custom related to "stoop sweeping," which not only keeps the dust and dirt down, but also cools the pavement off in the sizzling summer. "Water sprinkling" was a definite part of the rhythm of living on Kōyaku no Zushi, as both residents and business owners took care of the narrow street each morning and evening. Yet it is curious that in the government White Paper explaining the specifics of an infrastructure project a link is drawn to habits of hospitality and traditions of neighborhood etiquette.

In early July 2012, as the Gion Festival was starting to ramp up, the neighbors informed me that there was going to be an important ceremony to dedicate the renovation. I was invited to join them at the event, where Mayor Kadokawa would dedicate the new street. By the day of the ceremony, the streets around our house were starting to fill up with typical carnival booths with goldfish for visitors to catch and take home; games; traditional goods like *yukata* or paper crafts; and all kinds of summer foods like iced cucumbers, *warabi mochi, takoyaki,* and the like. On Saturday, July 15, the crowds for the festival were so thick that getting to our street was like swimming upstream. When Mayor Kadokawa arrived, dressed as always in formal *hakama* and kimono, bows were exchanged, the music stopped, and the event began as the head of the neighborhood association welcomed everyone and explained the decision-making process for the new road. Mayor Kadokawa spoke about how pleased he was with the hard work that this neighborhood had done together with the city and the university. He discussed this project as a part of the new age of environmental friendliness integrated in the "Walking City Kyoto" plans to encourage living well.[20] Throughout, he highlighted the *machizukuri* city planning projects as emblematic of Kyoto today. After the speeches, there was a ribbon-cutting ceremony, and the mayor walked through the narrow street surveying it all, with the other dignitaries, neighborhood residents, and musicians in procession.

Since 2012 the neighborhood has continued with renovations. Now there is even an official city street sign, in both Japanese and English, marking Kōyaku no Zushi and the Sugimoto Machiya—a traditional merchant's *machiya* on the south end of the street that is sometimes open for public viewings and tours. Older residences and small parking lots have been replaced by a Japanese chain hotel with a Kyoto-style entrance on Kōyaku no Zushi, and a Tully's coffee shop facing Shijō. As of 2019, another hotel was under construction along the south corridor. Likewise, a Japanese paper goods store and upscale restaurants and cafes have joined the restaurants, vintage kimono store, and traditional paper goods store that were there when we lived there. While the Tully's coffee shop and modern hotel (which opened in 2016) do not exude traditional Kyoto, the hotel entrance onto Kōyaku no Zushi was designed with Kyoto-style architectural features, and there is a small rock garden in the hotel lobby to fit the heritage atmosphere.

The neighborhood renovation project draws out several themes central to this chapter. For one thing, it is a perfect example of the city's tourism promotion plans and Mayor Kadokawa's vision of drawing on Kyoto's history and tradition to engineer heritage throughout the city. For another, this heritage renewal process uses high-tech, eco-friendly materials that give the appearance of tradition. There is no argument here that these materials *are* traditional, but they consciously and visibly create a heritage atmosphere for the old town. Furthermore, "Walking City Kyoto" is a significant part of each of the recent tourism promotion plans analyzed above, and this street renewal, creating a heritage atmosphere, adds a new off-the-beaten-path location for tourists to discover on their own, complete with signs marking a way through the narrow alleyway. It is an appealing place to stroll. At the ceremony in 2012, Mayor Kadokawa noted that the ambition to create a walking city leads to benefits for the citizens, as well as a beautiful townscape for tourists.

I have outlined this project not simply as an exemplar of Mayor Kadokawa's dream, although it certainly fits all the parameters. In fact, one of the critical aspects of this project is that it was both organized and coordinated by the local community to preserve a neighborhood in the face of increasing numbers of rental properties and shifting city economies. One resident of the street explained the neighborhood's goals to me, "We want to preserve the traditional atmosphere as new businesses and renters come in so that we can live in a beautiful location that retains the traditions that are important." To be sure, my family's presence, renting a traditional townhouse, was a part of this narrative; our neighbors to the left consisted of a Japanese mother and her two teenagers who were also renting, and the *machiya* to the right was vacant with a "For sale or rent" sign on it for our entire stay. In an interview for the *Yomiuri Newspaper* several years before the street renovation started, Mr. Kitanishi, the head of the neighborhood association, explained the goals for renovation: "Buildings should have an appearance that harmonizes with the beautiful townscapes; [we should] take care of our neighborhoods and cherish customs such as 'stoop sweeping'" (quoted in Masuda 2011). Since the outdoor units for air conditioners impaired the landscape, they were covered with traditional wooden lattices. Mr. Kitanishi continued: "As the era changes, if a new wind does not enter, the town stultifies. Yet there are things we want to protect no matter what. Without relying on the administration, I will improve my home with my own hands" (quoted in Masuda 2011). Two things stand out in these quotes. First, Mr. Kitanishi mentions "stoop sweeping," discussed above as a traditional feature of Kyoto neighborliness. At the same time, Mr. Kitanishi clearly points out that the local neighborhood took charge of the renovations, not leaving the task to city officials, exerting its autonomy and vision for the future.

In these statements by local residents, we see an articulation of the importance of keeping heritage alive for everyday living, not just for tourism. These comments fit with the city promotion plans, which emphasize experiencing Kyoto as heritage for local citizens and tourists alike. The juxtaposition of the front (Shijō side) and hidden (Kōyaku no Zushi side) entrances to the new hotel are prime examples, blending with and adding to the historic atmosphere but using new technology and adding new conveniences (a modern hotel and coffee shop). The comments embrace issues of identity and atmosphere, including what modern amenities should be disguised for the historic feel of a place. This example is an articulation of heritage for living in downtown Kyoto today. At the same time, within a few years, the addition of new historical marker signs explaining the historical significance to visitors was a part of this change. In the end, this neighborhood renewal was a heritage project attentive to atmosphere just out of the way in the city center.

Hospitality and Manners: Tensions in the Tourist City

I return now to the notion of hospitality. The ongoing upgrades at Kōyaku no Zushi highlight a shift away from a local residential street toward a commercial alley. In both architecture and content the businesses are largely in keeping with the heritage renovation—small cafes and shops specializing in vintage and resale kimono or traditional crafts, as well as a few high-end Kyoto restaurants surround the Takezasado, the woodblock print paper goods shop that has been there since 1891. Still, while this renovation has retained the atmosphere desired—it is a charming place to visit or stay—the neighborhood has gentrified. This is one example of the way that promoting the Kyoto brand to attract tourists in order to keep a neighborhood thriving has unintended consequences.

There is no doubt that there are distinct tensions inherent in welcoming large numbers of tourists into the city. This has always been true, but in recent years the problems of overtourism and sustainability have been at the forefront of UNWTO conversations. Yet as tourism rises in prominence as a global economic sector, city centers throughout the world are being renovated for it (Sorensen and Funck 2007; Spirou 2011). We see these tensions in Kyoto, where the central part of the city is also one of the main arteries of tourism. The very process of providing heritage experiences for tourists risks disruptions of natural, cultural, and religious locations. Beyond the debates about what kinds of venues are appropriate for Kyoto, debates have flared over the years about the benefits and costs of tourism, and conflicts have arisen between the city government tourism policies and popular tourist sites, especially large and wealthy Buddhist temples (Brumann 2012; Graburn 2004; Yamajō 2007). Most recently, there have been a host of news stories about the problems of overtourism. Bearing vivid images of overflowing trashcans and graffiti in the bamboo grove in Arashiyama, these stories tell of the ways too many tourists disrupt, even mar, the natural beauty of Kyoto. It is important to reiterate that there have long been throngs of tourists in Kyoto, especially in peak seasons, but beginning around 2017 a tipping point seemed to have been reached.

International tourists to Kyoto have increased threefold since I started this research, and the changes in the city are palpable. While the Hanamikoji area of Gion has always been a tourist hotspot, in the past few years it has become so overrun by throngs of tourists waiting to catch a glimpse of geisha that it is difficult to walk through. In fact, whenever problems of tourists in Kyoto appear in national news, as they do with some regularity, this area is the focus. The tension is felt acutely in Kyoto, a city that prides itself on etiquette and refinement. In the 2017 and 2018 Kyoto City Tourism Survey Reports, the top two complaints by Japanese tourists were "Too many people" and "Manners of foreign tourists are bad" (Kyoto City Tourism Office 2017, 2018). While "Too many people" has long been a complaint, in recent years it has consistently been near the top. Manners, however, constitute a new complaint. First appearing in the 2013 report, this complaint has risen steadily to the top. As of 2015 the complaint has specified "Manners of *foreign* tourists"; it is not surprising that the complaint coincides with the years in which the numbers of international tourists began to double (Kyoto City Tourism Office 2016).

To be sure, crowd management is simply a part of tourism management, itself a part of the hospitality industry, and Kyoto's approach draws on Japanese traditions of hospitality. In response to the problems of extreme numbers of tourists, pictographic signs prohibiting certain actions have popped up throughout high tourist areas. As seen in figure 2.3, these prohibitions typically pertain to problems such as sitting or leaning on the front of a building or littering but several new ones have popped up as well, such as "Be careful with selfie sticks" and "Don't touch *maiko*." These prohibitions are aimed at making crowds easier to navigate, as well as to make tourism more hospitable for locals. The need to teach tourists manners emphasizes the disruptions that tourism brings to the city, its citizens, and other visitors.

Signs that specify prohibitions, such as "Don't step on the grass" and "Don't feed the animals," are a part of crowd management in public spaces anywhere, yet Japan is notorious for the ubiquity and inventiveness of signs that regulate public behavior, such as the use of cell phones in public, running to catch a train, or even eating and drinking in public. In her work on museums and the creation of public spaces in the Meiji period, Noriko Aso (2014, 45–49) documents the ways that rules for public behavior were created in the shift from the rigid class strictures of the Edo period. In the Meiji period, as a part

Figure 2.3. Prohibition sign in Gion. Photo by author, 2017.

of new museum exhibits displaying national treasures to the public, rules for do's and don'ts were distributed and posted. In this vein, one curious solution undertaken jointly by the Kyoto City Convention Bureau and Trip Advisor is the release of several etiquette guides for Kyoto aimed at international tourists (available in English, Chinese, and Japanese). These guides are long, thin posters that are posted in tourist information centers, train stations, and sometimes on a public bulletin board, or they are sometimes laid out for pickup at various locations.[21] Titled "*Akimahen* Insider's Guide to Kyoto," the guides list behaviors to avoid in Kyoto in stylized and colorful glossy fold-outs. *Akimahen* means "no way" or "do not" in the Kansai dialect, and the term is used colloquially for behaviors to avoid. At the top of the poster a chef, *maiko*, a policeman, a priest, and a man in traditional dress are all frowning. Prohibitions and proper behavior are listed, along with a ranking of bad behaviors; they include, among others, "Don't smoke outdoors," "Be polite when asking *maiko* for pictures," "Don't litter," "Take your shoes off before stepping on tatami," and "Please line up in an orderly way." The posters also include the fines for ignoring such prohibitions, where applicable. As can be seen, some of the listings are common requests, some are specific to Japanese custom, and some are particular to Kyoto. In some ways, they are in perfect keeping with Kyoto, a city that prides itself on having exacting etiquette rules. In the travel sections of bookstores, there are whole series of guides to Kyoto etiquette in Japanese (for domestic tourists), highlighting local linguistic terms and customs (Tokai Seikatsu Kenkyu Purojekuto 2011).

Beyond being simple do's and don'ts signs, the *akimahen* posters must be understood in the context of the ways that Japan has been seen as inscrutable to international tourists. Part of the appeal of Japan for international tourists is a sense that the language and cultural differences are vast, especially between the West and Japan; but even within Asia, traditions like the use of tatami, taking one's shoes off at the door, or waiting in line in an orderly way are not shared customs. In this regard, there have long been signs or brochures to explain how to enjoy a Japanese inn, take a bath, enjoy a hot spring (*onsen*) properly, or enter and act in a temple. In contrast to the Kyoto etiquette books for domestic tourists, which serve to highlight the exoticism of Kyoto, the *akimahen* posters aim to teach tourists proper etiquette to help smooth relations between tourists and locals and between foreign and Japanese tourists. The *akimahen* campaign is the flip side of *omotenashi*—welcoming tourists, Kyoto style—aiming to suture the problems wrought by overtourism. This is a Japanese solution to the issues created by affective/experiential tourism, wherein tourists are welcomed into local life through Kyoto hospitality and taught to act accordingly.

Heritage Atmosphere and Hospitable Encounters

I end this chapter by drawing together the tensions that exist in the promotion of heritage experiences in a thriving urban environment. On the one hand, the fact that Kyoto has always been urban and the sense of its role as a historic "destination" are part of the city's charm, and these factors continues to draw tourists from across Japan and all over the world. But in the tourism promotion plans discussed here we see an attempt to balance a comfortable contemporary life for citizens with the preservation of the history and culture that is important not only to tourism; to be sure, being a heritage city is a point of pride for many citizens. The controversy about the new aquarium in Umekoji Park revealed some of these tensions, questioning what is appropriate for the Kyoto townscape. Likewise, one employee from the city tourism office, Mr. K—, said, "In order to attract more Asian tourists, they considered putting in a high-end mall specializing in national and regional designer goods, just south of the station. But in the end the idea fell through because it doesn't fit the Kyoto brand" (Mr. K— 2012). In each of these cases, a huge modern building in the middle of the city was deemed not only unnecessary, but also un-Kyoto. A similar set of issues can be seen in the *machiya* revival movement, which is guided by the loss of the traditional buildings throughout the city but open to a revival of traditional architecture in ways that enhance contemporary usage.

At one level, this chapter has been about the ways that the tourist industry in Kyoto produces experiences of heritage. Across the two tourism promotion plans of 2010 and 2015 the idea of more fully experiencing Kyoto stands out. In line with national tourism policies, this is a part of the city's strategy for spreading Japanese cultural soft power and increasing revenue by marketing hospitality and heritage. Entailed in this discussion are multilayered ways of visiting Kyoto: from a slow walk through the UNESCO World Heritage sites alongside throngs of tourists; to meandering through one of the historic preservation districts enjoying the atmosphere, stores and cafes, and temples and shrines; to following popular culture trends and visiting historic sites from one's favorite television drama—all of which will be examined in the chapters that follow.

Beyond particular building projects, landscape policies aimed at maintaining, restoring, and renovating historic districts shape the city's heritage atmosphere. The city's signage ordinances are strict, especially in the city center and near historic districts. For example, there was a controversy when a Lawson's (a prominent convenience store chain) moved into a storefront directly across the street from Yasaka Shrine (at the corner of Higashiyama and Shijō). A convenience store, the symbol of quick and easy modern life, across the street from a place of historical and spiritual significance to the city was considered unsightly, and yet tourists need a place to stop and rehydrate or refuel in this prime tourist district. There was a battle of the brands, as the bright blue and white of the Lawson's sign was deemed inappropriate—gaudy even—for this historic location.[22] A compromise was made to allow Lawson's to put a store there, but the sign's colors were changed to brown and orange to match the area's historic atmosphere. All these instances indicate conscious decisions about what to preserve, what to "create as though its old," and what to add that is new for the city to thrive. Rather than the concerns of the early critics of heritage tourism—that traditions were being created and passed off as actual history—here "authenticity" is not reducible to historical fact per se (although historical markers pepper the city) but rather to an ongoing, personal engagement with the past. Heritage in Kyoto pays homage to tradition and marks the city with historic signs so that the layers of history can be encountered by walking through the city streets, both in and out of the historic preservation districts.

This essence of Kyoto is not history but heritage—culture and tradition fashioned for the contemporary city and contemporary tourist. This broader sense that Kyoto symbolizes, represents, and embodies Japanese tradition is not easily located in any one place and does not represent just one moment in time. The various angles on heritage discussed here, from the most concrete to the most ethereal, demonstrate a sense that the city itself, not just a few districts or selected sites, is the heritage destination; Kyoto is a heritage city. As demonstrated in the chapters that follow, experiencing Kyoto heritage and Japanese culture and history is one of the driving vectors of tourism in Kyoto today.

Chapter 3

Seasonal Travel

The Culture of Nature in Kyoto Tourism

Kyoto, nestled amid rolling mountains, keenly reflects the changes of the seasons. The gaiety of Spring flowers turns to fragrant young leaves, followed by Summer, with riverside greenery providing a cool respite—changing at last to the crimson stain of Autumn colors. Recall dynastic tragedy, probe into the ambition of the brave generals of the Warring States period, follow in the footsteps of Edo artists, trace the events of the Restoration, savor the quaint charm of nameless thickets and narrow lanes. History and culture become one with the beauty of nature in the charm of Kyoto, where you will never tire of the changing seasons.

—"The Four Seasons,"
Kyoto City Official Travel Guide Website

One can argue that the seasons are important in all cultures, but what makes the Japanese culture of the four seasons particularly striking is the various and prominent ways in which cultural seasonalization—particularly the breaking down of nature into seasonal categories and phases with specific associations—occurs across a wide variety of media and genres over a millennium. The evolution of this poetic and artistic tradition paralleled the development of secondary nature in the metropolis, where nature took on multiple social, cultural, religious, and recreational functions.

—Haruo Shirane, *Japan and the Culture of the Four Seasons*

Nature affects the ways people travel. Most guidebooks start with an account of what the climate is like in the region, typically giving a range of temperatures and suggestions for the best months to travel there. Although travelers on business or those constrained by set vacation times are not always able to choose when they will travel, generally what to pack, what to expect, and how much to plan for the outdoors are dependent on the capricious designs of nature. This is one of the ways in which travel is embodied—that is, our bodily experiences are affected by the climate, food, and accommodations that pertain. Anyone who has traveled to Japan during the rainy season in June knows all too well that umbrellas become a part of the natural landscape. And in Kyoto, promotions for the fleeting beauty of new green leaves or moss in the rain pop up all over town. Like most places, the Kyoto tourism industry is organized around seasons, yet in Kyoto, discussions of nature and seasons are infused with references to traditional Japanese aesthetics. This chapter examines the ways that the Kyoto tourism industry markets itself through traditional aesthetics of nature, tacking back and forth between the pragmatics of dealing with the vagaries of the weather in Kyoto and the marketing of nature as culture; throughout I highlight the ways that these two realms—one practical and the other affective—intersect in tourism campaigns, festivals, and experiences of Kyoto today.

Part of Kyoto's natural beauty derives from its location in a basin surrounded by hills on three sides, ensuring that nearly every view has a verdant backdrop; most of Kyoto's famous sites include gardens and/or a view of the surrounding hills. At the same time, this very location makes the city damp and cold in the winter and hot and humid in the summer, as moisture is trapped in the urban basin. One of the oft told anecdotes about Kyoto is that people from northern Japan say, "I have never been as cold as I was in Kyoto in the winter!" In online forums, tourists warn each other away from the rainy season in June, when it rains nearly every day, and from the intense heat and humidity of July and August.

So, too, the tourist industry has its seasonal ebbs and flows of visitors. In an interview with me at the Kyoto Tourism Association in April of 2012, Mrs. A— used the tourism brochure for the winter campaign that had recently ended as an example of the ways that the association works with local businesses. The winter campaign focused on local foods. The imagery on the brochure was dark, black with gold and white highlights, and colorful images of Kyoto-style foods in subdued tones. "The winter and summer are our low seasons" Mrs. A— explained, "and then we are overflowing in the spring and fall. In the winter we try to arrange for temples to have special art or historic exhibits that are not usually on display. This winter we are also showcasing special Kyoto foods" (Mrs. A— 2012). In the years since my initial fieldwork, it seems that the winter campaigns always feature local cuisine and special temple exhibits.

Mrs. A—'s discussion of the winter campaign suggests several themes that set up the core issues in this chapter. First, there is the ebb and flow of tourists to Kyoto. According to Mrs. A—, some promotional marketing for winter and summer is necessary. From the tourism numbers gathered by the Kyoto City Tourism Office for the past decade, it is clear that Mrs. A—'s sense of the ebbs and flows is confirmed. Year after year, the lowest monthly numbers are in January, February, and July, while the highest numbers are in October, November, late March, and April (Kyoto City Tourism Office 2002–2019). This trend plays out for domestic excursionists and overnight guests, while the pattern for foreign tourists is largely affected by national holiday patterns. However, the influx of international tourists in the past five years has served to even out the numbers in months that were historically thin (Kyoto City Tourism Office 2019).

There are, of course, differences between domestic and foreign tourists, in terms of both ease of travel and patterns of vacation times. The winter campaign that Mrs. A— discussed was primarily aimed at a domestic Japanese audience, encouraging people to come to Kyoto for a quiet weekend in the winter. Over the course of our interview, though, Mrs. A— noted that in her interactions with tourist companies overseas—mainly in Taiwan, Korea, and China—she "encouraged tour companies to promote the Kyoto winter campaign because their clients could come at a time it was less crowded and not at peak prices. However," she continued, "the companies said that they would promote the winter campaign *if* we could guarantee blocks of rooms at top hotels during November and April" (Mrs. A— 2012). In Mrs. A—'s account this interaction was not a success because hotel rooms during November and April are booked a year in advance, and her association is not able to promise bookings.

The second thread embedded within this conversation about seasonal travel in Kyoto is the notion of the seasons themselves. Seasonal travel in Kyoto is not simply about the rhythms of inclement or pleasant weather, yet the prime tourist seasons in Kyoto are driven by nature—most prominently, leaves in color and the cherry blossoms in bloom. As witnessed by Mrs. A—'s hesitation about the availability of rooms in the peak seasons, the exuberance of cherry blossoms and changing autumn leaves throughout Kyoto's many gardens, as well the surrounding hillsides, has long been a draw for tourists.

The cherry blossom, *sakura,* has become a symbol of Japan both nationally and internationally. Untethered from spring, *sakura* have come to represent everything from the brevity of life, samurai and suicide bombers' dedication to the lord or emperor, friendship among nations, and more. The pink blossoms are beautiful and ubiquitous when they are in bloom, and they are so overused in marketing, popular culture, and national imagery that they have become synonymous with the image of "Japan." In Japan, as the *sakura* season draws near, weather reports in print and on screen throughout the nation include predictions as to when they will bloom, complete with maps overlaying tree icons in the same way that weather patterns are charted during the weekly forecast.[1]

Hanami (flower viewing) is a national pastime dating back to Heian-period aristocratic outings (Shirane 2012, 169). Still today, each year when the *sakura* bloom co-workers, couples, families, and friends gather in public parks under the blossoms for an evening of picnicking and drinking. In Kyoto, this is typically late March through early April. While this phenomenon can be found all over Japan, Kyoto has numerous nationally renowned locations for *hanami* including Maruyama Park, Kiyomizu Temple, Nijō Castle, Heian Shrine, and the Philosophers' Path; indeed, most major tourist spots have cherry blossoms integrated into their vistas. During this brief season, tourists—regional, national, and international—flock to the city, where souvenirs, sweets, and street corners alike are adorned with the famous pink blossom.[2]

While it is cherry blossoms that are world renowned, the busiest tourist season in Kyoto peaks in November, when the leaves turn brilliant red, magenta, vermillion, and gold. In Japanese, *kōyō* is the word for autumn leaves changing colors, and *momiji* refers to Japanese maples, which turn bright red each fall. These terms are used interchangeably to indicate more than just the fact of nature—the leaves are turning/have turned; they also refer to the yearly events of leaf viewing or going to see the leaves turning. Like *hanami,* viewing the leaves in autumn (known as *momiji-gari,* literally "hunting for leaves") is a part of the seasonal pacing of Japanese life; trips with family or friends to view the leaves are a common weekend event in the fall. Unlike cherry blossoms, autumn leaves are not uniquely associated with Japan; lots of places in the northern hemisphere in the fall attract tourists who gather to enjoy the crisp air, local warm drinks, and beautiful fall leaves. These things are all true as well of the tourists who flock to Kyoto to see the autumn leaves. Each fall social media take on the tones of autumn as countless images of Japanese maples are posted for general viewership across the internet. Kyoto is popular in the fall because of the vivid mixture of colors peppered throughout the hills that surround the city, as well as those carefully cultivated in gardens around the city. As a *meisho* (famous place) for autumn leaves, Arashiyama is still the top spot for viewing the fall colors along the Katsura River, though, as with the cherry blossoms, most tourist sites have vistas arranged particularly for the exhibition of fall leaves.

Beyond climate and colorful foliage, there is another way in which seasons are experienced in Japan, and that is through the comingling of nature and culture in Japanese aesthetics. As demonstrated in the epigraph above, Kyoto markets itself as the quintessential example of the beauty of the seasons, showcased through history and culture throughout the city. Every student taking Japanese learns that letters and greetings begin with a comment on the season, and nearly every account of Japanese aesthetics, or even Japanese culture, makes note of the importance of seasons as social lubricants and cultural tropes. The aesthetics of nature and the seasons that infuse daily life in Japan were cultivated first in Heian-period Kyoto, setting the scene for much of the later sense of the affect of the seasons. In some ways, traditional poetics and aesthetics about nature are themselves advertisements for domestic tourism in Kyoto today, whether encountered in school, on television, or social media.

This confluence of a historical relationship to nature that is intertwined with the Heian-period poetic tradition, the vagaries of travel at peak tourist seasons, and the role of the tourist industry (both official and entrepreneurial) in marketing seasonal affect frame my analysis in this chapter. In what follows, I discuss several features of Heian seasonal aesthetics in literature and architecture, emphasizing the cultivation of human sentiment in relation to nature. The final section of this chapter examines several new seasonal light-up events in which natural beauty is at the fore, created to attract tourists in the off-season and off-hours—Hanatōro (Flower and Lantern Pathways) and Kyō no Tanabata (Tanabata in Kyoto). These seasonal events draw on the earlier seasonal sensibilities linked to particular places in Kyoto while aiming to attract new tourists. I argue that these events work in three ways: quite simply they make economic use of the evenings, but they also draw on traditional aesthetics to create experiences for contemporary visitors, and they serve to link twenty-first-century tourists to a sense of Japanese culture that is neither simply exotic nor familiar.

Nurturing Sentiment

The Heian period looms large for Kyoto. This period, when the seat of both the ruling and military power were located in Kyoto, is lauded as the Japanese renaissance because it was a time when the literary, artistic, and governmental forms adopted from China in the preceding two hundred years were indigenized to fit the local culture. This was a time renowned for the development of the refined aristocratic culture of classical Japan.

Out of this flourishing aristocratic culture, several critical literary and artistic genres developed. As noted in chapter 1, the most influential literary texts in the Heian period were anthologies of poetry—the *Man'yōshū* (Collection of Ten Thousand Leaves, 759) and *Kokinshū* (Collection of Japanese Poems Old and New, 905). According to Haruo Shirane (2012, 27–32), the *Kokinshū* was the main source of poetic reference throughout the Heian period, and by the thirteenth century it had become the most influential classical text. Both poetry anthologies prominently featured themes of nature and the seasons. The symbolism and references to nature in these classical poems infused the development of Heian literature and aesthetics. Drawing on the imagery in the *Man'yōshū* and *Kokinshū,* aesthetically the seasonal cycle started with spring, symbolized by the bush warbler, spring mist, and plum and cherry blossoms. Summer was a transitional season of heat and humidity, symbolized by the mandarin orange, rain, and the moon, which shone at night when it was cooler. Autumn was the jewel of seasons in the Heian period, symbolized by beautiful leaves and ending with fallen leaves and chrysanthemums. Finally, the cold and damp winter was symbolized by a lonely landscape but graced with snow, and it ended with snow-speckled plum blossoms, the first signs that spring was coming (Shirane 2012, 34–45). In this way, references to plants that are symbolic of seasons and seasonal changes became a part of Heian literature, and these references became canonical symbols of the seasons.

In the Heian period, and still today, spring and autumn were the most lauded seasons, even though they were shorter than the more inclement seasons. Thus the aesthetic importance attributed to the seasons was in inverse proportion to the season in lived experience. Shirane writes, "Finally, when it came to the unpleasant or difficult seasons, summer and winter, aristocratic poetry and culture sought to depict not what nature was actually like but what it ought to be. For example, one of the most important summer topics in Japanese poetry (*waka, renga,* and *haikai*) was summer night (*natsu no yo*), which was thought to bring coolness and relief from the heat and was deemed to be all too short" (2012, 12–13). Thus in these early conceptions of nature, the ideal was being crafted over and above lived experience. Spring and autumn could be understood as transition seasons because of their brevity or as short harbingers of the oncoming heat or cold. Instead, their beauty was enhanced, drawn out in the aesthetics of nature that developed in the Heian period. At the same time, the transience or brevity of both seasons became a part of their aesthetic through the influence of Buddhist ideals such as impermanence and imperfection. Thus starting in the Heian period, spring and autumn are understood as being beautiful in color and in their transience. This aesthetic is vividly depicted in the literature and poetry of the period, and it was in Heian literature that nature came to represent emotion and human sentiments.

Two of the most famous literary classics from the Heian period demonstrate this view of nature astutely. *The Tale of Genji,* by Murasaki Shikibu, and *The Pillow Book,* by Sei Shōnagon, were the first instances of vernacular literature, and both were written by court women. These texts, while very different in style and focus, provide us with glimpses into the daily lives, rituals, and preoccupations of the aristocracy in the capital. Both texts reveal familiarity with the *Man'yōshū* and *Kokinshū* through an intertexual use of poems, a practice that had already become canonic in educated circles in Heian. Indeed, *The Tale of Genji* includes over seven hundred seasonally attuned poems and numerous references to poems from the

Man'yōshū and *Kokinshū*. And both texts make significant use of natural and seasonal imagery. The opening segment from *The Pillow Book* is a now iconic instance of Heian seasonal sensibilities:

> In spring, the dawn—when the slowly paling mountain rim is tinged with red, and wisps of faintly crimson-purple cloud float in the sky.
>
> In the summer, the night—moonlit nights, of course, but also at the dark of the moon, it's beautiful when fireflies are dancing everywhere in a mazy flight. And it's delightful too to see just one or two fly through the darkness, glowing softly. Rain falling on a summer night is also lovely.
>
> In autumn, the evening—the blazing sun has sunk very close to the mountain rim, and now even the crows, in threes and fours or twos and threes, hurrying to their roost, are a moving sight. Still more enchanting is the sight of a string of wild geese in the distant sky, very tiny. And oh how inexpressible, when the sun has sunk, to hear in the growing darkness the wind, and the song of autumn insects.
>
> In winter, the early morning—if snow is falling, of course, it's unutterably delightful, but it's perfect too if there's a pure white frost, or even just when it's very cold, and they hasten to build up the fires in the braziers and carry in fresh charcoal. But it's unpleasant, as the day draws on and the air grows warmer, how the brazier fire dies down to white ash (Sei 2006, 3).

Written most likely in the last few years of the tenth century, by Sei Shōnagon, a lady in waiting for the Empress Teishi, *The Pillow Book* provides witty anecdotes and lively commentary about the vagaries of daily life in the Heian court.[3] In the quotation above, Sei describes and extols the pleasures and pains of nature through the seasons.

Murasaki Shikibu was the daughter of a middle-rank aristocrat in the early years of the eleventh century. The fifty-four chapters of *The Tale of Genji* were written serially and circulated among the women of the court and even came to the attention of the empress herself. Murasaki was called to serve Empress Shōshi around 1006, most likely because of her talent at writing prose and poetry (Murasaki and Tyler 2001, xvii–xviii). While the oldest extant fragments date to the twelfth century, the text was well received in its own time, circulated within the capital and then beyond, and was beloved enough to warrant a set of *emaki* (picture scrolls). The story is about

Hikaru Genji, "shining Genji,"[4] a son of the emperor by a beloved, but lower, consort. Genji himself is always at once the court favorite and on the outs because of his birth and his many romantic indiscretions. The story continues thirteen chapters past Genji's death to follow the lives of two young rivals at court and in love, Niou and Kaoru.

Nature frames *The Tale of Genji* as most of the chapter titles are references to plants or locations. Furthermore, all of the central female characters have plant or nature images in their names: Fujitsubo (Wisteria), Aoi (Heartvine), Hanachirusato (scattering orange blossoms), and most notably Genji's beloved Murasaki (Lavender). In most cases, the women are named for a chapter that is critical to their characters, often the one in which Genji meets them or in which they die. Yet it is not simply that nature imagery is a large part of the setting in *The Tale of Genji*. In Heian texts like this one nature becomes representative of the emotional and physical state of humans. This technique first became apparent in the poetic tradition at this time, and it carried over into both the poetry and prose of Heian vernacular literature. Ivan Morris writes of the role of nature in poetry and its connection to emotion in Heian texts: "The inhabitants of the shining prince's world never try to cut themselves off from their natural environment; rather they strive to blend themselves with the nature that surrounds them, believing that thus they can learn to understand themselves and those about them. Sensitivity to the subtle moods of nature, indeed, was an essential attribute of 'good people.' Without such sensitivity it was impossible to enter into the 'emotional quality of things,' which was regarded as the basis of aesthetic, and even of moral, awareness" (1994, 20). This passage elucidates the sense that in Heian literature an awareness of the seasons was a part of demonstrating that one was refined or cultured. Moreover, nature imagery was used to index human emotions and sentiments. The connection with, rather than opposition to, nature bespeaks an ontology that is highly crafted during this period in Japan.

This sense of the emotion of nature is a critical component of poetic traditions in Japan, and the strong connection between emotions—love in particular—and nature was highly developed in Heian literature. Heian writers used nature imagery in poetry as a way to express emotions and thoughts indirectly. Especially in the works of women writers who flourished in this period knowledge of the poetics of nature allowed humans to both see and respond to nature and to each other (Shirane 2012, 7). The clearest example of the way in which the poetics of nature works to fuse the natural and the human is in the word *matsu*. *Matsu* (松) is the word for pine tree, but *matsu* (待つ) means "to wait." In poetic allusion, the long-lasting and hearty pine tree, which remains faithfully green throughout the harsh months of winter, represents waiting stalwartly (pining, if you will) for a traveling lover; whether the loved one is just away for the day or gone for years, the wait feels long. In this way, in Heian-period literature and poetry, nature came to be understood in its ideal form as a way to express refined human sentiments. Nature was an extension of the human, the ways that emotions could be expressed most poignantly.

Poetry was not simply written and circulated in print; it was frequently the creation of poetry parties, in which poems were written collaboratively and competitively. And nature was a main way to express emotions and to engage with the world and each other. In reference to this cultivation of natural aesthetics, which exemplify human sentiment, Shirane (2012) argues that seasonal references in Japan are "second nature"—that is, rather than being natural, they have been carefully and multiply crafted throughout the last thousand years. As has been highlighted here, this was not nature unrefined, nature in the wild, but rather a highly cultivated nature. Beyond literature and poetry this nature was cultivated in the architecture and gardens of the period as well.

Cultivating Nature

It is striking that the development of an aesthetics of nature is the product of an urban lifestyle. In the Heian period, Kyoto was a major city, in both prominence and size. Rather than a tale of increasing urbanization and the attendant loss of nature, Kyoto developed with a social understanding of nature. This sense of the beauty of nature, cultivated for contemplation, still infuses the city and is referred to implicitly and explicitly in tourist promotions and events. This section examines the ways that Japanese architecture and gardens are arranged to showcase a cultivated beauty of nature. Like so much that this book covers, this use of nature is not particular to Kyoto; it is the way that Japanese gardens are shaped. And yet this aesthetic sense has its roots in Heian culture, and it is exemplified in Kyoto today (Kuitert 2002, 1–54). In particular, Japanese gardens craft nature temporally, spatially, and conceptually through attention to the four seasons, the use of borrowed scenery, and the creation of a tableau.[5]

Framing a discussion of nature in Kyoto with examples of architecture may seem contradictory, but traditional architecture in Japan is rooted in the connection between nature and culture, and this can be seen first and foremost in Heian-style architecture. The *shinden-zukuri* style of Heian aristocratic mansions included an open layout in which the central building was connected to smaller quarters by verandas. This architectural style is known for the ways that the outside world is incorporated into the inside. Rather than small internal "pocket gardens," for which Japanese-style homes are known today, in the *shinden-zukuri* style the gardens surrounded the buildings. With the long, flowing layout linked by verandas, each room could have a different view of a garden; even in inclement weather, the eaves over the outer hallways shielded the occupants from the vagaries of the seasons. Our living spaces shape our lives, and this style of house, wherein all the main rooms open through sliding doors or blinds to views of gardens, created a culture in which the boundaries between inside and outside, the natural and the human, were indistinct (Morris 1994, 33; Shirane 2012, 89–92).

While most of the aristocratic mansions in the *shinden-zukuri* style were destroyed in the city's long history of fires and architectural styles changed over the centuries, there are depictions of such mansions in *emaki* scrolls and texts like *The Tale of Genji*. These images make it clear that the boundaries between inside and outside were not only permeable through corridors and views of the garden, but also that nature was brought inside through architectural features, artistry, and clothing. *Shinden-zukuri* houses had sliding doors leading to the outside but also separating rooms. The internal doors and screens were frequently decorated with artwork featuring nature. Just as a garden's scene changes with the seasons, so too the interior screens could be changed to represent the season. In each of these cases, both the interior decorations referencing nature and the seasons and verandas that blurred the lines between inside and outside sought to infuse Heian social life with nature.

While nature was brought into Heian interiors through the use of screens, art, clothing, and architectural style, gardens were the feature around which a house was constructed. The gardens of Genji's Rokujō palace, with its homage to the beauty of each season, provide the archetypal vision of a Heian garden attentive to and cultivated for the seasons. About halfway through *The Tale of Genji*, Genji has built a mansion to bring all his most beloved ladies under one set of roofs; each lady has her own quarters, showcasing the season that suits her temperament. While the Rokujō mansion never existed, its depiction idealizes the importance of seasons and cultivated natural vistas in Heian culture.[6] The description of the southeast quadrant, where Genji's favorite wife, Murasaki, would reside, is telling:

> With construction completed, the move to the Rokujō estate took place in the eighth month of the following year. The Umetsubo Empress was expected to occupy the southwest quadrant because that had been the former residence of her mother. Genji and Murasaki occupied the southeast quadrant. The northeast quadrant was given to Hanachirusato, who had been living in the east annex of Nijō, while the northwest quadrant was being reserved for the Akashi lady. Some of the hills and ponds originally on the four parcels of land were not in a proper or pleasing location, so Genji had them excavated and shifted; by reshaping the appearance of the streams and the position of the hills, he was able to build each quadrant elegantly in accordance with the tastes and wishes of his ladies.
>
> The southeast quadrant was notable for its tall hills, and every kind of tree that blooms in the spring was planted there. The design of the pond was particularly appealing, and the garden in front of the residence was planted in five-needle pine, red plum, cherry, wisteria, mountain rose, rock azaleas, and other spring plants. Though the garden was planned with the spring season in mind, unobtrusive clusters of autumn plants were also set about here and there (Murasaki and Washburn 2015, 455).

This scene bespeaks the crafting of nature for which Japanese gardens have come to be known. Not only is there an attention to plants and scenery that exemplify each season, culminating in the grandeur of fall and spring, but also Genji's attention to the view from each quadrant and the peppering of plants that will flower or add color even in the off-season is important. The placement of each plant aims at the construction of a particular view and a particular season. This is true both temporally and spatially. This attention to the seasonal changes in the garden is part and parcel of the ways that Japanese gardens have been constructed beginning in the Heian period.

Japanese gardens craft vistas not only according to the seasons, but spatially as well. In addition to botanical elements, they integrate a range of other features, including the use of rocks, water, bridges, and paths as central elements. They even incorporate elements from outside the garden proper: *shakkei,* or "borrowed scenery." *Shakkei* borrows from the beauty of a mountain backdrop to enhance the beauty of a garden vista. While the word *shakkei* came into common usage in the Edo period, sources point to Tenryūji in Arashiyama as the first instance of the use of this notion of "capturing nature from a distance" in a garden dating back to the mid-fourteenth century (Hendry 2004, 88; Kuitert 2002, 176–178). Gardens in Kyoto all take advantage of this feature, especially when cherry and maple are scattered throughout the tree-covered hillsides in both Higashiyama and Arashiyama (the eastern and western sides of the city). Thus borrowed scenery is a feature of Japanese gardens that is put to good use in Kyoto.

Finally, the cultivation of nature in Japanese gardens is not concerned with merely temporal and spatial views of nature, but also with a conceptualization of nature.[7] The cultivation, which incorporates plants, paths, water, and rocks, often seeks to recreate a natural scene writ small. This can be seen in the final passage describing Genji's Rokujō winter garden: "Nara oaks, seemingly proud of their red leaves, which were in tune with the present season [fall], had been transplanted along with various other trees—the names of which were unknown—brought from deep in the mountains to create the impression of a shaded grove" (Murasaki and Washburn 2015, 456). In this garden various trees of unknown species—that is, uncultivated trees—were planted in the garden in order to create the effect of a wild mountain grove. Thus in the middle of the city a secluded mountain grove reminiscent of the seaside was created to suit the personality of the Akashi princess. As this instance exemplifies, the cultivation of nature in a garden can elicit the feeling of a very different landscape or season or place.

Today this practice of recreating nature through a garden tableau is seen in many gardens in Japan, but it is perhaps most famously imagined in Zen temple gardens, which are plentiful in Kyoto. Epitomized by patterned white rocks, combined with larger rocks, moss, and trees or bushes often in the background—a style called *kare-*

sansui (dry landscape)—Zen gardens often represent nature in miniature. While it may seem surprising that a garden without plants at its center can be said to represent nature, dry landscape gardens "encapsulate nature at large and bring it close" (Shirane 2012, 99). Zen gardens may represent an ocean with islands or mountains and fields through the technique of *mitate,* or "allusion." According to Shirane, *mitate* "means something like 'to see X as Y' [and] does not refer to the replication of a distant object or landscape so much as it is evocation through one or more physical features, such as a figuration of rocks and sand" (2012, 96). The goal is to recreate the basic elements of nature on a smaller scale. This is, perhaps, the epitome of cultivating nature, rallying natural objects (rocks, moss, stones, water) to create a tableau that evokes a larger natural scene.

Just as nature came to represent human emotions through poetry and literature, in Japanese gardens nature is cultivated to evoke the natural order through human artifice. In all of these ways, in Japan nature is crafted in dialogue with architecture and the pace and pathos of human lives. Today Kyoto is a modern metropolis, and Kyoto tourism is urban tourism; yet many of the most famous tourist sites, from temples to gardens, exhibit the cultivation of nature in the ways discussed here. In particular, attention to the seasons, *shakkei,* and views of nature from various angles along a veranda are all a part of the tourist experience in Kyoto. Many of the most recent landscape policies (discussed in chapter 2) were driven by attempts to preserve the borrowed scenery by restricting the height of buildings. Maintaining the surrounding scenery and vistaed view is one of the five main elements implemented in 2007. The Vistaed-View-Creation Ordinance aimed to conserve the thirty-eight vistas of Kyoto by setting the maximum height of buildings so that views remained unobstructed; it also specified the color of roof tiles that were visible in the view (Kyoto City Landscape Division 2007; 2014, 41–84). In this recent example, the natural environment of urban Kyoto is cultivated by city planners. In all of these ways, nature infuses Kyoto through the ever-present view of the surrounding hills as well as through the cultivation of seasonal aesthetics historically and culturally imbricated throughout the city.

Seasonal Attractions

The seasonal sensibilities examined above are a part of what attracts visitors to Kyoto, and they infuse tourism in the city today.

It was clear from my conversation with Mrs. A— that her own sense of tourism in Kyoto was organized seasonally and driven by natural phenomena—cherry blossoms and autumn leaves. The traditional "three viewings"—cherry blossoms, leaves, and the moon—remain fixtures of tourist promotions and events in in the city. These three viewings date back to Heian poetics of nature, where they originated in aristocratic outings to write poetry under the blossoms or leaves or moonlight. By the Edo period, such outings had become a part of the seasonal pattern of life in the urban culture more broadly (Shirane 2012, 168–174). In contemporary Kyoto the cultivation of nature and the seasons is a part of tourist offerings both old and new. In this section I examine the ebb and flow of seasonal tourism by analyzing several seasonal events that have been set up in recent years and that draw on traditional sensibilities to attract tourists during the evenings of the off-season.

As demonstrated thus far, in Kyoto tourism, nature looms large because of the surrounding hills, the traditional aesthetics that evolved from Heian court culture, and the sheer number of gardens at temples and shrines in the city. A part of signifying seasons includes the plants that are in bloom: cherry blossoms in spring, hydrangeas in summer. Whether one stops in at the Tourist Information Center in Kyoto Station or checks the city's tourism website, "What's in Bloom" is a primary feature. Just on the right as one enters the tourist information center is a small sign labeled "*hana dayori*" (Flower Tidings) with a list of the flowers in bloom updated daily (in Japanese). The term means news or tidings of flowers, and it has become almost synonymous with "news of the cherry blossoms," although in Kyoto, all blooming flowers are included in the forecast. Likewise, on the Kyoto City tourism website for domestic tourists there is a tab titled "*hana dayori*."[8] The tab displays a four-column chart listing the types of flowers in bloom in a given month, locations where they can be found (often temples and gardens), the number of trees/plants there, when they usually bloom, and how far in bloom they are: "not yet," "just opening," "best viewing," "waning." While this may seem like specialized knowledge of interest only to garden aficionados, the fact that these charts are in prominent tourism locations signals the role nature plays in domestic tourism in Kyoto.

During my 2012 *hanami* excursions, I wandered around the Okazaki Park area amid the throngs of cherry blossom visitors enjoying the sunny day. I headed to the Shin'en Garden in the Heian

Shrine.[9] There was a line to reach the tables arranged as an entrance for this busy time of the year. Along with entry tickets to the garden, one could buy postcards, shrine charms, and a few cherry-blossom-related souvenirs. Inside the garden, narrow paths snake through the foliage, never straight so as to ensure good views, and traditionally to confuse demons. While I have never visited this garden when it was entirely empty (simply a feature of Kyoto tourism), on this day the crowds were thick, and I was carried along by a current of people. That year the cherry trees bloomed early, something everyone commented on. Furthermore, it was uncharacteristically hot and humid for late March and it had rained hard the previous day, so both the sky and the ground were peppered with pink petals. To get out of the crowd a bit, I decided to participate in the tea ceremony, which is available in the teahouse situated conveniently at the end of main *sakura* area.[10] Fortuitously for the anthropologist, there were talkative people with me that day. The two women performing the ceremony looked tired but chatted with us amicably. The older of the two, a woman in her fifties, said they were exhausted because there had been nonstop guests that day; they had served tea to more than four hundred people, and our group was close to the last as they were closing soon. The hosts commented that due to the rain the day before, today had been unusually busy, even for the peak season. They added that this was the busiest time of the year for the shrine. I was joined by a group of five women, all in their forties, in town for the day from Osaka. Another woman, visiting on her own for the day from Osaka, said she was making the most of her day by visiting Maruyama Park, Nijō Castle, and the Imperial Palace (Gōsho); the Heian Shrine was her last stop. Finally, there was a group of three young women office workers (two of whom were wearing kimono) who said that they came to Kyoto from Okayama every year to see the cherry blossoms, but this was their first time at the Heian Shrine. This glimpse, albeit small, encapsulates a range of domestic tourists to Kyoto for the cherry blossoms—tourists who traveled from a few hours away to view the blossoms at their peak. As mentioned above, *sakura* bloom vividly throughout Japan, but for domestic tourists who want a day's excursion, Kyoto provides famous cultivated views of the blossoms throughout the city. And these events require no advertising.

Tourism in Kyoto is frequently marketed with natural imagery that goes beyond the details that appeal to flower enthusiasts.

Seasonal plants grace almost all of the marketing for Kyoto tourism sites. Throughout the year, posters advertising different tourist venues are adorned with cherry blossoms and wisteria for spring; iris and lotus, along with moss, for summer; ginkgo and maple leaves for fall; and snow and pine trees for winter. While none of these natural phenomena are unique to Kyoto, the tourist industry has cultivated and capitalized on all of them. Kyoto is the only place I know of that markets the viewing of nature in the rainy season. An oft mentioned example is the muted beauty of the golden hues of the Golden Pavilion in the rain or on a cloudy day, said to epitomize the aesthetic of *wabi sabi* (rustic beauty). Even so, it is the seasonal attractions of flowers and foliage that enhance the main tourist seasons of the year. Indeed, during *hanami* season the hotels are all booked a year in advance, and roads are so congested that daily life can be trying in the center of the city, and traffic is notoriously difficult during the leaf viewing season in the fall. Throughout my time in Kyoto, everyone with whom I chatted—from cab drivers and tour guides, tourists (both domestic and international), and a host of industry personnel—complained about the constraints on transportation and housing in April and November.

It is curious that in all of my interviews with industry personnel these two popular tourism seasons were not a main topic of interest. April and November are the prime tourist seasons for Kyoto, and yet they require little to no direct marketing because of their national prominence. In my interviews both cherry blossom and leaf viewing came up only in passing, in lists of the busiest times. Conversations were much livelier when it came to the challenges of attracting tourists in the off-seasons and off-times. Thus rather than focusing on the throngs visiting temples and shrines to view cherry blossoms or leaves, this final section examines several new citywide tourism events, paying attention to the ebb and flow of tourists in Kyoto, the city's tourism promotion plans, and the ways that traditional aesthetics are integrated or used to frame new events.

Both the tourism promotion plans discussed in chapter 2, Future Kyoto Plan 2010 and Yearning for Kyoto Plan 2015, emphasize the need for evening events for tourists when most of the major tourist attractions are closed (usually around 4 or 5 p.m.) (Kyoto City 2010, 2015). The Rakutabi Kyoto guidebook, *Guide to Kyoto Evening Tourism,* begins with this pronouncement: "'Night comes early in Kyoto'; somehow we have come to embrace such an image. That is as it should be; a number of temples, shrines, and long-established Japanese confectionery shops in the familiar tourist spots finish their work of the day relatively early. Therefore, many people who come to enjoy shopping and wandering around temples don't know what to do in the evening." The book goes on to suggest that there were lots of events from ancient times that were intended for the evenings. The book continues: "If you select the season and time right, you can have a significant experience of 'evening time, Kyoto style'" (2009, 4–5). Each of the new light-up events discussed in this section aim at just that: drawing tourists and locals alike to the tourist districts after hours, seeking to make evenings in Kyoto livelier and more eventful.

Hanatōro: Off Peak, on the Beaten Path

In May 2012, Mr. I— (2012), a longtime employee in the tourism industry, and I discussed some of the seasonal activities that bring people to Kyoto, including the four big events (大行事 *daigyōji*) each year: Jidai Festival in October, Aoi Festival in May, Gion Festival in July, and Gozan-no-Okuribi (Daimonji Fire Festival) in August. "Beyond these famous festivals, in the twenty-first century Kyoto has created several new annual events to attract tourists in the off-season," Mr. I— added. In collaboration with business groups and temples and shrines, the city created the Hanatōro light-up events in early December and March and the Kyō no Tanabata evening light-up in August. These new events take place outside of the peak tourist seasons, and each takes advantage of the quiet evening hours in the main tourist districts to showcase local crafts, artwork, temples, shrines, and the city itself.

The Hanatōro events have been held every year since 2003 in Higashiyama and 2005 in Arashiyama in early March and December respectively.[11] Both events run for ten days in the evenings, when the streets of the heritage tourist districts are usually dark and quiet. The Hanatōro events line the evening streets with lanterns to light the paths strategically throughout the route, and large-scale *ikebana* displays (flower arrangements) from the top schools in Kyoto are showcased. Event descriptions on fliers, websites, and official reports draw on themes that have been addressed throughout this chapter. The report from the 2014 events states the following: "Along with the temples and shrines, the historical and cultural heritage, nature and townscape, all of which symbolize Kyoto, we have combined '*akari*' [light] from the glow cast by lanterns around the *roji* paths, signifying Japan's abundant spirit and 'hana,' from *ikebana,* to create the *miyabi* feeling of Kyoto" (Kyoto Hanatōro Promotion Council 2015). Here there are references not only to nature and the townscape of Kyoto, but also to the traditional aesthetics of *miyabi* (the Heian-period aesthetic of courtly elegance), sensed in the soft light of lanterns in the narrow streets in the evening. The Japanese website for the event makes similar references to the history of the city, traditional aesthetics, and a new evening tradition:

> Kyoto is colored with a long history of 1,200 plus years; it has numerous excellent traditions and cultural features, including world heritage sites, yet it is an international cultural tourism city with a unique personality and attraction that boasts a cityscape surrounded by beautiful nature that brings out the unique flavor of each season.
>
> Aiming to promote Kyoto evenings as a new tradition of *fūbutsushi* [風物詩] for the twenty-first century, starting in March 2003 a new set of tourism resources businesses was created for the Kyoto Hanatōro with the theme of "light" in Higashiyama (Kyoto Hanatōro Promotion Council, "Kyoto Hanatōro").

Fūbutsushi refers to "things that evoke memories or anticipation of a particular season" and originally referenced poems, although it is used more broadly today. The 2014 Hanatōro report romantically refers to these new events as evocations of early winter and early spring. Thus the Hanatōro Promotion Council aimed to create a new seasonal tradition, one that promotes two off-seasons in the contemporary tourism cycle.

In the case of the Arashiyama Hanatōro in December, the famous bamboo walkway and bridge are both lit up from 5:00 p.m. until 8:30 p.m. each evening. This winter event brings people to Arashiyama in the off-season, just after the leaf viewing season. The text accompanying the announcements for Hanatōro 2015 and 2016 in English read as follows: "Light and Blossoms Pathway: Taking advantage of nature, the waterfront, the bamboo forest and historical cultural assets of the Saga-Arashiyama region, a walkway totaling approximately 5 km is rendered from the light of open air lanterns, whose shades and shadows imbue a Japanese sentiment alongside the blossoms of voluminous flower arrangement pieces. The created effect is a pathway that beckons you to walk down it" (Kyoto Hanatōro Promotion Council 2015). Here, too, the links between traditional crafts and aesthetics and the charm of an evening walk in Arashiyama are all highlighted. Amid the lanterns and flower displays, there are booths selling souvenirs and food, crafts corners with events for kids, and areas where one can learn about traditional Kyoto crafts. The area temples are also open for special evening hours and have light displays throughout the grounds during the ten days of the event.

As noted, the second major Hanatōro event is in Higashiyama in early March before the peak *hanami* season. The Higashiyama Hanatōro brings people to the eastern hills before the main tourist season has started. The website advertising the 2019 events in English reads as follows:

> ROHM co. produces "Light and Blossoms Pathway"
>
> A lot of lanterns decorate the 5 km walking path that leads to the foothills of Higashiyama Mountain. From the north, the path goes through Shoren-in Temple and Maruyama Park, and then through Yasaka Shrine to Kiyomizu Temple in the south. Enjoy the striking charms of Kyoto streets. Faint lights that beautify the store fronts of Monzen-machi, soft lights that reflect off the stone pavements, lights swaying amongst the trees, white and earthen walls (Kyoto Hanatōro Promotion Council, "Kyoto Higashiyama Hanatōro").

Like for the Arashiyama event, this description highlights the charm of Kyoto evenings, nature, light, and crafts, tourist sites, and the city.

In March 2012 my family and I attended the Hanatōro one evening. Lanterns lit a path from Kiyomizu Temple all the way north to Shōrenin near Sanjō. We entered right in the middle at Yasaka Shrine, where the atmosphere was eerie and festive, the trees and shrine grounds lit by low lanterns. As we walked toward Kōdaiji, the streets were lovely, lined with different lanterns, a new style every block or so, always with a sign about the company who made or sponsored them. As one young woman from Osaka commented, "I like the atmosphere; it feels both old and new." Key landmarks were lit with special lights, all to highlight the features in the dark. Yet despite the careful attempt to craft a refined nighttime atmosphere, it was hardly serene due to the throngs of people.

Two features link the two Hanatōro events, evidenced in the name: flowers and light. These two features highlight Kyoto crafts, both old and new, through showcasing *ikebana* exhibits and the incorporation of LED technology in traditional-style lanterns. The art of flower arranging is another example of the cultivation of nature discussed above. Developed as a craft in the medieval period, alongside tea ceremony and bonsai, *ikebana* is the practice of arranging natural elements into a display that captures the feeling or mood of the practitioner or event for which it is created. In fact, the term "flower arrangement" is a bit misleading because the focus of the display is not always on the flowers. Like for rock gardens, natural elements are used and carefully arranged to elicit the feeling of fall or spring or joy or sadness. According to Shirane (2012, 98), the rules for standing-flower arrangements were formalized by the 1600s, and the earliest books about the subject set out the main elements (center, augmentation, and base) and tools, as well as lists of which plants and features were appropriate for which season. Rokkakudo in central Kyoto is known as the birthplace of *ikebana,* and the three top schools are still located nearby. The *ikebana* arrangements along the Hanatōro paths were large scale and lit up, events in and of themselves for decoration and contemplation. In this way, a traditional art, which has ties to the city, is showcased in this new celebration of early spring and early winter. The displays at both Hanatōro events are not merely examples of past tradition, but they also exemplify the best of contemporary *ikebana* in Kyoto.

Light is also a feature of these two events; various temples and shrines host special evening light-up events. The lantern path that winds through the historic district is sponsored by Rohm, a semiconductor company located in Kyoto that showcases new LED technology by sponsoring a variety of light-ups throughout the city. Thus rather than traditional lanterns with their attendant fire risk, the lanterns in Hanatōro use the latest lighting technology in a traditional aesthetic.

While walking the main paths is free, the temples that feature special light-up events charge their usual entrance fees. Inside the temple grounds there may be lanterns lining the paths, views of the lit-up areas outside their walls, and a view of a famous garden at night. But there is also a special set of lights on the main garden feature. In 2012 we went into Kōdaiji because its advertising featured a dragon.[12] The front entrance was lit with an eerie blue light as we wandered among a thinned-out crowd. The dry landscape garden was lit with red and blue lights that illuminated rocks arranged to look as though a dragon was swimming in the garden. One large object, made from traditional roofing tiles, made the hump of a dragon's back, and in the northeast corner the dragon's head emerged out of the sand. Similarly, in other temple gardens different lighting techniques are used, not simply to illuminate a dark garden, but also to produce a particular effect through use of color, shading, or projected light designs. Such special features with the theme of light attract evening visitors to temples in the off-seasons. Thus, the Hanatōro events weave together three key threads central to this chapter: the city promotion of off-peak travel; the appeal of nature in Kyoto; and the cultivation of natural sentiments throughout the urban landscape.

One of the features of the recent tourism promotion plans was to attract new demographics of tourists to Kyoto. In particular, many of the domestic tourists who flock to Kyoto year after year are over the age of fifty, so attracting younger tourists who will be repeat visitors is important to such efforts (Kyoto City 2010; Mr. K— 2012). The Hanatōro Promotion Council website released a report on the results of a survey for the 2014–2015 events. According to this report, 929,000 people visited the December Hanatōro over the course of the ten-day event in 2014; more than half (57 percent) of the visitors were under the age of forty, while 40 percent were under the age of thirty. The following spring, 1,128,000 people visited the Higashiyama Hanatōro. Similar to the data for the December event, 58 percent of the visitors were under forty, and 43 percent were under thirty (Kyoto Hanatōro Promotion Council 2015). This is a significant shift from the city's average tourism demographics, indicating that perhaps the Hanatōro does attract younger audiences and families. Indeed, the annual tourism survey reports list the start of Hanatōro as a factor in increasing tourism numbers in 2003 (see figure I.1) (Kyoto City Tourism Office 2019, 2). Furthermore, of the domestic tourists, who made up 70 percent of the tourists in December and 74 percent in March, more than half were from the Kansai area, and just under half stayed in a hotel for at least one night for both events (Kyoto Hanatōro Promotion Council 2015). Finally, of those surveyed a little over 50 percent came just for this event and did not visit any other tourist location. Thus it seems that these events have been relatively successful at attracting new, younger tourists to Kyoto in the off-season, albeit for short excursions.

Tanabata: Evoking the cool summer evening

Summer is a difficult season in Kyoto; it is warm and rainy for most of June and then oppressively hot and humid throughout July and August. The Gion Festival, held each July, was originally created in the Heian period to ward off pestilence in the stifling heat of the summer. If we refer back to the traditional associations of summer exemplified by the passage from Sei Shōnagon quoted above, we see that in the hot summer months, evenings and nights are the primary aesthetic references. This sense about summer is mirrored in the Kyoto City Official Travel Guide web page: "Summer is the season when the rain in Kyoto is most beautiful. This section [of the web page] introduces sightseeing courses for enjoying the beauty of hydrangeas, which is a typical flower in the rainy season, and the tranquil atmosphere of temples in summer"(Kyoto Convention and Visitors' Bureau). Flowers in the rain and cool spots in the summer heat are highlighted in promotions of Kyoto in summer, fitting with the traditional symbols of summer. So, too, throughout Japan in July and August, summer festivals are a mainstay of many localities seeking to enjoy the summer evenings. The final light-up event examined here is set in the heat of the late summer around the traditional Tanabata festival.

Kyō no Tanabata is celebrated each August simultaneously in the east and west of the city, but unlike Hanatōro, which was invented for Kyoto tourism, it is a well-known tradition. Tanabata, or Star Festival, was brought to Japan from China in the Nara period. Typically observed on the evening of the seventh day of the seventh month, Tanabata celebrates the summer night sky. A folktale holds that two stars—the herdsman Hikoboshi (Altair) and the weaving princess Orihime (Vega)—were lovers, but their love distracted them from their work (herding cattle and weaving cloth), so Orihime's father caused the Milky Way to separate the two. Orihime was so distraught that she convinced her father to let them meet once a year. Tanabata celebrates the yearly meeting of these two lovers in the night sky. References to Tanabata celebrations can be found in the *Man'yōshū* and in Heian literature, but the festival became a major holiday when it was embraced by the commoners in the Edo period (Shirane 2012, 158–159). By the Edo period, the tradition of writing poems and praying for weaving and other craft skills were common; in this period the practice of writing poems on colorful strips of paper tied to a tree was started (Shirane 2012, 159). Today, people still write wishes on colorful pieces of paper and hang them in places of celebration on July 7.

First created by the Kyoto City Tourism Office and the new Kyoto Tanabata Executive Committee in 2009, Kyō no Tanabata features many aspects of this traditional myth, best described through the committee's English-language website:

> Kyo-no-Tanabta is a collection of events held in August, which is when Tanabata falls in the lunar calendar. The events are designed around the theme of "Wishes," in honor of the tradition of "making a wish once a year." It is a ten-day event full of magical productions of bamboo and light, where visitors can enjoy the tradition of Tanabata in true Kyoto style. . . . At each site, visitors can purchase "Picture Postcard Strips" (100 yen each) for writing wishes and attaching them to bamboo leaves. In addition, many temples and shrines in the area will be putting up Tanabata decorations and offering special nighttime admissions (Kyoto Tanabata Executive Committee).

Fitting with the theme of the night sky in the myth and traditional Tanabata festivals, Kyō no Tanabata takes place in the evening, from 7:00 to 9:30 p.m., for ten days in early August. Tanabata is typically celebrated in early July, yet in the lunar calendar the date falls close to a month later. Kyō no Tanabata makes use of this difference because in July the Gion Festival takes up much of the city's energy and attention. Since Kyō no Tanabata is held a month later, it falls during one of the lowest tourism months of the year.

Originally there were two main locations for the Tanabata events, on opposite sides of the city—the Horikawa and the Kamo River. The Horikawa is a much smaller river that has been fully channeled into a canal. It runs north to south near Nijō Castle on the western side of the city; it is a popular local place for walking and running, with paths out of the main pedestrian and bike traffic. The Kamo River, Kyoto's famous river on the east side, is a much larger venue, featuring a variety of booths and events all along the riverfront. In recent years locations have been added in the north and south of the city, as well as at Amanohashidate, on the coast in Kyoto Prefecture.

Two themes emerge in this evening event tying it to the traditions of Tanabata festivals and to Kyoto in particular: love and crafts. The festival involves a myth about star-crossed lovers—star lovers who can be together only once a year by crossing the Milky Way. With two simultaneous events along two prominent rivers in Kyoto, that crossing is highlighted. In the Horikawa Kyō no Tanabata event cables of lights are strung across one section of the narrow canal almost like a canopy.[13] The constellations and Milky Way are illuminated above as one walks along. Drawing on the theme of love, the Kamogawa event features a "Love Cam," where couples can take a picture of themselves in front of a Tanabata background with print club-like (*purikura*) like embellishments.[14]

In the Tanabata myth, Orihime weaves beautiful cloth near the Milky Way. Kyoto is known for its cloth weaving and dyeing industries, which developed to provide the elaborate robes of the court and aristocratic circles. In the northwestern quadrant of the city center, near the Horikawa, sits Nishijin, an area renowned as the center of weavers and cloth craftspeople. Nishijin is known for several kimono craft industries, including *yūzen* dying. *Yūzen* is a method of painting/dying detailed scenes on silk for kimono; it uses rice paste to control where the dye sets and where it washes off. The method was developed by fan painter Miyazaki Yūzensai (1650–1736) in response to sumptuary laws aimed at limiting the use of intricate stacked embroidery and gold thread. The *yūzen* technique enables an artisan to paint a scene on silk using a washable adhesive to achieve a similarly detailed texture for images on kimono (Dalby 2001, 40; Yuzo 2019, 75). Traditionally the long pieces of cloth were set up to flow in the river to wash out extra die. Since the *yūzen* technique is associated with Kyoto, as a part of Kyō no Tanabata, cloth streams down in both rivers, and *yūzen* demonstrations are featured as a way to promote local and traditional crafts.

These new Tanabata events draw on some of the earlier imaginings of summer, focusing on water and the enjoyment of the cool(er) evenings in the heat of the Kyoto summers. The description for the Kamo River event on the website explains (in Japanese), "Various events are offered, centered on the area from 'Oike-Shijō' along the darkened, Kamo River. Walking paths staged with bamboo and light, full of Tanabata sentiment; water art projections; an open *maiko* teahouse; and a demonstration of the flow of *yūzen* in the Kamogawa all incorporate elements of the summer evening" (Kyoto Tanabata Executive Committee). One of the events held over the weekend is the Kamogawa Nōryō (Festival for Enjoying a Cool Evening), a celebration of summer on the stretch of the path between Sanjō and Shijō. The use of the word *nōryō,* which means enjoying the cool of the evening, harkens back to the seasonal sentiments crafted in an earlier time, evoking the aesthetics of summer.

In the report released after the 2015 Kyō no Tanabata events, the executive committee described the events as follows: "Blessed by the weather throughout the time, at both places we had more than 760,000 people visit, the second-highest number on record, thanks to the tourists, the Tourism Office, and everyone in the prefecture and city. From almost all of the people, we received a good response, and [Kyō no Tanabata] has steadily become established as a summer *fūbutsushi* of Kyoto" (Kyoto Tanabata Executive Committee).[15] From the less poetic part of the report, it is clear that the demographic for this new event, like for the Hanatōro, is primarily regional. In 2015, 53 percent of tourists were from Kyoto Prefecture (mostly Kyoto City itself), and another 32.5 percent were excursionists from the Kansai region. Like for the Hanatōro, visitors come to Kyoto for this new tradition of summer, but Kyō no Tanabata draws fewer overnight guests. Thus while the report assesses that Kyō no Tanabata is becoming synonymous with Kyoto in August, it is primarily attractive to locals, not as a major draw of new tourists for long visits.

Each of the new events discussed here was created to attract regional tourists in the off-season and when the main tourist sites have closed for the evening. And all of these events last several days, like a festival, and showcase a range of lighting displays, as well as traditional crafts. While Kyō no Tanabata directly incorporates elements of the summer tradition of celebrating Tanabata that have evolved over the centuries, the two newly created Hanatōro events likewise take advantage of the nighttime atmosphere in the temples, shrines, and cityscape of Kyoto. This is highlighted by visitor posts and comments on social media.[16] There are recurring references to the atmosphere created by lanterns in the heritage districts at night in comments such as the following: "It looks even more historic lit up in the evening!"; "Kyoto is enchanting lit up at night"; "The twilight effect of the lanterns at night is amazing!"; "So romantic at night." While each of these evening events draws on traditional aesthetics (like *miyabi,* courtly elegance) and each features traditional crafts (like *ikebana* and *yūzen*), these are not historical displays preserving a craft but rather exhibitions of contemporary crafts. Here, too, we see an example of living heritage, discussed in chapter 2. In fact, each of these events creates a heritage atmosphere in the evening hours through lights and displays, taking advantage of new ways to see these historic districts. In this case, a new event is invented not only to bring tourists into the city in the off-season and off-hours, but also to promote and support innovations in the traditional craft industries by drawing on traditional aesthetics (Yuzo 2019).

The Affect of Seasons in Kyoto Today

One of the threads throughout this book is the sense in which Kyoto tourism is urban heritage tourism, and in this chapter the heritage harvested is one of nature and seasons. From classical tradition to contemporary events for families and younger visitors, this chapter has examined tourist events in Kyoto that cultivate nature, imbuing seasons, plants, and places with human sentiments. By drawing links back to traditional poetic associations with nature and Heian literature and aesthetics, my aim is not to reify a romantic sense of the Japanese as having an innate oneness with nature, but rather to demonstrate how human relations with nature have been constructed in Japan in ways that are mobilized in promotions of Kyoto for domestic and international tourists today. Reading tourist events through the lens of prior narratives and aesthetics of the nature of Kyoto allows us to think about the ways that Kyoto, a twenty-first-century urban metropolis, promotes tourist experiences of nature and the seasons.

As I hope has become clear in this chapter, the role of Heian aesthetics in the city is complex. On the one hand, for domestic audiences no advertising is required to associate Kyoto with autumn leaves, cherry blossoms, and poetic sentiments; the associations of spring in Kyoto and autumn in Arashiyama are planted early as the Japanese learn about traditional poetry and literature. On the other hand, these aesthetic traditions are presented as living history to be experienced even in small ways by international tourists, who are drawn often by the stereotype and marketing of the Japanese sense of the seasons or a Japanese connection to nature. While there is much more to Kyoto than nature and Heian aesthetics, still that sense of a traditional sentiment is part of the appeal for many tourists, both domestic and international, even if they understand it in different ways. Indeed, the bulk of tourism in Kyoto involves views of nature. In tourist venues from the smallest cafe to the largest temples and shrines seasonal accents are a part of the decor, products for sale, and overall atmosphere. One can buy almost anything (from fans, to teacups, to incense, to Hello Kitty key chains) with a silhouette of cherry blossoms on it. These souvenirs seek to capture the feel of seasons in Kyoto for visitors to take home with them; this is marketing pure and simple. And yet, like the events discussed in this chapter, they index the seasonal associations with a long history. New seasonal events that seek to attract tourists to the city in the off-season are perhaps a new form of the cultivation of nature, what Shirane (2012) calls "second nature." In these events, seasonal sentiments are mobilized to attract tourists and provide fun events for locals in the heart of contemporary Kyoto.

Aiming to promote the atmosphere of Kyoto's traditional streets in the evenings, as well as to entice new visitors with the charm of contemporary urban Kyoto, both Hanatōro and Kyō no Tanabata re-imagine traditional aesthetics and seasonal associations for contemporary tourists. These events are new creations; there is no pretense that they are long-standing traditions, yet both draw on traditional understandings of the seasons as affective experiences that cultivate human experiences. In these new events, nature is understood as an extension of human emotions, exemplified in Kyoto and commodified as both trinkets and experiences that index tradition. In the end, these events seek to cultivate sentiments in the contemporary cityscape by drawing on aesthetics of nature and the seasons, traditional crafts and myths, and setting these events in prime tourist spots but after hours. With the creation of events that integrate nature and traditional aesthetics into the contemporary cityscape, visitors experience the seasons of Kyoto affectively.

Chapter 4

Bakumatsu Vacation

Sakamoto Ryōma and Heritage Contents Tourism in Kyoto

"Ryōma-sama, thank you for all you have done for Japan. I hope you are as close to Oryō as ever."
"I want to find someone like Ryōma!"
"I hope to be as successful at love and work as Ryōma-sama."

—Messages to Ryōma from visitors to the Teradaya in Fushimi

The personal messages left for Sakamoto Ryōma (1836–1867) at the Teradaya exemplify the turn to experiential tourism discussed throughout this book. Framed by these voices, this chapter moves away from large-scale tourism promotion plans, organized festivals, and World Heritage sites to examine tourism in Kyoto from the ground up. Walking around Kyoto, one cannot help but encounter historic markers and placards, including old stone pillars and new wooden signs, demarcating sites where historic events transpired or historic figures resided. As noted in the introduction, the layers of history are palpable all over the city. But references to historical events in Kyoto are not relegated to official historic markers. Alongside the markers one is likely to find contemporary popular images, ranging from posters to manga- or anime-style illustrations, both professional and amateur. Retelling stories of heroes and villains from the past is the stuff not only of legend, but also of popular culture. Moreover, with the advent of heritage contents tourism, popular historical fiction, whether in print or other media, reinvigorates interest in heritage

Figure 4.1. Messages to Sakamoto Ryōma at the Teradaya. Photo by author, 2017.

sites and encourages local entrepreneurs to mark and market ties to history. In order to examine the connection between history, tourism, and popular culture, this chapter analyzes tourism sites in Kyoto that commemorate the life and death of Sakamoto Ryōma, focusing on how one popular *bakumatsu* hero's story is retold in ways that promote personal connections with the past while speaking to contemporary anxieties. As I will argue, the sites examined here cast Ryōma as a young hero who persevered for the birth of the modern Japan at a time of national upheaval; it is a message with particular resonance in the wake of thirty years of economic and social precarity.

In Kyoto, locations that best exemplify this way of commemorating the dramatic (and dramatized) events of history can be seen in the scattering of local sites dedicated to *bakumatsu* events (1853–1868), which gained renewed popularity in the twenty-first century. As noted in the introduction, *bakumatsu* refers to the last few decades of the Edo period, highlighting the revolutionary events that led to the Meiji Restoration in 1868. As home to the emperor, in whose name the plots to end the Tokugawa rule were proposed, Kyoto was an important location in the *bakumatsu* period. Stories of intrigue, mystery, and murder—plots hatched and foiled in the teahouses, alleyways, and inns of Kyoto at this time—abound. The Teradaya Incident, Sakamoto Ryōma, the Shinsengumi, and the Ikedaya Incident (to name a few) are all variously commemorated in spots around the city. Examining these small-scale sites give us a glimpse of tourism beyond the must-see tourist spots and hyper-marketing of the traditional beauty of Kyoto.

The sites analyzed in this chapter are all situated along an informal pilgrimage route that commemorates the life and death of Sakamoto Ryōma. Ryōma is one of the most popular heroes of the *bakumatsu,* remembered for his youthful daring and diplomatic acumen. While scholars debate about how influential Ryōma actually was, his youth, swordsmanship, and martyrdom at the cusp of the creation of modern Japan are well known. The first biography extoling Ryōma's virtues came out less than twenty years after his death, and his story has been retold in novels, television shows, and movies in the ensuing years. This was brought home to me during my preliminary fieldwork for this book in the summer of 2010; Japan was in the throes of Ryōma fever. Everywhere one went, it seemed, there were posters of Ryōma, including historic photos or images from *Ryōmaden* (Ryōma's Tale), the Taiga drama that year.

The *Taiga dorama* (Big River Drama) is an important cultural icon of postwar Japan. The year-long historical drama series produced by NHK, the national broadcast company, has been running since the early 1960s, enticing audiences across Japan every Sunday night at prime time. The television series dramatizes important historical events, featuring top actors and elaborate sets. Dramatic national moments like the Warring States period, the unification of Japan in the late sixteenth century, and the *bakumatsu* period comprise a large part of the Taiga drama oeuvre. Not only are these dramas popular, but they are also an industry in and of themselves, tied to travel promotions with Japan Railways (the national railway) and tourist industries in locations featured in the show that year. Philip Seaton's (2015) research on Taiga drama tourism demonstrates that the factors that make these dramas successful at inducing local tourism are complicated and uneven; yet *Ryōmaden* was one of the most successful at boosting tourism, especially in Kochi (Ryōma's hometown), Nagasaki (where he founded the Kaientai, an early trading company), and Kyoto (where he was assassinated) (see also Seaton et al. 2017, 33, 89). In *Ryōmaden*, Ryōma was played by pop idol Fukuyama Masaharu; still today posters of Fukuyama's Ryōma can be found around Ryōma sites, alongside photos of Ryōma himself. That decade-old posters still decorate the informal Ryōma tourism route speaks to the longevity of these media recastings and the ways that they inform heritage tourist sites.

Yet *Ryōmaden* is not the first time that Ryōma's story has taken on a new life through popular retellings. Christian Tagsold's (2013) analysis of twentieth- and twenty-first-century Ryōma historical novels argues that Ryōma has become what Pierre Nora (1989) calls a "realm of memory." That is, Ryōma's story is not simply an account of historical events, but he has also become a site for collective memory, the contours of which change depending on the context of the retelling. Tagsold (2013, 48–51) demonstrates the ways that Ryōma's story shifts attendant to contemporary concerns—he is cast, in turn, as democratic, patriotic, peace loving, or a businessman. In short, his heroism does not remain in the 1860s; rather, he is a hero for contemporary Japan as well. Building on these narrative versions of Ryōma's story, the tourist sites examined here add to his story, casting Ryōma as a young hero who dedicated his life, fought, and died for the birth of the modern nation—a sentiment with a particular resonance today.

Finally, the sites examined in this chapter are good examples of the ways that heritage and contents tourism can be enmeshed. As noted in the introduction, contents tourism is a branch of media tourism, wherein places and scenes from media like television, anime, or video games induce tourism (Beeton, Yamamura, and Seaton 2013; Masabuchi 2010, 2018; Okamoto 2015, 2018a, 2018b; Seaton and Yamamura 2015; Seaton et al. 2017). Today one cannot attend this cluster of sites and ignore the pop culture references, including *Ryōmaden* posters and goods emblazoned with *bakumatsu* manga, anime, video game characters, and the like. As Seaton and colleagues note, "Many of our case studies are tourism to heritage sites induced by the representation of history in popular culture. If we think of history as a story, with historical characters performing important deeds in various locations, we can think of *history as contents*" (Seaton et al. 2017, 10; emphasis in original). The sites analyzed here do exactly this: they present history as contents engaging new visitors with stories from the past brought back to life in the present. Yet it is clear that an exacting historical account of these events is not the story that these stakeholders are telling. Indeed, the sites analyzed in this chapter—the Teradaya and the Kyoto Ryōzen Gokoku Shrine—do not tell Ryōma's story at all; attendees must know it before they arrive. Both sites claim a version of authenticity that does more than commemorate this hero or his times. Rather, these locations, which were important in Ryōma's life and death, provide ways for contemporary tourists to experience and interact with that history. This is one feature that stands out in contents tourism: fans seeking to connect with the places and people in the stories they love (Okamoto 2018a; Sugawa-Shimada 2015). This notion of a personal connection to heroes and events of the past is another way that experiential tourism manifests itself today. This face-to-face history is being both cultivated and sought out in these sites through the staging of events and the encouragement of personal connections with the characters in this historical story.

The first half of this chapter takes the reader on a tour of several important Ryōma sites in Kyoto—the Teradaya in Fushimi, where Ryōma narrowly escaped an assassination attempt in 1866, and then two locations in Kyoto proper, where he was assassinated and buried in 1867.[1] In examining these sites, I pay attention to the way Ryōma's story is told through brochures, signage, exhibits, and souvenirs. The second half of this chapter pulls together the threads that emerge in the analysis of the sites themselves, emphasizing the ways that these small-scale *bakumatsu* sites reveal a nostalgia for the modern in post–"lost decade" Japan (Prough 2018). This analysis stands in contrast to earlier accounts of historical tourism, which emphasize the ways that nostalgia often aimed at what was lost in modernity. In her examination of the Japan National Railways' "Discover Japan" campaign, Marilyn Ivy (1993, 251–253; 1995, 29–65) argues that this popular campaign from the 1970s was a part of a wider elegy for the premodern, prevalent in the high-growth era. Similarly, Millie Creighton (2009) analyzes the Rekishi Kaidō (History Highway) tourism campaign of the 1990s, which featured sites across Japan that commemorated Edo; she argues that the representations of a neatly unified Edo Japan are symptoms of nostalgia in an era of increasing globalization. Both scholars posit locations evocative of Edo Japan marketed as palliatives to the problems wrought by modernity in late twentieth-century Japan. As demonstrated in this chapter, however, Ryōma tourism in Kyoto today is likewise nostalgic tourism about the Edo period, yet the sites examined here are nostalgic for the hope of the turn to modernity, a hope for a renewed national strength and global prominence. These sites laud Ryōma as the iconic young modern hero who embodied new values for the nation at a time of national precarity.

Ryōma's Kyoto History

The *bakumatsu* period was a time of increasing discontent with Tokugawa rule and especially with the way the *bakufu* handled the Western encroachment. The fundamental threat to 250 years of seclusion that started with Commodore Perry's arrival in 1853 paved the way for growing dissatisfactions with the status quo among low-ranking samurai. Critiques of shogunal competence and legitimacy raised the issue of a return to imperial rule. As home to the emperor, by the early 1860s Kyoto was rife with young samurai loyalists who had left their domains to fight for the emperor (Jansen 1961, 100–102). As the plots to capture the palace and restore the emperor to power developed over the last decade of the Edo period, the shogunate put into place several militias to quell plots against the *bakufu* in the name of protecting the emperor from harm. The Shinsengumi was one such group from Kyoto. Housed in the Mibu area of the city, these samurai were trained to police the city on behalf of the *bakufu,* using the same kinds of ruthless and cunning tactics as the loyalists themselves. Accordingly, Kyoto became the veritable staging ground for the new nation, and accounts of these years depict the city as teaming with samurai fighting for the future of their country.

Sakamoto Ryōma was a fairly low-ranking samurai from a wealthy but marginal domain, Kochi, the capital of the Tosa domain on Shikoku.[2] During his short life, Ryōma joined the ranks of many young samurai who sought to change the political structure of late Edo Japan (Jansen 1961, 77–84). At this time, young samurai from across Japan met and interacted through swordsmanship schools. Ryōma, a renowned swordsman, took full advantage of these opportunities (Jansen 1961, 115). Indeed, both of the events in Ryōma's life that are commemorated in Kyoto involve swordfights. But Ryōma is renowned for his versatility as much as his swordsmanship. To start with, he is known for being a nascent politician who worked with Nakaoka Shintarō (1838–1867) to broker an alliance between the Chōshū and Satsuma domains, an alliance that eventually led to the Meiji Restoration. Ryōma was also a proponent of adopting

Western-style governance and technology as a means to maintain sovereignty. Moreover, Ryōma is heralded as an entrepreneur due to his role in founding the Kaientai(Jansen 1961, 223–270). Finally, Ryōma is known for his forward thinking; just a few months before his death, he outlined an eight-point plan that anticipated several government initiatives that would become a part of the new Meiji state, including the restoration of the emperor, the establishment of an assembly, and the creation of a constitution and a modern military system (Jansen 1961, 295–296). Thus Ryōma is legendary for both his samurai prowess and his modern sensibilities on the eve of the birth of the modern Japanese nation-state.

Most of Ryōma's life was not spent in Kyoto, and yet the sites examined in this chapter commemorate critical events in his short life: the attack on his life at the Teradaya and his death on Kawaramachi. The first incident occurred on March 9, 1866, in Fushimi, just south of Kyoto. Ryōma was staying at the Teradaya, an inn he frequented, with a friend from Chōshū. He had just returned to the inn with news that the alliance between Chōshū and Satsuma was successful when the famous scene took place. Ryōma's letter to his brother vividly describes the events of that evening:

> There was one man, Miyoshi Shinzō, with me. We had come up from the bath and were on the point of going to bed, when we thought we heard something strange; it sounded like the footfalls of someone sneaking around below us (we were on the second floor). Then, in the same way, we heard the clattering of six-foot staves. Just at that time the woman I've told you about earlier (her name is Ryō [Oryō] and I have since made her my wife), with no thought of her own safety, came running up to us and warned 'Look out! The enemy have invaded unexpectedly, and men with spears are coming up the stairs!' At that, I jumped up, grabbed my *hakama* and the two swords, along with a six-shooter pistol, all of which I had left in the next room, and crouched down towards the rear of the room. Miyoshi Shinzō had on his *hakama,* put on his two swords, and grabbed a spear; and then he too crouched down (quoted in Jansen 1961, 228).

In the skirmish that followed this attack, Ryōma shot several rounds with his Smith and Wesson revolver, but he was injured. As the attackers regrouped, Ryōma and Miyoshi ran out the back and down the side streets until they found a storehouse in which to hide. As soon as it it was safe, Miyoshi went to the Satsuma compound to get help for Ryōma, who was too wounded to run further. When Ryōma finally arrived at the Satsuma compound, Oryō was there waiting for him (Jansen 1961, 227–230).

Just a year later, in November 1867, the second incident took place in Kyoto proper: Ryōma was assassinated by Tokugawa loyalists, along with his colleague Nakaoka Shintarō. The two were staying at the house of a friend—the Ōmiya soy sauce shop and residence. As the story goes, Ryōma was feeling ill, so he and Nakaoka had moved to the warmer main house. They usually stayed in a room above the storehouse at the back because it had an escape route to a small temple nearby, a detail that indicates that caution was necessary. Feeling ill, Ryōma sent for comfort food from home, a chicken dish called *shamo* (an oft-repeated detail in his story). A knock at the door, assumed to be the delivery, revealed three men who attacked Ryōma and Shintarō. The attack happened so quickly that they barely had time to draw their weapons, and Ryōma was killed instantly. Shintarō survived just long enough to recount the evening's events (Jansen 1961, 343–344). This event took place just a month before the Meiji Restoration, so neither man lived to see the emperor restored to the throne.

These two sword fights on the eve of the birth of the modern nation are the focus of the sites dedicated to Ryōma in Kyoto. In what follows, I turn to these tourist sites, focusing on how Ryōma's story is being told today and why. Each of these sites commemorates events that combine the bravado of samurai culture with the import of modern ideals; yet these sites also cultivate personal connections with these heroes of old, making this a living history for twenty-first-century tourists.

Intrigue at the Teradaya

Situated just south of Kyoto on the river from Osaka, Fushimi served as a major transit route into Kyoto by ferry. As such, several inns and teahouses to accommodate travelers were located along the river in Fushimi. During the Edo period the Satsuma compound was nearby, making Fushimi an attractive place for loyalists to meet just outside the capital. The Teradaya was just such an inn. Through its affiliation with Satsuma it provided lodging for guests who had local business with Satsuma, and in the *bakumatsu* era this included groups of loyalists (Jansen 1961, 227). In fact, in 1862, four years before Ryōma's famous stay, a group of loyalists was attacked at the Teradaya, halting an early plot to restore the emperor.[3]

In Fushimi today, Ryōma's presence is unavoidable. A life-sized cardboard cutout of Ryōma greets visitors as they exit the train station. Next to this figure is a local-interest sign highlighting Fushimi's main attractions: *bakumatsu* history and name-brand sake. From the station, it is just a short walk to the river, where a bridge leads to the Ryōma-*doori shotengai* (shopping area) and the Teradaya. It is surprising that the route to the Teradaya is not overtly marked, but along the way references to Ryōma can be spotted in the nooks and crannies of the streets of Fushimi. Storefronts and even residential windows frequently feature a small image or figurine of Ryōma, and there is at least one bar that bears his name. On the river, just across from the Teradaya, is a small pier where ferries arrived from Osaka in earlier days; today, tourists can take a scenic boat ride starting from this same landing.

The Teradaya looks like a traditional inn, featuring *machiya* architectural elements (discussed in chapter 2). The large, traditional lantern with "Teradaya" inscribed on its side, as well as the Kyoto City historical marker in front, are the main indicators of the inn's significance. The sign explains the 1862 attack on the loyalists but curiously not the attack on Ryōma, which is the central story told inside the inn. A small, family-run business, the Teradaya is less polished than institutions like the Ryōma Museum in Kochi or the Ryōzen History Museum in Kyoto. In fact, while the inn is filled with exhibits, commemorations, and paraphernalia honoring Ryōma, there is little explanatory text to be found inside, and what text there is is primarily in Japanese. While a small pamphlet in English is provided upon request at the entrance, it is clear that the target audience is Japanese; moreover, it is assumed that visitors know the story of the events at the inn. Rather than introducing visitors to the story, the exhibits aim to bring tourists into the spaces where these events happened. Lending to this air of authenticity, the inn is still owned and operated by the Terada family. Although the inn was severely damaged in fires during the post-Restoration skirmishes, the brochure assures visitors that "Today, the inside has been renovated, but the layout and style have not changed, thanks to the careful historical investigation and restoration conducted by the 14th generation, Terada Isuke" (Teradaya). Instead of a history lesson, it is clear that the appeal here is to experience firsthand the environs that Ryōma himself inhabited. Those seeking an immersive experience can book a room at the historic inn for the night, although Ryōma's room is not available.

As one first enters the building, there is a ticket booth on the left-hand side of the inn's *genkan* (foyer) and a display of books and a few goods for sale. After paying the entry fee, there is a place to remove one's shoes before stepping into the inn proper. The first room is lined with old photos of the Teradaya and posters of Ryōma, and the walls are lined with glass display cases featuring Ryōma-related goods—from file folders to good luck charms to small scrolls of Ryōma's writings.[4] At the far end of this long, narrow room, the route takes visitors up the stairs to the guest rooms where the action took place. Just to the right of the stairs, the room where Ryōma was staying is clearly marked. It houses a small shrine to him and an alcove with an image and statue. The alcove also houses a Smith and Wesson revolver—a critical artifact in Ryōma's story. Replicas or representations of this gun are featured at almost every Ryōma-related exhibit, and the Teradaya is no exception. Finally, upstairs here and there on the walls, small slashes and a small round hole are marked for visitors as sword and bullet damage from the attack on Ryōma. These reconstructed sword slashes and bullet hole raised a controversy within the tourism community in recent years, prompting the Teradaya to make the reconstruction of the inn more prominent in its brochures and website. As of 2017, the signs for these features remained in the inn despite the controversy because they are a critical part of the story. These features indicate an attention to recreating a kind of "authentic" atmosphere for visitors interested in Ryōma's story, even though the building has been reconstructed.[5] There are three more rooms upstairs, each of which is filled with historical artifacts and photographs, information about the two attacks at the inn, and tourist maps pointing out other *bakumatsu* sites in the Kyoto area.

After wandering through the upstairs, seeing Ryōma's shrine and and the site of the attack, the visitor is guided downstairs through a final set of rooms filled with artifacts about Ryōma and an eclectic set of images of the inn throughout the past century. One room includes a small area for people to leave *ema,* which can be purchased at the inn desk. *Ema* are small wooden plaques most frequently found at Shinto shrines. The purchaser writes a wish or prayer on the small piece of wood and hangs it up on stands. Periodically, the shrine priests burn the prayers and wishes to send them to the gods. *Ema* at shrines commonly include prayers for success—on exams, in health, in love, or in one's career; at the Teradaya similar messages were all left in honor of Ryōma himself, as seen in the epigraphs to this chapter. For example, in May 2013 there was one by a Chinese family, who "love Ryōma" and "hope to come again." The young couple, Chie and Koji, asked to be as close as Ryōma and Oryō; and a couple on their honeymoon promise to "persevere in their relationship like Ryōma and Oryō." Others dream of love or meeting the right person or for fortitude at work or on entrance exams. Yet not all of the *ema* are so serious; in 2017 one young woman wrote, "Yep, it is a new year, and I still love Ryōma!" The *ema* was replete with a hand-drawn manga-style image of a girl in kimono with Ryōma.

The inn may seem a surprising place to find these religious items, but *ema* have moved beyond their original religious use to become a tourism practice. With the contents tourism boom, *ema* have become a popular form of fan engagement with heritage sites (Seaton et al. 2017, 22, 45–47; Sugawa-Shimada 2015). In part, the presence of such messages to Ryōma indicates a younger demographic of tourists. According to the staff with whom I spoke in 2013, older couples and groups of men have long comprised the main visitors to the inn, but in recent years young people too have come to love Ryōma. Older male history buffs still visit the inn, but they do not tend to leave *ema*. Yet in line with the ways that the Teradaya seeks to keep Ryōma's story alive, the sentiments exhibited on *ema* indicate contemporary visitors' desire for a personal connection with this historical figure. In her research on women contents tourists, Akiko Sugawa-Shimada (2015, 47–50) found that *ema* and similar personal messages are an important way that female fans connect with favorite characters at heritage sites related to the video games Sengoku BASARA and Hakuōki. Likewise, Henry Smith (2007, 111–114) found similar personalized messages to Ryōma on tiles for purchase at the Ryōzen Gokoku Cemetery in Kyoto. These personal messages enable a face-to-face encounter with history, forging a connection between the past and the present.

As seen in this discussion, the Teradaya is filled with objects that reference Ryōma through the years. Historical artifacts and photographs tell the visitor what the inn looked like in Ryōma's time, but the inclusion of photographs from later eras, and posters from recent dramatizations like *Ryōmaden,* draw this history through time. Here we see history amplified and visualized by later representations in the twentieth and early twenty-first centuries. Seaton and colleagues find a similar pattern of layering at other contents tourism heritage sites. Describing the Akiyama Brothers' Birthplace Museum in Matsuyama, they write, "Visitors to the museum, therefore, are presented with a complex interplay between real historical figures and the television drama, realms of memory and places of the imagination, authenticity and inauthenticity" (Seaton et al. 2017, 31). At the Teradaya the implicit assumption, that visitors know the story and want to experience the places where these historic events unfolded, shapes the ways that the proprietors pay careful attention to keeping the inn "authentic" in layout, despite its reconstruction and renovations to open new portions of the building. At the same time, exactly how visitors know the story—whether from school, historical fiction, television dramas, or a combination of these—shapes what they want "authenticated." Thus the exhibits in the Teradaya ensure that Ryōma's story is not relegated to the past. The curation of photographs and artifacts augments the feeling of walking in Ryōma's footsteps, while the *ema* allow visitors to connect personally with Ryōma and his story. Moreover, the juxtaposition of historically attentive curation, photographic images from different moments in time, alongside media representations from across the past century bring Ryōma's story into the present. Thus this history is made real for contemporary visitors to the Teradaya today.

A Modern Ryō-mance

One cannot visit the Teradaya without noticing the emphasis on Ryōma and Oryō's story. At the Teradaya, Oryō is an important character. In fact, above the door of the front room on the second floor, there are two images of Oryō—one as a young woman just after the Restoration and one as a much older woman. These two photos can be found in much Ryōma literature. Not much is known about Oryō, but she is said to have been "a famous beauty" (Jansen 1961, 228; Rakutabi Bunko 2009b, 36). Ryōma's letters to his siblings describe her as beautiful, strong, and courageous. Moreover, he highlights the ways she helped the loyalist plots. It was on account of her strengths that Ryōma secured her a job at the Teradaya (Jansen 1961, 225–228). Perhaps most compelling are Ryōma's own words about Oryō's role in his brush with death in the Teradaya (quoted above).

As the story goes, Oryō ran up the stairs, from the bath, to warn Ryōma of impending danger, saving his life that day. When I visited in 2017, the stairs near the back of the second floor of the Teradaya had been opened up, allowing visitors to descend the staircase that Oryō ran up to warn Ryōma. Small handwritten signs on the walls authenticate this important location. The bath where Oryō would have been is open for viewing as well (next to a newly added guest restroom). This part of the lore, where the young maid runs out of the bath to warn Ryōma, is critical to the story. The recent evolution of the exhibit space, with the addition of the stairway she ran up and a replica of the bath itself, augments ways that the remains of these historical events can be experienced by visitors to today, but it does so in a way that emphasizes Ryōma and Oryō's love story.

Ryōma and Oryō's story is celebrated as a modern romance. The contours of this famous love story include the similarity of their names, their reunion after the Teradaya escape, and their "honeymoon in Satsuma." Most popular accounts of the lovers mention the fact that the character "ryō" (龍) in both their names means "dragon," an auspicious symbol linking the two lovers. Perhaps the clearest commemoration in honor of this romance is the statue of Ryōma and Oryō situated just across the river from the Teradaya (figure 4.2). The statue is labeled "Ryōma and Oryō's, Love Journey Statue" and was erected by the Fushimi Lions Club in 2011 (a year after *Ryōmaden* aired), marking the spot where they embarked for Kyūshū on a ferry soon after the 1866 incident. In the Ryōma lore there are frequent references to this trip to Satsuma. In fact, this trip is often referred to as "Japan's first honeymoon" (Rakutabi Bunko 2009b, 34–35; Seaton 2015, 94). Ryōma and Oryō did get married and travel to Satsuma for some rest and relaxation. After all, Ryōma was injured, and he was a wanted man. Yet this notion of "Japan's first honeymoon" demonstrates the ways that this romance is frequently couched in terms that reference the influx of modern Western ideas. Beyond the romantic narrative found in guidebooks and tourist campaigns, this is perhaps best exemplified in the romantic sentiments and prayers for love left on the young couple's *ema* at the Teradaya. In the end, the combination of samurai courage, young romance, and hope for the modern nation, embodied in the way these Fushimi sites tell Ryōma's story, infuse these historical events with contemporary concerns. Here, fated young love is the stuff of legend, popular culture, and contemporary fantasy.

Figure 4.2. Ryōma and Oryō's love journey statue, Fushimi. Photo by author, 2014.

Mysteries of History in the Streets of Kyoto

Unsolved mysteries from the past make for good stories, and accounts of Ryōma's death fit the bill. Dramatic accounts of his assassination in Kyoto appear in three different Rakutabi guides to Kyoto replete with possible escape routes and other sundry details (Rakutabi Bunko 2008, 2009b, 2013). As outlined above, in November 1867, Ryōma and Nakaoka Shintarō were staying at the house of a friend when they were assassinated. The Ōmiya residence and shop was located on Kawaramachi, between Shijō and Sanjō, right in the heart of a busy shopping district. Unlike the Teradaya, the Ōmiya establishment is no longer there. Today, the location is almost invisible amid the hustle and bustle of shoppers and tourists in the area. The storefront at this location has changed hands multiple times during the course of my research—morphing from a Circle K convenience store to a travel agency to a sushi restaurant. Like many *bakumatsu* sites in Kyoto, the site of Ryōma's death is identified by a small stone marker and a Kyoto City historical site sign.

Walking north on the left-hand side of Kawaramachi, an attentive observer can see a stone marker, a wooden Kyoto historic site sign, and a map to Ryōma's gravesite, located in the Kyoto Ryōzen Gokoku Shrine not too far away. These historic markers are situated just in front of an ever-changing storefront, and they are most visible when the foot traffic is blocked by a history buff, curious tourist, or media camera crew stopping to read and take pictures of the signs. The layers marking this spot are clear, as can be seen in figure 4.3. The stone pillar on the left has marked this spot for a long time, while the wooden sign is a more recent version; finally, the image of Ryōma and map to the cemetery were added in 2013 or 2014 by the Kawaramachi Shopping District Association. This recent addition, by a neighborhood commerce group, signals local interest in the commemoration of Ryōma as a part of Kyoto's past and this district's history.

With the map at the site of the former Ōmiya house, Ryōma's gravesite can be found at the Kyoto Ryōzen Gokoku Shrine in Higashiyama. Just off Ninenzaka, between Kiyomizu Temple and

Figure 4.3. Site of Ryōma's assassination, Kyoto. Photo by author, 2014.

Maruyama Park, there is a road known as Restoration Way. At the intersection, a large concrete *torii* directs the visitor up a steep hill. About halfway up is a bend in the road with a Kyoto City historical marker; on the left is the Ryōzen Gokoku Shrine and Cemetery; on the right, the Ryōzen History Museum.[6] The text reads as follows:

> Officially recognized by the national government, this museum is a center for display of artifacts and research associated with the Meiji Restoration, the turning point for the modernization of Japan. The purpose of the museum is to convey the will and determination of individuals involved in the creation of the modern nation.
>
> In 1868, the first act of the new government was to establish a monument to fighters for the new nation here in the Ryōzen district. The Ryōzen Patrons Society was established 100 years later, in 1968. Restoring the area, the society opened the museum in 1970 and continues to operate it today.

The shrine was established as a resting place for the souls of those who devoted themselves to the Meiji Restoration, but Ryōma's and Shintarō's gravesites are the central attraction.

The Ryōzen Gokoku Shrine is the most official of the sites discussed in this chapter. As a religious site of national significance honoring the war dead (*gokoku* means "defense of the country"), it might be surprising to find the trappings of a contents tourism site here. When I first entered the shrine grounds in the summer of 2013 on my informal Ryōma pilgrimage, I found myself facing a typical shrine building. It was quiet and empty, but there was a group of middle school students chatting and buying drinks and souvenirs from a smaller building to my immediate right. Upon closer inspection, I saw that this building served as the entryway to the cemetery proper, as well as a small store for souvenirs. The shrine and cemetery entrance looks like many tourist sites: there are vending machines, *bakumatsu*-themed gotcha-ball machines, and two turnstiles requiring 300 yen to enter the cemetery. Upon entering, one can wander through the cemetery, but the route that is well marked leads to Ryōma and Shintarō's gravesite, just above the entrance on the hillside. The gravesite houses a small shrine with two grave markers, a recently added statue with descriptions of Ryōma's and Shintarō's brave deeds, and an official Kyoto City historical marker (in Japanese). It is one of the oldest Ryōma sites, and yet even here the layers of Ryōma's changing image are on display as signs, statues, and other features have evolved over the years (Seaton et al. 2017, 90–91). High on the hillside, the site serves as a scenic overlook with a sweeping view of the city. As Rakutabi Bunko's *Ryōma's Guide to Kyoto* (2009b, 108) romantically highlights in reference to the view of the city from the vantage of the statue of Ryōma and Shintarō, these two heroes "have a view of the land that was sacred to the *bakumatsu* leaders." This romantic vista of the city is always featured in guides to this site, fitting with the wider representations of Ryōma, as well as with traditions of tourism in Kyoto that frequently highlight views of the hills from the city or of the city from the hills.

Unlike a typical shrine booth offering religious items such as charms for ailments or successes and votive cards and candles, the shrine souvenir store by the entryway is filled primarily with Ryōma goods, as can be seen in figure 4.4. There are a few *ema* and a charm or two (on the left), but mostly there are images of Ryōma on postcards,

Figure 4.4. Ryōma goods at the Kyoto Ryōzen Gokoku Shrine. Photo by author, 2013.

T-shirts, and folders, alongside books and DVDs of stories about him, and once again the Smith and Wesson is featured prominently.

This eclectic selection of goods, while atypical for a shrine or cemetery, is par for the course at heritage contents tourism sites and speaks to a younger demographic. The Ryōzen shrine and museum are just up the hill from one of the most popular tourism areas of Kyoto; the path of cobblestone streets leading from the Kiyomizu area to Maruyama Park is lined with souvenir shops that cater to school excursion students who come to Kyoto in droves. Moreover, each year around November 15, Ryōma's birthday, the Ryōzen shrine hosts a Ryōma Festival (Ryōma Matsuri). According to the shrine's website, as well as a description in the Rakutabi Bunko (2009b) guide, the Ryōma Festival attracts a wide range of students and fans. The festival honors Ryōma and Shintarō by serving *shamo,* the chicken dish that Ryōma ordered just before he was killed. It also features a dance competition called Ryōma Yosakoi." *Yosakoi* is a traditional dance from Kochi, Ryōma's home prefecture, and each year twenty teams of college students from around Japan travel to the Ryōzen shrine to perform the dance (Kyoto Ryōzen Gokoku Shrine Website 2014).[7] *Ryōma's Bakumatsu Guide to Kyoto* muses, "It is said that Ryōma and friends can see the energy of today's youth from heaven" (Rakutabi Bunko 2009b, 109). This youth-oriented festival formalizes the ways that the Ryōzen Gokoku Shrine and Cemetery have become a *bakumatsu* contents tourism site. And the festival shapes the souvenirs and goods available at this shrine; there is even a full Ryōma *yosakoi* outfit for sale at the shrine store year round, as seen in the upper right corner of figure 4.4. Like the Teradaya, this is a heritage site, a shrine and cemetery; nonetheless it draws from popular stories about the *bakumatsu* period, both new and old. The shrine not only commemorates, but also recreates and celebrates a connection in the present to this particular past. In this way, Ryōma tourism in Kyoto draws in varied audiences and enlivens history by bringing it into the present.

Heritage tourism sites are multivalent: they commemorate an event from the past, whether it was located at the actual site or elsewhere; they allow visitors to follow the footsteps of beloved heroes or villains; and, in the case of heritage and contents tourism sites, they integrate images from mediated versions of the story and encourage visitors to engage with the historical figures or characters by leaving personal messages.[8] In the case of the Teradaya and the

Ryōzen Gokoku Shrine, I have demonstrated the ways that Ryōma's story has been renewed in the second decade of the twenty-first century in ways that emphasize the perseverance, vigor, and passion of youth in times of national upheaval.

The Passion of Youth in Times of Precarity: *Bakumatsu* Tourism for Twenty-First-Century Tourists

The central question in this chapter is, "What is appealing about Ryōma's story for contemporary tourists, as exhibited in sites dedicated to him in Kyoto?" This close reading of these sites draws out the ways that this is heritage tourism aimed specifically at the turn to modernity. In this final section, I gather the threads that have emerged in the ethnographic portion of this chapter to theorize across this set of small-scale heritage contents tourist sites. I want to begin by emphasizing that these are stories whose contours are true; historical events are remembered in each of these sites. And yet, as I have tried to make clear above, in these sites, the stories are romanticized and amplified through their connection to contemporary popular culture. Sites commemorating historical events, as seen here, are one aspect of heritage tourism, and they instigate strong reactions. The fundamental problem arises when we mistake heritage for history, and that certainly happens when tourists learn history primarily through such experiences.

Throughout this chapter I have emphasized the ways that Ryōma's story has been recast for the present to attract new demographics of tourists: the montage of posters, era photos, artifacts, personal messages, and souvenirs from across the twentieth century, found in both the Teradaya and the Ryōzen Gokoku Shrine. The layering of *bakumatsu* narratives builds on the notion of heritage that has emerged in the previous chapters. In the examples in chapters 2 and 3, the heritage created through branding, landscape and urban planning policies, and new events that draw on traditional aesthetics is atmospheric and affective. Heritage atmosphere in these examples combines the material and immaterial to create places for touristic experiences that bring the past into the present. In the case of sites commemorating Ryōma, a similar process can be seen, but this time it is a historical narrative that is retold as neither mere past nor trivial present. Through these sites, Ryōma is recast as a hero for modern Japan writ large, not relegated to the events of the Meiji Restoration but a hero for today.

In some ways this is not new. As I alluded at the beginning of this chapter, Ryōma's story has always been about the making of modern Japan. As Tagsold writes about Shiba Ryōtarō's popular novel *Ryōma ga yuku* (Ryōma on the Move), "The novels of Shiba Ryōtarō can only be understood from the perspective of disconnecting Meiji modernism from the slide into militarism and ultra-nationalism in the Shōwa era, and portraying Sakamoto as the embodiment of a bright, modern history" (2013, 56).[9] According to Tagsold, exactly what that "bright, modern history" is changes in the context of the retelling. In the case of Ryōma, Tagsold (2013, 48–51) argues that the story has shifted throughout the twentieth century, from an emphasis on democracy, to patriotism, to peace, to business acumen. In the sites analyzed here, I argue that this emphasis has shifted once again through the prominence of Ryōma's Smith and Wesson and the young couple's romance and "honeymoon," both of which are decidedly modern in this context. These elements are woven throughout the sites examined in this chapter, telling a story about the role of youth in Japan on the cusp of change. Today, in the wake of nearly three decades of economic and social malaise, Ryōma tourism in Kyoto lauds the role of youth in the creation of the modern nation.

The ways that these *bakumatsu* sites in Kyoto are heritage contents tourism sites speak to tourist demographics as well. As mentioned above, the demographic for *bakumatsu* sites during much of the twentieth century was older couples or groups of older men. Similarly, the Kyoto Ryōma fan club is comprised of middle-aged and older businessmen (Henry Smith 2007, 116; Tagsold 2013, 51–53). However, Ryōma's story has drawn female audiences in the late twentieth century precisely because of some of the modern features discussed here (Henry Smith 2007, Tagsold 2013). Henry Smith (2007) notes that women are an important element of Ryōma's story because of his romance with Oryō and his close relationship with his older sister, Otome, both of whom are often highlighted in accounts of his story. This was made clear in the Fushimi sites, which put Oryō at the fore. Tagsold (2013, 52) argues that this demographic trend was fueled in part when *Ryōma ga yuku* was made into a Taiga drama for the centennial of the Meiji Restoration (1968). This trend has been renewed in recent decades, as a part of the *rekijo* (history girls) trend. Surprisingly, at the start of the twenty-first century, young women in Japan were flocking to Warring States– and *bakumatsu*–related events and museums, and their interest was fueled by popular culture. Akiko Sugawa-Shimada argues that the phenomenon of women traveling for heritage contents tourism has roots dating back at least to the 1970s, but they were only recently seen as an important market: "In the 2000s, female history fans were 'discovered.' They were named *rekijo* in a postfeminist context and were expected to become potential customers helping Japan out of its long-lasting recession" (2015, 54). She goes on to argue that the *rekijo* are different from their predecessors in their desire for connection with their favorite historical characters from video games and anime. She writes: "Historical facts and historical sites (tombs, temples, shrines, castles and so on) stimulate the imaginations of *rekijo,* through which they can perceive and construct psychological connections to their favorite historical figures. A desire to construct a spiritual connection is more conspicuous in *rekijo* tourism than in men's contents tourism" (2015, 51). It is clear that the personalized *ema* to Ryōma left at the Teradaya are a part of this trend, although there the messages were not exclusively by women. Perhaps what we see in these sites dedicated to Ryōma in Kyoto, is that this *rekijo* practice is no longer the sole purview of young women or younger tourists but has become a broader part of contents tourism.

The new audiences of contemporary Japanese youth engaging with this story about Ryōma as the quintessential modern hero raises the notion of heritage as cultural production with recourse to the past (Kirshenblatt-Gimblett 1995). Despite its roots in contents tourism, the visibility of a younger demographic of Ryōma fans is not entirely owing to the desires of young fans to connect with Ryōma. In fact, the rhetoric of youth persevering for the nation is central to the ways these stories are being curated and retold in twenty-first century Japan. The text from the Ryōzen Shrine and Cemetery's website reads: "Try to trace the way and feel the will of the pioneers who established the foundation of modern Japan and died young" (Kyoto Ryōzen Gokoku Shrine Website 2014). Likewise, the Ryōzen History Museum explains the Meiji Restoration as a time when young people embodied the spirit and will to reform in Japan. At the top of the staircase at the start of the main restoration exhibit the follow text is printed boldly on the wall in both Japanese and English:

> The Spirit of Japan—About 150 years ago, around the time Japan's Shogunate system was coming to an end, ships from overseas,

notably the American "black ships," arrived in Japan and demanded that the country open up to foreigners. Suddenly, Japan was exposed to trends in the world at large. Amidst strong pressure from overseas and confusion within Japan, the Meiji Restoration took place, bringing reforms that widely encompassed politics, culture, and industry in just a half a century.

Most of the people who accomplished this mighty task, laying the foundations for a modern Japan, were young, in their twenties and thirties. Those people dedicated their lives to such courageous actions in keeping with traditional Japanese attitudes. Under the teachings of pioneers and 2000 years of Japanese history, that attitude has been one of taking in the outstanding aspects of foreign countries, and nurturing them skillfully, in ways well suited to Japan. It is precisely such an attitude that can be described as the "Japanese Spirit."

Now that we have reached the 21st century, we need to develop that spirit further and contribute to a peaceful, prosperous world. At the Ryōzen Museum of History, our earnest wish is that visitors may follow in the footsteps of the people who brought about the end of the Shogunate and the Meiji Restoration. We hope you find our exhibits helpful in this regard.

The materials at both the Ryōzen Shrine and Cemetery and the Ryōzen Museum of History are written as invitations to visitors to experience the paths trod by these young heroes, but they also charge contemporary youth with following in those footsteps. These sentiments must be understood through the current fears about the declining birthrate and concerns about the malaise of youth in contemporary Japan that have pervaded public discourse for the past two decades (Allison 2013; Brinton 2011; Leheny 2006). These historical stories, which have regained popularity through twenty-first-century popular culture, are all set in a chaotic and yet hopeful time over one hundred years ago. A parallel is not lost on the proprietors of the two Ryōzen sites. Both are actively encouraging, if not calling on, youth, who have been cast as unambitious, to act for the nation. Although each of these demographics—proprietors and visitors, young and old, male and female—is likely drawn to Ryōma's story and *bakumatsu* sites for different reasons, the connection is a historical lesson about crafting a nation in turbulent times.

Face-to-Face History in *Bakumatsu* Tourism

Through an examination of a handful of small-scale sites dedicated to Sakamoto Ryōma in Kyoto I have tried to highlight the ways that particular heritage sites—in this case sites that commemorate the birth of the modern nation—produce personal experiences in the present with recourse to the past. In each of these sites, a kind of face-to-face history is being both cultivated and sought out, enabling tourists to make personal connections with the characters in historical stories. Both the Teradaya and the Ryōzen Gokoku Shrine are linked to historical events that have long attracted tourists. Both have presented romanticized popular representations of Ryōma since the early Meiji period, driven by popular culture retellings and contemporary concerns. The visitors to these sites participate in this cultural production by the kinds of experiences they seek, be it following in Ryōma's footsteps, staying at the inn where Ryōma and Oryō "fell in love," leaving personalized *ema* to their heroes, or attending a Ryōma festival. And each of the sites discussed here is fostered by a loose network of local entrepreneurs and proprietors—the owners of the Teradaya, Fushimi residents, the Ryōzen Patrons' Association, and Fushimi City and Kyoto City—who are invested in this particular history. These various actors combine historical narratives and popular culture contents to create sites that connect the then and now. In Fushimi the story that is curated for the present is one of a brave young couple shaping their nation's future. In Kyoto the story is one of brave young men fighting to create a modern nation. Through the casting of Ryōma as a modern samurai, imbued with values modern and Japanese, romantic and revealing, these sites promote a nostalgia for the modern. This nostalgia does not mourn the loss of premodern mystery, but rather something that feels lost in the "lost decades"—excitement and hope for Japan as a modern nation. These sites suture together historical details and contemporary popular representations of *bakumatsu* events in order to generate narrative(s) about youth and nation and hope for twenty-first-century Japan.

Chapter 5

Kimono Crowds

Inhabiting Heritage on the Beaten Path in Higashiyama

Things I want to do in Kyoto. 1. See World Heritage! 2. Walk in the landscape of the former capital 3. Relax in a Japanese style cafe.

—JTB Publishing, *Kyoto. Tabihana Kansai 1*

Discover Kyoto's New Autumn in Kimono: On a relaxing day of autumn, put on a kimono and feel your spirit rise as you enjoy sightseeing in Kyoto. While wandering through the small city streets, temples, shrines, historical buildings, and the famous geisha district, try stopping for a green tea parfait. (About 7 hours.)

—Kyoto City Convention and Visitors' Bureau, "Kyoto City Official Travel Guide."

In the spring of 2017, throughout the ever-congested tourist areas of Higashiyama in the east and Arashiyama in the west, groups of tourists in vividly patterned kimono filled the narrow roads, shopping, eating, and stopping to take selfies or group photos. The boom for seeing Kyoto while wearing kimono has been one of the most visible, puzzling, and provocative changes in Kyoto tourism over the past decade. This chapter sets down in the center of the most on-the-beaten-path district of Higashiyama to examine *in situ* the ways that heritage is constructed and experienced in Kyoto today. The epigraphs that open this chapter are drawn from two different guides to Kyoto. Each suggests a walk through a heritage district to take in the atmosphere through sights, sounds, and snacks as a way to experience Kyoto. The first epigraph is from the JTB's *Tabihana* series of guides to Kyoto.[1] Written in the first person "voice of a young woman," the quote casts Kyoto as rich in heritage, landscape, and Japanese style (*wafu*). The second epigraph, written for international tourists on the Kyoto City website, suggests that the experience of putting on a kimono adds to the mood of sightseeing in an historic district. These small suggestions for tourists echo many of the themes discussed in this book—walking through Kyoto, enjoying the scenery (natural, historical, and cultural), and experiencing the heritage atmosphere—but this time wearing kimono. Moreover, this new way of experiencing Kyoto has flourished particularly among Asian tourists, the newest demographic of tourists to Kyoto. Thus this final ethnographic chapter adds one more layer to the emerging picture of tourism in contemporary Kyoto: the embodied experience of heritage atmosphere.

Structuring this chapter around a walk in the Higashiyama district grounds it in the experiences craved and crafted by tourists and tourism personnel alike.[2] The focus on kimono rental allows me to zoom in to quintessential Kyoto products and contemporary trends, highlighting the ways that tourists are invited to experience and perhaps even inhabit Kyoto heritage. Perhaps more than any other example in this book, kimono are iconic representations of Japan, alongside Mt. Fuji and cherry blossoms. Indeed, kimono are an integral part of tourism imaginaries of Japan. Anthropologist Noel Salazar (2012) coined the term "tourism imaginaries" to theorize the ways that tourists and local mediators create, internalize, recreate, and mobilize representations and understandings of places and cultures. Salazar and Graburn write, "We conceptualize imaginaries as socially transmitted representational assemblages that interact with people's personal imaginings and that are used as meaning-making and world-shaping devices" (2014, 1). More than simply stereotypes, make believe, or ideology, imaginaries articulate the ways that we make sense of peoples and places through prior discourses (whether academic, promotional, or crowd sourced), a wide range of media, and experiences both personal and perceived. Furthermore, tourism imaginaries are not all in our heads; they can be materialized—manifested in practices, embodied or reinforced through objects, and captured "on film" or "in image." There is no doubt that kimono loom large in tourist imaginaries of Japan, and they have material roots in

Kyoto. Because Kyoto housed the imperial court for a thousand years and was home to famous geisha traditions kimono images are a part of the landscape of the city. Indeed, such images saturate Kyoto, as everyone from *maiko* (apprentice geisha) to Hello Kitty wears them in promotions of Kyoto. As this chapter attests, today kimono have been put to various new uses in contemporary Kyoto.

While kimono or *yukata* (light cotton summer kimono) have long been purchased by international tourists as souvenirs, the instances examined in this chapter are experiential. They are embodied and consumed during one's time in Kyoto, brought home through memories, picturesque photos, and posts on social media. This examination of kimono tourism in Kyoto draws on the "performance turn" in tourism research, which aims to move beyond the semiotic or visual approaches of earlier models (MacCannell 1999; Urry 1990) to emphasize the multiple, embodied, and multisensory ways that people travel (Bærenholdt et al. 2004; Coleman and Crang 2002; Haldrup and Larsen 2010; Urry and Larsen 2011). As Michael Haldrup and Jonas Larsen theorize, "We need a *circuit* of performance model that blurs the distinction between production (choreographing) and consumption (acting) and instead see them as interrelated and overlapping in complex ways. Tourist performances do not exist independently of structures of 'production' and wider societal discourses" (2010, 4; emphasis in original). We will see in this chapter the circuit of performance, wherein rental shops both craft and cater to tourist desires through marketing the heritage experience of walking in kimono, and we will also see locals' responses to this touristic practice shift. Moreover, the phenomenon of kimono tourism in Kyoto is an apt demonstration of the ways that tourists are often co-producers and/or co-marketers of tourist experiences through exhibition and crowd sourcing in today's social media milieu.

Finally, framing this chapter with an *in situ* walk through Kyoto in kimono allows me to tease out the embodied experience of tourism in the most popular heritage district. As noted in the introduction, the Japanese term for these kinds of tourist experiences is *taiken* (体験). Comprised of the character for "body" (*tai* 体) followed by the character for "experience" or "trial" (*ken* 験), *taiken* is usually translated to mean "personal experience," but the body is critical to the experience. The touristic experiences discussed in this chapter are somatic—they come through the senses and the body, and they appeal to emotions or feelings more than to reason. Thus this chapter aims to unpack the ways that walking in a heritage tourist district, sightseeing, and taking a break in a *matcha* cafe—and doing so all in a rented kimono—provide a Japanese-style experience. I argue that walking through Kyoto in kimono demonstrates a shift in tourism practices from "seeing" to "being." This shift moves from an older model in which tourists saw new sites and took souvenir pictures to take home and show friends to a newer variant in which tourists are able to feel a part of the heritage atmosphere through costume. And selfies shared on social media capture the kimono-clad tourists as a part of the sites, emphasizing the immediacy of their experience.

Perambulatory Tourism: Wandering through Kyoto Heritage Districts

I begin this view of Higashiyama as a tourist might begin a trip—by looking at guidebooks aimed at domestic tourists in Japan. While people increasingly plan their trips by turning to online sources (including websites, social media, and travel blogs), guidebooks remain a prevalent feature of domestic travel in Japan. Indeed, the Kyoto City Tourism Survey Report shows that 30–40 percent of domestic tourists consistently say they used a guidebook in planning their trip or while they were traveling, even today (Kyoto City Tourism Office 2018). While this statistic may reflect the number of older tourists in Kyoto, any bookstore in Japan has a large travel section filled with books, magazines, and pocket-sized travel guides, ranging from city or prefecture resources to those with a thematic focus like hot springs, romance, or modern towers. A quick scan of the Kyoto section of the travel section identifies a range of books that target specific themes like world heritage, *matcha* (powdered green tea) cafes, trendy souvenirs, or mysteries of history. This variety points not only to the sheer number of people who travel to Kyoto, but also to the number of repeat visitors, who are more likely to try to tailor their next trips in fresh ways in order to see something new.

Rather than being organized by utility—sights, restaurants, hotels, entertainment, etc.—Japanese guidebooks and travel magazines tend to be experientially organized—that is, they are structured around an itinerary or set of activities that may take a few hours, a day, or a few days. An itinerary typically includes a main site or two, as well as select local delicacies and souvenirs all within walking distance. This pattern of what I call "perambulatory tourism" recalls earlier travel practices, discussed in chapter 1. *Monzen machi* (temple towns), surrounding the entrances to popular temples and shrines, would include lodging and places to eat, relax, and be entertained after a hard day's journey. Early guidebooks included suggestions for places to stay and play before and after visiting a *meisho* (famous place), and they also listed local delicacies to be sampled. Today's Japanese guidebooks retain this approach, starting with the grandeur of a famous site, followed by a local map and an invitation to wander around the area. Guidebooks typically note historical sites as well as trendy cafes, traditional crafts, snacks to be sampled, and souvenirs of interest. This perambulatory approach ties together historic or cultural sites with local crafts and gustatory pleasures. In this mode of travel, we see several elements central to this chapter: walking in the old city, visiting a heritage site, and stopping for refreshments at a trendy Kyoto style cafe—all organized experientially.

Strolling through Higashiyama

My focus in this chapter is on the Higashiyama area (eastern hills) because it is the most well-traveled tourist area of Kyoto, featuring one of Kyoto's UNESCO World Heritage sites, Kiyomizu Temple. Established as a temple to the Buddhist deity of compassion, Kannon, at the Ōtowa Waterfall in 778, Kiyomizu Temple is famous for its views of the hills and the city from its veranda, which stands nearly thirteen meters high. According to the Kyoto City Tourism Office (2008–2020), Kiyomizu Temple is the most visited location in Kyoto, ranked number one by foreigners and Japanese alike year after year; over the past ten years 20–50 percent of tourists surveyed spend time there.[3] Higashiyama is also one of Kyoto's oldest tourist districts, built up around the entrance to the temple. As such, it is a heritage preservation district featuring temples and shrines linked together by narrow stone streets lined with traditional wooden shops, restaurants, and cafes. As argued throughout this book, heritage in Kyoto always looks both backward and forward, and the Higashiyama tourist district exemplifies this dynamic. Heritage in Kyoto is not confined to strict preservation but emphasizes the use of traditional materials and techniques. In fact, most of the buildings in this preservation district date back only to the Meiji period due to fires that raged through the city over the centuries. Despite strict landscape preservation laws, which ensure a historic atmosphere featuring traditional wood architecture, not all of the stores and restaurants have a long history in Kyoto. Along the winding, cobblestone, pedestrian-friendly streets one can find restaurants, shops, galleries, and historic sites both old and new; for example, alongside centuries-old pottery shops both Sanrio (the makers of Hello Kitty) and Studio Ghibli character goods stores can be found.

As the largest swath of heritage preservation area, the Higashiyama district plays an outsized role in the city's tourism plans, serving as a model for other areas. The opening description of the projects under "Walk to understand Kyoto" in the Future Kyoto Plan 2010 states: " 'Walking' is an environmentally friendly means of transportation suitable for everyday life, but in Kyoto its value goes beyond mere transportation. Today, the five senses can be satisfied by the history and tradition that live in the city, making walking nothing less than the most luxurious style of tourism to enjoy" (Kyoto City 2010, 20). This goal to create walking zones upholds wider tourism trends wherein cities seek to renovate the urban core; it also ties into the eco-friendly motif aiming to cut down on traffic for both tourists and citizens while highlighting how safe Kyoto is. Pragmatically, the "Walk to understand Kyoto" project listed new services, such as a kiosk at Kyoto Station to facilitate easy check-ins for major hotels and a luggage storage and delivery service so that tourists could enjoy immediate "hands free" tourism. The Yearning for Kyoto Plan 2015 continues such efforts, creating more scenic walking routes to and from major sites, putting more benches and rest areas along main routes, and lining streets with flowers that display the four seasons. Thus the "Walking City Kyoto" campaign is both pragmatic and atmospheric. It does more than simply solve traffic issues; it also dovetails with the turn to experiencing Kyoto personally. While it encourages tourists to save bus fare and reduce environmental costs, "Walking City Kyoto" projects also open opportunities to discover (see and feel) everyday Kyoto, its history, culture, and citizens. The Higashiyama district offers an apt example of these efforts. As a historic preservation district, traffic is restricted in much of it, and it features numerous sights that one can easily walk among. All along the way the vibrant green of the eastern hills provides the backdrop to the panorama.

Stretching up to Kiyomizu Temple are narrow streets lined with shops, restaurants, and cafes. Almost always packed with tourists, both domestic and international, the area is an eclectic mix of traditional Kyoto food shops, stores selling pottery (for which the area is famous), and those selling every possible tourist souvenir from fans, to T-shirts, to traditional textiles, to pickles, to key chains and phone accessories. One cannot miss the area's most well-known sweet, *yatsuhashi,* one of the *meibutsu* (famous foods) from Kyoto. This small, cinnamon-flavored biscuit, made of rice crackers, is bent into a bridge shape and baked. While the baked version is traditional, raw sweets, folded into triangles and filled with flavored bean paste—*matcha,* strawberry, peach, chocolate, etc.—are the most popular today. Virtually all souvenir stores in Kyoto carry *yatsuhashi,* but five stores from three top brands specialize in them; all are located just outside of Kiyomizu Temple's main entrance, and some of them boast eight hundred years in the same location.

After a visit to Kiyomizu Temple for spectacular views of the city, heading back down the hill chock-a-block with wooden storefronts, stopping for samples of *yatsuhashi* or a *matcha* ice cream cone, one reaches a junction of several roads. To the right is a picturesque *roji* known as Sannen-zaka (as seen in figure 5.1) that leads to Ninnen-zaka. These two quaint roads allow one to wander through Higashi-yama in a pedestrians-only zone, where the traditional and

Figure 5.1. Tourists in Sannen-zaka shops. Photo by author, 2019.

contemporary shops thin out a bit, leaving room for a host of other temples, small museums, and restaurants.

Japanese guidebooks, city tourism policies, and tourist districts like Higashiyama are all organized by the desires of tourists to see and feel history and culture. They envision active engagement: a visit to a famous temple or world heritage site, a pause for a snack and a rest along the way, and a stop for souvenirs. As the fictional young woman's voice of the *Tabihana* guide to Kyoto exclaims, "I want to relax in a Japanese-style cafe. Kyoto is the place for chic [*suteki*] Japanese-style cafes. [I want] to be in a *machiya* atmosphere entranced by an artisanal [*kodawari*] *matcha* parfait. Blissful moments in the home of the Japanese sweets" (JTB Publishing 2010, 6). While stopping for a snack in the midst of a long day of shopping or sightseeing is nothing new, the Kyoto flavor added here is a *wafu,* or Japanese-style, atmosphere of *matcha* in a *machiya* cafe. The term *wafu* (和風) emerged in the Meiji period as Western goods and concepts flooded into Japan, making it important to demarcate what was indigenous and what was imported from the West—*yōfu* (洋風 Western style), *yōfuku* (洋服 Western clothing), *yōshoku* (洋食 Western food). The styles and objects newly called *wafu* in the Meiji period are all good examples of "invented traditions"—newer versions of items, styles, or aesthetics codified as Japanese in the face of imports from the West. Yet, while *wafu* means "Japanese-style," it is also translated in English-language tourist guides as "traditional." This notion of traditional does not mean a stagnant or unchanging remnant from the past but something with roots in the past. Alongside other examples throughout this book, this emerges as a kind of timeless Japaneseness. Traditional Kyoto townhouses (*Kyō-machiya*) exemplify this well. As discussed in chapter 2, they were on the decline until the 1990s, when a community organization began a movement to conserve the traditional townscape. It is important to note that their survival was not due to a process of converting them into museums; rather they were put to new use as houses, rental homes, restaurants, cafes, and shops. Today, *machiya* represent the visual heritage aesthetic of Kyoto, and they line the streets of Higashiyama.

Matcha, too, contributes an important imaginary of Kyoto. The potent, powdered form of green tea developed in Japan as a part of the tea ceremony, but it has become a globally popular beverage and flavoring for sweets in the twenty-first century. And Kyoto is infused with it. The vivid green powder was originally whisked in order to help Buddhist monks stay awake in long vigils of sutra readings as early as the eighth century; it also refreshed weary travelers throughout the Edo period (Pitelka 2003; Saberi 2010). It is not surprising that there are deep connections between *matcha* and Kyoto. The first tea house for the tea ceremony was Kyoto's Silver Pavilion, built in 1482 as a retirement villa by the eighth Ashikaga Shogun, Yoshimasa (Saberi 2010, 48). The tea ceremony flourished in Kyoto, and all three tea schools in Japan in the tradition of Sen no Rikyū—Omotosenke, Urasenke, and Mushanokojisenke—have their headquarters in Kyoto still today. So, too, Uji, in Kyoto Prefecture, just south of the city proper, is the most famous area for tea cultivation in Japan. Both *ujicha* (tea from Uji) and *matcha* are popular souvenirs from Kyoto today. The Rakutabi Kyoto guidebook *All Things Matcha in Kyoto* refers to Kyoto as the *matcha* capital, noting, in reference to the dark green stripe of the city buses, that "even the buses are painted with the *matcha* color" (Rakutabi Bunko 2007, 1). Thus stopping for a *matcha* treat (whether tea and a traditional sweet or a parfait) in a Japanese-style cafe is marketed as a Kyoto-style break in a day of sightseeing; and places to do just that are easy to find in any of Kyoto's tourist districts. Rather than an authentic tea ceremony experience (although such an experience can be found in Kyoto on a variety of scales), these cafes recast Kyoto style as traditionally modern and culturally chic. Thus, *matcha,* with its connotations of tradition, the precision and discipline of Zen meditation, and tea ceremony, has been modernized for a Kyoto-style break in the hustle and bustle of a tourist's day.

Moreover, this *wafu* atmosphere is advertised—indeed romanticized—for domestic tourists as well as international tourists in Kyoto. What is for sale, alongside a drink and sweet, is a *wafu* escape from the vagaries of daily life. Guidebooks and city tourism promotions alike encourage tourists to experience "with all five senses" the sights, sounds, smells, and crowds of Kyoto as they walk the paths trod by countless others over the centuries. Indeed, the Higashiyama district evolved as a *monzen machi* and has been cultivated by landscape policies in recent years to provide a heritage atmosphere for tourism. Thus there are layers of history and culture, fantasy and policy, that create the kind of heritage tourist district suited to perambulatory travel.

Embodying Heritage: The Kimono Rental Boom and Experiential Tourism

The notion of perambulatory tourism—in this case walking through Higashiyama to see and feel the heritage district—emphasizes an embodied approach to tourism. Yet in recent years the bodily experience of walking in Kyoto has morphed. Taking a stroll in a historic district in kimono has become an "authentic" way to experience Kyoto heritage. To be sure, kimono-clad figures are common in promotions of Kyoto, from the colorful *maiko*, to the stately kimono of a *ryokan* (Japanese inn) employee, to Mayor Kadokawa, to Hello Kitty (who wears kimono when in Kyoto). However, everyday Kyotoites on their way to work or out for the evening do not regularly wear kimono. Rather, in recent years the explosion of kimono-clad figures in Kyoto is comprised largely of tourists. The practice of renting kimono, complete with hair styling and accessories for three hours, half a day, or a day, is all the rage in Kyoto today. This trend is an apt example of the turn to experiential tourism.

In the initial stage of my research in 2012, kimono rental shops were well advertised and visible but nothing compared to today, where every corner near the main tourist areas seems to have a rental shop, if not two. Early in my fieldwork, kimono came up in a variety of ways: they were an important product of Kyoto through the Nishijin weaving district; they were a way of dressing for tour guides "to fit the atmosphere of the city"; and they were a fun way for young Japanese couples to enjoy seeing the cherry blossoms or fall leaves of Kyoto. By 2017, international tourists, and Asian tourists in particular, had embraced this way of experiencing heritage Kyoto. By 2019, the streets of Higashiyama were filled with brightly colored kimono and *yukata,* bringing a playful but puzzling addition to the overcrowded heritage atmosphere. Sightseeing in kimono adds a layer of embodied experience to walking, shopping, and imbibing the heritage atmosphere in contemporary Kyoto.

Kimono in Kyoto: Evolving Traditions

Since Kyoto was the imperial capital from 794 to 1868, much of the craft industry revolved around creating goods for the court, from luxury, to ritual, to necessity. It is not surprising that textiles developed as one of Kyoto's traditional industries (*dentō sangyō*). The term "kimono" means "object to wear," and the kimono as we know it today did not take center stage until the Meiji period, when it was codified in juxtaposition to Western-style dress (Dalby 2001, 59–62; Slade 2009, 127). Kimono are comprised of a long robe, open at the front, with wide sleeves. They are customized to a wearer's height by folds at the waist, fastened closed by wrapping left over right, and secured with a thick belt called an *obi.*

While silk cultivation and weaving predate the founding of the Heian capital, Kyoto's first courtiers were renowned for their colorful layered robes (Dougill 2006, 2). Heian-period court dress for women is known as twelve-layered robes (*jūni hitoe*), although the number of layers varied depending on rank and occasion. There were formal guidelines as well as aesthetic norms about what colors and patterns to choose for each of the layers, depending on the season. Liza Dalby writes, "The most interesting aspect of Heian colors was their set combinations, called *irome no kasane.* These sets had poetic names that referred to natural phenomena, especially flowers. . . . The colors used in each named combination were generally consistent, though the absolute number of combinations and the fashions of layering changed over the centuries" (2001, 225). The biggest shift in the overall form of kimono occurred in the medieval period, when the many layers were gradually reduced to one, the innermost layer, called a *kosode;* at this time robes began to be held closed with an *obi* as well (Dalby 2001, 36). In the fifteenth and sixteenth centuries, kimono made of silk, the most luxurious fabric, had trickled down from the courts to samurai and courtesans. This style of dress spread to wealthy merchants, who could afford it by the 1700s (Hareven 2002, 28; Slade 2009, 53). In the 1800s, the *obi* gradually became wider and thicker, making it more than a mere fastening mechanism. According to Dalby, "From this time on, the obi became more highly elaborated and eventually came to demand as much attention as the gown itself. The modern kimono/obi combination is heiress to this trend—so much so that it sometimes seems the kimono is merely a backdrop for the obi" (1983, 290).

Two traditional industries in particular have helped keep kimono alive in Kyoto: the *hanamachi* (geisha districts) and Nishijin. There is no doubt that the cultivation and preservation of geisha arts and culture is important to the ways that kimono are understood in Kyoto. Geisha are purveyors of the traditional arts, including music, song, and dance performances; tea ceremony; and, as Dalby (1983) observes, the wearing of kimono. Though fashion trends have shifted over the years, since the early twentieth century geisha (or *geiko* as they are known in Kyoto) have come to be associated with kimono, even though the style and form of kimono that geisha wear differ from those of the average Japanese woman, were she to choose to wear a kimono for a special occasion. The five geisha districts in Kyoto have survived in tandem with traditional craftspeople who cater to their sartorial needs, as witnessed by the shops selling *kanzashi* (hair ornaments), *geta* (wooden lacquered sandals worn with kimono), and the like, located around each geisha district.

The weaving district in Kyoto, Nishijin, is in the northwestern quadrant of central Kyoto, beginning at the intersection of Imadegawa and Horikawa. Nishijin is renowned for two specific types of kimono-related textiles: Nishijin *obi* and *yūzen* silk dying (discussed in chapter 3). Nishijin has been an important textile district since the fifteenth century, when weavers returned to the city after the Ōnin war (Hareven 2002, 26; Yuzo 2019). The streets in this area have long been lined with *machiya* featuring the distinct window lattice indicating a weaving household. Nishijin is often used as the prime example of an important heritage industry on the decline for the past half century or more and a decline in kimono wearing is a part of this story. As Jenny Hall notes, "The kimono's image today is a garment that is beautiful but expensive, impractical, difficult to put on and daunting to wear in terms of adherence to the strict rules of etiquette that have developed since World War II" (2015, 78). In postwar Japan fewer people wear kimono regularly, in part because kimono are expensive. Increasingly, more and more people rent them for a one-off occasion such as a graduation, wedding, or funeral.

The Nishijin *obi* is registered as a cultural property, and Kyoto City promotes this traditional industry to showcase heritage arts through the Nishijin Textile Center for tourists; the city also commissions textiles for important events (Hareven 2002; Yuzo 2019). Nishijin products, renowned for their intricate patterns and use of gold and silver threads, are considered luxury items. Finally, the textile crafts associated with Kyoto all emphasize artistic ways to decorate kimono fabrics through weaving or dying.

Despite a general decline in kimono use in postwar Japan, Sheila Cliffe (2017) calls the recent uptick in kimono wearing a "kimono renaissance." This is due in part to the birth and growth of the kimono rental industry, which began in the late 1980s (Ogata 2015). In the twenty-first century, more Japanese consumers are making kimono visible by renting them for special events. For example, Cliffe (2017, 158, 201) notes that until around 1999 almost no Tokyo high school or college graduates wore kimono for their graduation ceremony, but today almost all the young women wear kimono for such occasions (see also Ogata 2015). Similarly, renting kimono for Coming of Age Day (Seijin no Hi) each January has also become a trend throughout Japan.[4] In fact, many of the companies that flourished in renting kimono for these events have recently branched into the kimono rental for tourism business as well. Ogata Michimasa (2015) argues that the ease of renting a kimono for special events has increased the wearing of kimono, but at the same time it has led to kimonos' becoming increasingly mechanically produced items rather than crafted pieces of clothing.[5] In response to this decline in the traditional industry, Hall's (2015, 2018) recent ethnographic work on the kimono industry in Kyoto demonstrates important ways that designers and craftsmen are finding new techniques and uses for kimono fabrics in order to make it easier to both produce and use them. While both Cliffe's and Hall's work on the increase in kimono magazines and shops, as well as new creative designers and styles, demonstrates an uptick in interest in kimono in recent years, to date, kimono are primarily rented to be worn for ceremonial or special occasions. Consequently, while kimono may be becoming trendier, they are not seen as functional everyday wear in Japan today.

Kimono Experience (Kimono Taiken) *in Kyoto*

While Kyoto is famous throughout the world for its geisha, in promotional materials, souvenirs, and advertisements, it is actually the figure of the *maiko,* a geisha apprentice, that adorns objects from postcards to the foam on a cappuccino in Kyoto. With their white face, archaic hairstyle, red collar, long sleeves, tall shoes, and elaborate trailing *obi, maiko* are the real celebrities of Kyoto. Spotting one walking quickly through the crowds of Gion's Hanamikoji—the most famous, visible, and crowded geisha street in Kyoto—has long been a tourist dream. A quick search on Facebook or Instagram results in pages of photos of a *maiko* on the move. Today, the crowds are so thick on Hanamikoji in the evening that geisha and *maiko* heading to their evening parties must take cabs to avoid them rather than walk the short distance. With this exotic and romantic image in mind, it is not surprising that dressing up like a *maiko* has been popular throughout the twenty-first century.[6]

In fact, the precursor to today's kimono rental is *maiko henshin taiken* (*maiko* transformation experience), in which a guest is made up like a *maiko* from makeup through accessories, and then provided with a photo shoot;[7] one can also then walk around the area for a few hours in costume. Indeed, almost all the "*maiko*" one encounters in the busy tourist district are actually makeover customers, especially if they are stopping for lots of photos rather than hurrying along with their heads down. The three "*maiko*" figures curating photos in figure 5.2 are *maiko* makeover customers from the summer of 2013.[8] It should be noted that it is not easy for an unhabituated woman to walk smoothly, much less properly, in kimono and *geta* (sandals), so the first versions of these try-on studios were all focused on an inside-the-studio photo shoot. While this option is still available at some of the rental shops, in recent years the shift has been made to walking in Kyoto in kimono.

More recently, for a price starting at around thirty dollars, a guest can dress up in kimono or *yukata,* including the underrobe, *obi, tabi* (socks), sandals, and one or more accessories like an *obi-*

Figure 5.2. Tourists taking photos of their *maiko* transformation experience. Photo by author, 2013.

nori (decoration over the *obi*) or a handbag in kimono fabric. Depending on the price, customers can get more accessories, get their hair done properly, walk around for three hours to all day, get photos at a studio onsite, or (for a hefty fee) have a photographer follow them as they walk through the heritage district. In recent years, many of the shops have added the service of having the kimono and accessories sent to and/or returned from a hotel's front desk.

Over the ten years of my research kimono rental shops have proliferated all over the city at a mindboggling pace, advertised with mannequins dressed in basic kimono in front of the shops. In fact, in recent years kimono rental for tourism has taken off in tourist districts throughout Japan, although it started in Kyoto. Wargo, one of the larger companies, with nineteen shops in Japan (eight of which are in Kyoto and four in Tokyo), advertises on its website that in 2019, 167,513 people rented kimono from the company. Similarly, Okamoto, the company that claims to have started the "sightseeing in kimono" concept at its store at the foot of Kiyomizu Temple, proclaims that it rents to 200,000 customers each year in its six shops, all located within the Higashiyama tourist district of Kyoto. In 2012, kimono rental was visible through ads and occasionally through kimono sightings. One typically saw two or three young Japanese women visiting Kyoto together or a young couple seeing the cherry blossoms or leaves in kimono. Yet by 2017 the terrain had changed significantly, and Higashiyama was filled with groups of tourists in kimono, riding rickshaws, carrying their phones or cameras on selfie-sticks, and stopping for pictures and snacks.

Feeling Kyoto: Embodying Heritage in Higashiyama

Like all forms of clothing, kimono dictates the way the body can move. In particular, the long and narrow skirt demands short steps, and the wide *obi* ensures erect posture. Dalby (1983, 286) notes that kimono is perfectly suited to Japanese architecture, where the activities of daily life are conducted close to the floor. It is said that the narrow skirt makes kneeling in a traditional *seiza* style (kneeling with the buttocks resting on the feet) the most comfortable way to sit, and the wide thick *obi* helps keep the back straight, enabling one to keep this posture for longer. Conversely, the bulky *obi* makes actions of modern life, like sitting on a chair and riding in a car, challenging (Dalby 1983, 287; Hall 2015, 60). As discussed above, most Japanese women today will have worn kimono once or twice for a special occasion and thus are unskilled at putting them on; furthermore, how to do so requires patience and knowledge. In fact, there are schools and classes available to help Japanese women learn how to put on and wear kimono properly.

In my earliest conversations about tourism in Kyoto, I met several private tour guides who saw wearing kimono as a part of their profession—and one that they had grown to enjoy. To be sure, even today, most guides do not regularly don kimono, but the views of the guides with whom I spoke are illustrative of what it is like to wear kimono in Japan today. All six of the guides who talked about kimono were female and all were Japanese, but none were born or raised in Kyoto; they ranged in age from twenty-two and just out of college to mid-forties with children in college. All of these women brought up the practice of wearing kimono as a part of our conversation about being tour guides in Kyoto; each noted that she had very little experience with kimono before she started wearing them as a guide. Ms. N—, who had been giving tours for more than ten years, said she had worn kimono only once before, when she turned twenty, and did not own any before this. Mrs. H—, who lived in Osaka, laughed as she told me she first got the idea because of the Kimono Passport, which gives discounts on public transportation and at some shops and restaurants to anyone dressed in kimono. "The first day I did it, everything took me so much longer and felt harder. But I got used to it, and now I feel better when I wear kimono—more proper and feminine and cheerful," Ms. N— said. Ms. W—, who now works as staff at a *ryokan* in town, said she went to college in Kyoto, and when she graduated, she wanted a job where she could wear kimono. "It really feels different to be in kimono; all my movements, my body, and my attitude are more refined and livelier in kimono. But I don't want to be a *geiko*!" she laughed. Mrs. I— made a similar point: "Kimono changes your comportment immediately, but it also changes your whole attitude; something is transmitted about being a Japanese woman when you wear kimono." Across these comments, several points stand out: the ways kimono makes one feel, Japanese womanhood, a sense of embodying culture. Perhaps the most striking conversation about kimono came up when I was talking with Mrs. H—, who often gives private tours to wealthy tourists from Europe.

> JP: What kinds of questions do your guests ask frequently? Any that surprise you?

Mrs. H—: They always ask about geisha and want to know whether or not geisha are prostitutes. It is hard to explain their history and get across that they are not prostitutes, even though in the past it was different. But sometimes . . . they ask me why I wear kimono when it makes it so hard for women to walk. . . . Then I feel uncomfortable. They sometimes even ask about foot binding. But that's China! (Mrs. H— 2012)

Here the romance with kimono is tainted for Mrs. H— when it is compared even indirectly to unsavory practices like prostitution and foot binding in the minds of tourists. What becomes clear in each of these conversations is the ways that kimono wearing was new to these women, each of whom learned how to do so as a part of becoming a tour guide in Kyoto, apart from upbringing and everyday life, and each saw it as a way of feeling Japanese.

Advertisements for kimono rental in Kyoto, in both Japanese and English, reiterate many of the sentiments that guides themselves articulated. Okamoto Rental Kimono includes this excerpt as a part of the front page of its website (in Japanese and English):

> When you hear [the term] kimono, you imagine something very troublesome and cumbersome. However, our shop will totally change such perceptions, as our customers enjoy an easy-to-wear kimono experience. Although there was not such a concept of wearing a rental kimono for walking in the past, we wanted our customers to feel more comfortable with kimonos, and this is the form which we finally came up with. We'd like to preserve the Japanese tradition in various forms as nowadays we have fewer occasions to wear kimono (Okamoto Rental Kimono).

Here the company allays potential consumers' fears about the difficulty of dressing properly in kimono. It notes that it wants customers to be more comfortable in kimono and is interested in helping to preserve the tradition today. As a store that started in 1830 by selling kimono fabric goods near Kiyomizu Temple, Okamoto wants to keep the kimono industry and tradition alive. This attitude correlates to other citywide efforts like the Kimono Passport. Of course, not all rental shops or staff have such grand dreams of returning kimono to everyday life. The popularity of kimono rental for tourists does lead to the visibility of kimono in and around Kyoto, although to the trained eye, the materials are not of a high quality and the kimono are often not worn correctly or discreetly.

One of the biggest surprises of my research is that kimono rental boomed with international tourists, especially from Asia (South Korea, Taiwan, Hong Kong, Singapore, Thailand, and China), in the past five years. In 2012, industry personnel were already talking about the increase in Asian tourists, but the general assumption was that Chinese tourists were not interested in Kyoto. Everyone with whom I spoke reiterated the same refrain: Chinese tourists come to Japan for high-end shopping, and they like Osaka and Tokyo. One tour guide mused, "[Chinese tourists] are not interested in Japanese history, and that is what the Kyoto brand is about. If they want to go to temples or gardens, they can do that in China." Thus while there was a sense that tourists from Asia were increasing, no one foresaw the threefold increase in Asian tourists to Kyoto that came in the following years.

As discussed in the introduction, over the past decade, the number of Asian tourists to Kyoto has increased dramatically due to a combination of the rising affluence in the region and Tourist Nation Japan policies. In 2008 Asian tourists comprised about 30 percent of the international tourists to Kyoto, and as of 2017 that figure had risen to 59 percent for three years running. The figure for Chinese tourists alone rose from 6 percent (44,100) to 29 percent (1,146,100) between of 2006 and 2019 (Kyoto City Tourism Office 2007–2019). To put this into perspective, in 2012 Asian tourists comprised 74 percent of international tourists to Japan, and as of 2017 that number was up to 85 percent. So while an increase in Asian tourists to Japan is a part of this story, to quote Mrs. A—, from the Kyoto Tourism Association, "Asian tourists have discovered Kyoto" (2017).

Parallel to these shifting demographic trends, tourists and the tourism industry alike turned their attention to experiential travel. Beginning in 2012, the Kyoto City Tourism Survey Report started asking about what "traditional cultural experiences" (*dentō bunka taiken*) international tourists had tried.[9] Over the past five years the top experiences were tea ceremony, kimono or *yukata* experience, and Japanese cooking classes or walking tours. On average 21 percent of the international tourists surveyed said they had rented or planned to rent kimono/*yukata* while in Kyoto; over the past five years the average for Chinese tourists has been 36 percent, and for the Taiwanese, 30 percent; North America, Australia, and Europe combined average 12 percent. In contrast, an average of 21 percent of Westerners participate in tea ceremony—more than participate in kimono rental and more than their Asian counterparts at 14 percent (Kyoto City Tourism Office 2013–2019).

As I returned to Kyoto in the summer of 2017, I was struck by the increase in the number of tourists wearing kimono, especially in the Higashiyama area. In a conversation at one of the Okamoto Kimono Rental shops during a lull in the crowds, two staff women in their thirties talked about how kimono rental had boomed. One woman, who had been working there for several years, said, “Of course, it varies, but we have about 150–200 guests a day.” “Some days there is a huge line, and all the space is full that so you can barely move,” her colleague added. When I arrived that day, there wasn’t anyone in line. Four tourists, speaking Chinese, were headed into the studio with the photographer; the staff was tidying up kimono and *obi* that had been cast off in a quick changing session. One of the clerks continued, “Most of the guests are Asian, from China, Korea, or Thailand, and there are all kinds of groups, from just two to over ten. But not many Japanese tourists rent kimono these days.” The clerks highlighted that rentals varied from season to season. “During *hanami* in the spring and again when the autumn foliage is at its best in the fall, young Japanese couples will rent kimono for a romantic date. That is the most that Japanese do it,” one clerk. When I returned in the spring of 2019, this trend had evolved further as young Japanese couples, as well as groups of middle school students on school excursions, donned kimono and *yukata* throughout Kyoto. The number of male tourists dressed in *yukata* seemed to have risen as well. Kimono rental has become a significant feature of Kyoto tourism, and it is on the uptick in other parts of the country as well.

Watching crowds of kimono-clad tourists enjoying shopping, snacks, and selfies (as seen in figure 5.3), I found myself wondering about what this new trend might mean. I asked a young woman selling *warabi mochi* (a traditional Kyoto sweet) a bit away from the main throngs what she thought of the kimono rental boom. She replied, “At first I was surprised. But now I love seeing kimono. It makes the whole atmosphere lively.” Similarly, a kimono rental employee who was a college student working part time said, “Kimono just fits the Japanese atmosphere of Kyoto perfectly.” A group of girls

Figure 5.3. Tourists in rental kimono shopping and eating ice cream in Higashiyama. Photo by author, 2017.

from Taiwan who were eating ice cream in rental kimono talked to me about their experiences. One said, "It makes me feel different [gestures standing up straighter]. My clothing fits the atmosphere of the city. It makes it fun to walk around."

As I spoke with shop staff, citizens, and tourism personnel about the growth in tourism in Kyoto during my visits in 2017 and 2019, all commented on the new kimono trend, expressing mixed opinions. Almost all said that kimono rental was the newest trend, then trailed off with, "Chotto . . . ," a way of hedging that shows concern or disapproval. Several were quick to point out that the rental kimono were not real Kyoto kimono but were produced with cheaper fabric, often "made in China." Many laughed at the ways that foreigners would take lots of pictures of people dressed in kimono, mistaking other tourists for geisha or at least for Japanese people. The plethora of slightly derisive comments surprised me given that they were in the context of short conversations; these kinds of comments are not the standard polite small talk, indicating the pejorative feelings about this new trend. In fact, as of 2019 at least one of the major kimono rental companies picked up on critiques, marketing its rentals through slogans like, "Isn't kimono rental lame? 150,162 dressings in 2017" and "Kimono rental is out of fashion isn't it? 150,162 dressings in 2017" (Wargo 2019). It is not surprising that opinions would fluctuate around a tourist phenomenon as pervasive as kimono rental, and the perspectives I heard throughout my research ranged from puzzled curiosity to sarcasm to bemused acceptance; in the backdrop of all conversations was a sense that tourism is an economic driver through which many in Kyoto make their livelihood but it is also a disruptive part of daily life in the city.

Somatic Tourism: Analyzing Kimono Experiences

There is no doubt that a host of tourists in traditional dress is quite surprising. In this final section, I turn to examine what this new trend of tourists walking through the heritage districts in kimono might mean. There is a range of ways to analyze this trend: as historical re-enactment, cultural appropriation, cosplay, the theme-park-ification of Kyoto, or a playful way to experience the city. All these approaches grapple in different ways with a sense of Japaneseness and the goals or interests of tourists. One of the clear difficulties in conducting this kind of analysis on tourists is that it is hard to get into in-depth conversations about what this kind of experience might mean to people in the long run. Thus my analysis here is not aimed at determining a concrete sense of what this means to individual tourists, but rather what the larger pattern means for tourism in Kyoto.

Tourism in costume is not an unusual phenomenon in the era of experiential tourism. A widespread phenomenon today, historical reenactment encompasses a range of forms, from highly produced historical reality television shows like *The 1900 House* or *Pioneer House,* to groups of fans in Civil War reenactments in the United States, to historical museums like Colonial Williamsburg or Plymouth Plantation, where staff members are dressed in historically appropriate clothing (McCalman and Pickering 2010; Schlehe et al. 2010). This approach to local and national history for tourists has been called affective history, where participants seek to feel, not just to read about, a different place and time.[10] This is an integral and increasing part of the experience economy today (Pine and Gilmore 2011). In living history museums, docents who staff exhibits often enact a character, sometimes an actual historical figure, as they impart information about the time and place to visitors. While the extent of the reenacting—from period costume, to the addition of an accent, to an entire backstory—varies from location to location, many of these sites employ history buffs and aspiring actors as docents. Yet kimono rental in Kyoto is driven by a different set of interests. While female staff at a high-end *ryokan* or tour guides often wear kimono to work, tourism industry personnel are not renting kimono en masse; rather it is tourists who are in costume and walking around the historic district.

Aside from staff or docents at museums, reenactment is also performed by history buffs. For history fans who enjoy reenacting a beloved event or era, attention to getting the details of dress, setting, and experience exactly right is at a premium. As Vanessa Agnew puts it, "Reenactors take their history seriously—their credibility is measured by their conversancy with period minutiae and their fidelity to the 'authentic'—and they uniformly believe that reenactments both 'bring history alive' and test common assumptions about the past" (2004, 330). Such attention to details is not the case for most tourists in kimono in Kyoto, where expertise on kimono is neither required nor promised. Furthermore, kimono rental is not promoted as a way to learn about history; there are no narratives, factual or fictional, that attend this tourist experience. While there are a few historical costume experiences, like dressing in the twelve-layered Heian robes for a photo shoot or renting the modern Taisho-style *hakama*, the kimono that tourists rent are generally mass-produced versions of what stores rent for graduation and coming-of-age ceremonies. In addition, although dressing in kimono is marketed and discussed as "traditional," the kimono that most tourists rent today are in contemporary colors and patterns. The use of the term "traditional" for kimono is tricky. For one thing, it is not a garment from a precise historical moment; rather, what tourists rent are cheaper versions of contemporary kimono, which evolved over centuries to take their current form. At the same time, few Japanese wear them regularly. What makes kimono feel "traditional" is that a sense of Japanese style or heritage has come to be associated with it. As has been discussed throughout this book, rather than heritage understood as a strict preservation or crass recreation, heritage in Kyoto refers to the use of traditional materials even when utilized in new ways. Thus while the mastery of historical knowledge is not a part of kimono rental for most, tourists renting kimono in Kyoto share with reenactors around the world a desire to inhabit the spaces of Kyoto's historic district a bit differently.

As we shift lenses from historical costume to cultural costume, the notion of international tourists dressing in traditional or indigenous costume brings charges of cultural appropriation to the fore. As seen in the discussion of kimono above, forms of dress are ways in which individual bodies are shaped by cultural practices. In particular, the term "cross-cultural dressing" is often used when Westerners dress in the traditional clothing of non-Western cultures (Guth 2000; Mayer 2012; Miles and Neath 2016). As Melissa Miles and Jessica Neath explain, "As a form of cultural appropriation, cross-cultural dressing reduces other cultures and peoples to costumes that can be 'tried on,' effacing histories of colonial oppression and denying the specificities and complexities of cultural identities" (2016, 548). Charges of cultural appropriation are used when items of indigenous material culture—most often clothing, music, or material objects—are adopted by another group, whether for fashion, art, or political purposes.

An extreme but apt example is the "Kimono Wednesday" controversy at the Boston Museum of Fine Arts (MFA) during the summer of 2015. That summer, as a way to showcase the Monet painting "La Japonaise," which features Monet's wife posing in a kimono and surrounded by Japanese fans, the museum featured "Kimono Wednesdays," where visitors could view the painting while trying on a kimono. Quickly, a group of Asian Americans began protesting this as at once glorifying and reifying the orientalism of Monet and his painting. The museum's own description, crafted for a public conversation about the controversy, sums it up as follows:

> Last summer, the MFA offered programming focused around Claude Monet's "La Japonaise," with the goal of exploring the painting with visitors, as it documents both Monet's interest in Japanese art and his reaction to the fad of "Japonisme" in Paris. Reproduction kimonos made in Japan for a Japanese audience were available for visitors in Boston to try on, an experience intended to engage them both with the garment and Monet's rendering of it. The framing of the event through a Western lens sparked protest, counter-protest and much conversation and debate about issues including Orientalism, racialized iconography, institutional racism, representation of minority groups, and cultural appropriation (Boston Museum of Fine Arts 2016).

What is most interesting for our purposes is that the kimono at issue were made in Japan for visitors to the Tokyo exhibit of Monet's "La Japonaise." As Julie Valk (2015) points out, the kimono were commissioned by NHK for a try-on experience aimed at Japanese visitors to the traveling exhibit; the exhibit went on to Paris and then Boston, where the protests erupted. It is easy to see why a kimono experience that targeted a contemporary Japanese audience reads differently in Boston, which has its own history of *japonisme*,[11] although, as Valk (2015) aptly argues, it is critical to note that not all cultural appreciation is pejorative appropriation. Kimono rental in Kyoto is a good example of this difference in two ways. On the one hand, the kimono rental companies that started these promotions originally targeted domestic tourists, only adding international tourists as a way to expand their business. On the other hand, while there is some critique of international tourists in kimono, as mentioned above, the complaints in Kyoto were never about cultural appropriation. Critiques centered on the poor quality of the kimono tourists were wearing (without knowing it) and tourists' lack of proper comportment or decorum when in kimono. Even when comments were bemused, tourist kimono rental was understood as a kind of fascination with this quintessentially Japanese clothing—that is, as appreciation, not appropriation. Moreover, the notion of cultural appropriation is not one that comes naturally to Japan, a nation known for creative borrowing and adaptation.

Still, since conversations about cultural appropriation involve postcolonial or post-imperial cultural borrowing, we cannot ignore the fact that kimono tourism blossomed among Asian tourists, especially Chinese tourists. Certainly, tensions between Japan and China, two global powers, wax and wane, with the atrocities of World War II, comfort women, and war crimes in the background. Yet in recent years, China became the fastest-growing tourist demographic globally just as Japan embarked on its Tourism Nation Japan policies as solutions to decades of economic stagnation. Stereotypes of Chinese tourists as loud, pushy, and unwilling to follow the rules threaded many of the conversations I had with tourists and industry personnel alike throughout my research. These tensions are real and can be felt in the most crowded areas in recent years. Yet this image of walking in the historic district in kimono is understood as a timeless and apolitical Japanese style, distinct from the imperial aesthetic of the early to mid-twentieth century. Indeed, this tourist imaginary carries across national tensions as a romantic and exotic *wafu* experience for Asians tourists as well.

To be sure, a better comparison for kimono rental in Kyoto is the practice of cosplay—dressing up in costume and attending a convention, party, or event. Cosplay is a combination of costume and role-play, developed out of manga and anime fan cultures in Japan beginning in the 1980s, although the practice can be found throughout the world today.[12] Like historical reenactment participants, cosplayers care deeply about getting the details of a costume just right and wearing it to an event where other fans will appreciate the reference, affection, and hard work in creating it; only in the case of cosplay the world and/or events replayed are from popular manga and anime titles. In the most common example of cosplay, a fan makes a costume and wears it to a manga or anime convention. At the largest conventions one will see cosplayers walking around amid regularly clad fans, but there is always a cosplay area where cosplayers are allowed to gather to take pictures of themselves or each other and where fans can go to get pictures of or with their favorite characters or the best costumes. Indeed, photography plays an important role in these events. Michal Daliot-Bul writes, "This practice differs greatly from role-playing games, in which players assume the role of a character. In posing for photos, a costume player tries to embody the character that she performs, expressing in a frozen posture and a penetrating look the essence of that which the characters stands for" (2014, 93–94). It is important to note that scholars of both reenactment and cosplay take seriously the ways that such experiences by fans shape their sense of self long after a particular event is over (Agnew 2004; Daliot-Bul 2014; McCalman and Pickering 2010; Schlehe et al. 2010; Winge 2006). In recent years, as experiential tourism has increased, cosplay is emerging in tourist locations as well, especially fueled by the rise of contents tourism (Seaton et al. 2017; Sugawa-Shimada 2015). A prime example is Yamamura Takayoshi's (2009, 2015) research on fans of the anime *Lucky Star* who started showing up at sites in Saitama related to the anime, often in costume, and the subsequent development of local contents tourism in that region.

While kimono rental is not exactly cosplay, there are similarities between the two. In her work on recent developments in kimono as fashion in Kyoto, Hall (2015, 78–79) suggests that kimono rental places in Kyoto allow for a wider range of cosplay through newly themed kimono and new fashions such as putting kimono or kimono fabrics together with more modern accessories. She (2018, 303) demonstrates the various ways that designers and magazines aim to "speed up" kimono, making it attractive to contemporary Japanese women. Hall argues (2015, 78) that young women who rent from Kimono Hearts—a company that provides a nostalgic and/or hip newer style of kimono for young women to rent—are examples of a new kind of cosplay, both historic and modern. In contrast, sociologist Ogata Michimasa (2015, 115) notes that one of the main critiques of Japanese youth renting kimono for graduation and coming-of-age events is that such rentals seem like it is "just cosplay" for them. That is, contemporary youth, especially in Taishō or Shōwa antique kimono, seem out of place. Ogata (2015, 125) argues that the problem is not in youth wearing kimono incorrectly but rather in the mass production of kimono paired with the practice of having a stylist help coordinate an outfit, hair, and makeup. In this way, it is the performance of "trying on kimono" that makes this practice playful and ephemeral. While the bulk of the kimono rentals found in Kyoto are not cutting-edge fashion but cheap polyester or cotton contemporary kimono in Japanese-style prints, I find Hall's introduction of a broader sense of cosplay to be useful for thinking about kimono rental for tourists in Kyoto. Indeed, one of the differences between cosplay and historical reenactment is the transitory nature—that is, cosplayers do not typically stay "in character" all the time. In cosplay, most of the time, there is an actual character, or a character type, who is being performed. Yet in kimono rental there is not a particular time, character, or even type of character that is being embodied. In tourist kimono rental in Kyoto today, one is not a *geiko* or *maiko,* samurai or merchant, salaryman or *shōjo;* one is oneself on holiday in kimono.

In addition, the practice of dressing up in a costume and posing for photos connects cosplay and kimono rental for tourism. In cosplay, it is in the act of posing for a photo that the character's essence is performed, a technique that Daliot-Bul (2014, 94) connects to *kata* (set movements or poses in the martial and performing arts). The photo is an essential part of the performance. So, too, posing for the perfect photo or selfie in the historic district in Higashiyama is a big part of the appeal of kimono rental. A quick scroll through images on Instagram or Facebook reveals a nearly endless set of the same photo in front of iconic scenery. Indeed, it is hard to get a picture in the area without accidentally catching someone taking a posed shot. Photography has long been a part of tourism, capturing the sights seen and experiences had (Bærenholdt et al. 2004; Haldrup and Larsen 2010; Urry 1990; Urry and Larsen 2011). As Haldrup and Larsen (2010, 122–153) emphasize, digital photography involves both the production and consumption of images—one can take a photo, check it, edit it, but also consume it, enjoy it, and share it immediately. They write, "Digital photography transforms not so much what tourists' picture as how they picture, i.e. how they perform photography" (2010, 140). I think of this act as "mobile curation"; and it is one that is further enhanced by the spread of smart phones and social media. In the case of perambulatory tourists dressed in kimono, the combination of social media, heritage atmosphere, and the embodied experience curate iconic moments to be captured and shared in real time.

The way that dressing up in kimono, even for a few hours, shapes the ways one can move, stand, and walk, adds a somatic element to walking through a heritage district. Across this evolving phenomenon, wearing kimono is clearly seen as quintessentially Japanese. This is apparent in some of my earliest conversations about dressing up for a romantic getaway to Kyoto, in which wearing Japanese-style clothes and eating Japanese-style treats while in the heritage district is a part of the romance for a young Japanese couple. More than experiencing history, young Japanese tourists are playing at/experiencing a kind of timeless "Japaneseness." Just as Kyoto sells a heritage atmosphere, here the tourists' clothing matches the aesthetic. What is being bought and sold is a way of "feeling Japanese" for modern travelers. But there is no doubt that international tourists who dress up in kimono and walk around Kyoto draw on a different set of sentiments. While there certainly are, and have long been, Japanophiles who would like to feel as Japanese as they can and seek out a kimono experience while in Japan, this group is too small to account for the kimono rental boom in Kyoto today. So, too, the kind of identity work that cosplayers and reenactors are likely doing through performance does not seem applicable to this hyper-commercialized tourist experience. Kimono rental in Kyoto is at once too popular and fleeting to really shape a sense of self, even when the participant returns to everyday life, both as a tourist and at home. Here we encounter the limits of touristic experience. And yet the embodied experience of walking in the historic district in kimono is affective; it shapes how one feels and moves for the day in ways that play to tourist imaginaries (desires and materials) of what "Japan is like." It is the somatic experience of walking differently, more slowly, perhaps clumsily, through the heritage district, in fabrics and patterns that match the endless stream of images from Kyoto online and in print that drives this tourist experience. Kimono rental for tourists in Kyoto creates a fleeting experience of contemporary heritage.

Embodying Heritage in Kyoto

The tourists eating ice cream, shopping, and looking at their smartphones in kimono in figure 5.3 capture the dynamism and complexity of kimono tourism in Kyoto. This chapter has provided an analysis of the experience of heritage tourism in contemporary Kyoto *in situ* through an examination of tourists walking through the Higashiyama district in kimono. From "Walking City Kyoto" tourism promotions, the perambulatory tourism that dominates Japanese guidebooks, and the new trend of seeing Kyoto in kimono we have seen how an embodied experience of heritage is created and consumed in contemporary Kyoto. The Higashiyama heritage district is cultivated and protected by some of the city's strictest landscape preservation laws, and much of the area discussed here is open only to pedestrian traffic. Perambulatory tourism encourages a more personal experience of a place, allowing one to find new nooks and crannies, stop into a small temple, try a traditional snack, or buy a souvenir. There is no doubt that our travel is affected by our somatic and sensory experiences—taste, sound, smell, humidity, and even crowds affect our experience of places. The most oft-heard comment in any popular tourist district is "There are so many tourists here." The experience of crowds is physical as they jostle and vie for the best views, photo ops, food samples, and places in line. Moreover, in the examples analyzed here, tourists' bodies are shaped, even if for a few hours, by the experience of seeing world heritage sites and stopping for a Japanese-style snack while walking in kimono in Higashiyama. Building on the affect of the seasons and personal encounters with history discussed in prior chapters, the somatic experiences, *taiken,* of walking through the heritage district in kimono provide new ways to experience Kyoto, drawing on identifiable imaginaries of Japan, practices not experienced in daily life in modern Japan. While the experience of walking through the heritage district in kimono is fleeting, captured in photos or a post on social media, tourists in kimono have become a part of the heritage atmosphere in Kyoto.

Epilogue

"Experience Kyoto—Making Kyoto the World's Hometown"

Toward a Conclusion

"Experience Kyoto—Making Kyoto the World's Hometown." This slogan caught me off guard when I saw it front and center on the newly designed Kyoto City Official Travel Guide website in the summer of 2014.[1] Of course, the focus on "experience" was not surprising; but what does it mean to posit that Kyoto is both distinctly Japanese and a hometown for the world? I imagine those in charge of this slogan were thinking about a place that is welcoming, comfortable, and familiar when they came up with the notion of a "hometown" in marketing to international travelers. Yet while Kyoto tourism promotion plans aim at being welcoming, Kyoto's appeal is that it is particular: it embodies Japanese heritage. After all, Kyoto is famous for being the birthplace, incubator, and even repository of traditional Japanese culture. If this slogan was marketing hometown Kyoto to domestic tourists, it would fit with twentieth-century tourism campaigns marketing rural Japan as everyone's hometown (*furusato*); I suspect "hometown" is a translation of this Japanese term.[2] Yet if one can imagine a domestic tourism campaign framed by "Kyoto: Japan's hometown," one can scarcely imagine that a regional campaign framed by "Kyoto: Asia's hometown" would be successful. Although the slogan noted above was just a promotional tagline that appeared for only a few years, I use it to frame this epilogue because it raises issues that have emerged throughout this book: international, national, and local cultural tourism; a turn to personal and embodied experiences (both domestic and foreign); and the role of Kyoto in (re)presenting Japanese heritage. And it raises issues that have been at the forefront of scholarly, political, and cultural conversations for more than thirty years: the relationship between the global and the local.

ж ж ж

There is no doubt that we live in a globally connected world. As early as the 1980s scholars began to theorize the speeding up and closing in of time and space that come with postmodernity and globalization (Harvey 1990; Jameson 1995; Jameson and Miyoshi 1998; Yamajō 2007); these have further collapsed in the twenty-first century through the explosion of the internet, social media, and smartphones. Decades of globalization have ensured that global economics, commerce, politics, and health are inextricably interconnected. Even the recent rise of xenophobic populism, which attempts to reclaim national sovereignty, is both a symptom of the threats felt by such entanglements and proof that national boundaries are more porous than ever. Zygmunt Bauman's (2000) notion of "liquid modernity" aptly characterizes the fluidity with which we craft lives today. Liquid lives require flexibility and adaptation; we are no longer scripted by institutional expectations. But they also entail uncertainty; we have to pull together our sense of selves, life paths, and social lives from seemingly endless choices.[3] For Bauman, like for many social theorists, the tourist is an apt metaphor for the ways we live today. As tourists and postmodern subjects, we live in an experience economy—consuming people, places, and things in the construction of ourselves and our sense of the world around us (see also MacCannell 1999, 2011; Urry 1990, 2006; Urry and Larsen 2011).

Yet tourism is more than a metaphor for modern life. Tourism is one of the fastest-growing economic sectors, and the host of industries that support it—hotels, travel agencies, event venues, heritage sites, museums, destination marketing, transportation infrastructures, restaurants, translation services, tour companies—comprise a wide swath of global employees. According to the UNWTO, in 2018 one in ten people were employed in the tourist industry in some capacity, and tourism comprised 10 percent of the global GDP (direct and indirect) (World Tourism Organization 2018b). With this scope, there is no singular way that people travel. Even those who do not travel physically live mobile lives. Through our ever-present devices we can read about, chat with, learn from, and connect to people from across the globe on a daily or even hourly basis (Elliott and Urry 2010; Germann Molz 2012; Sheller and Urry 2004). If it was not always clear, it is now: our understanding of the global and the local cannot be disentangled.

Olympic Heritage

Perhaps the most recognizable example of global and local entanglements can be found in the Olympic Games. Beyond international sporting events, the Olympics are important national moments on the global stage. This is symbolized most poignantly in Olympic opening ceremonies, wherein the host nation welcomes visitors, viewers, and athletes through choreographed performances. These performances showcase national traditions, telling stories of cultural and historical uniqueness, modern progress, and technological prowess. Indeed, until the games start, one could almost forget that these are sporting events; once they start, a different national display commences—this time of physical prowess through medal counts.

As I write, Japan is again preparing to host the Summer Olympics and Paralympics in Tokyo in 2021. While much has changed since Japan first hosted the Olympic Games in 1964, the parallels involved in planning an event of this scale are undeniable.[4] The 1964 Olympics were a watershed moment for Japan on the global stage, signaling the nation's rebirth after the devastation of World War II—a chance to demonstrate its rapid recovery (economic, political, and spiritual). The Tokyo Olympics in 1964 recast Japan as peace-loving and international while at the same time showcasing the newly renovated Tokyo, as well as technological innovations like satellite broadcasting and the world's first high-speed rail. Tokyo constructed modern facilities for the Olympic Village, whose contours still shape the Yoyogi area through the stadium and park, large housing complexes, and a Parisian-style shopping avenue—all built to exhibit postwar Tokyo as a city on par with those in the West.

As seen here, preparation for the global games is not all about sports facilities. Indeed, the Olympics are major tourist events. Leading up to the 1964 games, new hotels were built, streets were modernized, and English was added to the names of train stations throughout the city. The bullet train debuted in order to bring Olympic tourists to Kyoto and Osaka, highlighting technological advancement and the nation's cultural history all at once. In anticipation of the influx of tourists, the 1963 Basic Tourism Law called for the establishment of eight tourism routes within Japan; it also liberalized travel policies, making it easier for Japanese to travel outside the country again (Funck and Cooper 2015, 42; Leheny 2003, 92; Soshirodo 2005, 1110). In 1964, the first national tourism agency, JNTO, was established to promote Japanese tourism abroad. In the end, only 50,000 international visitors attended the Tokyo Olympics, well shy of the anticipated 130,000 (Wilson 2012, 161), but global viewers could take in the transformation of Japan through television coverage using the latest broadcast technology.[5]

Certainly, much has changed since 1964, and yet discourses surrounding the Tokyo Summer Olympics 2020/2021 similarly offered hope for renewal in the wake of nearly thirty years of recession. More than half a century after the end of World War II, the Peace Clause (Article 9) of the Japanese Constitution is still in place, even if it is being whittled away. Technological prowess in transportation and consumer electronics has driven Japan's economy to competitive heights, making Japanese cars and consumer electronics global household names. Japanese business practices emphasizing a closer connection to consumer demand (like "just-in-time" delivery) have shifted global production and distribution models; and Japanese popular culture has garnered global fans for three decades, becoming a top national export. Yet since the bursting of the economic bubble in the early 1990s Japan has struggled to find equilibrium economically and socially in the ensuing lost decades (Allison 2013; Brinton 2011; Leheny 2006). Moreover, post–World War II regional tensions continue to simmer, even as economic and political relations evolve. In this context, Japan's hosting the Olympic Games in 2020 was seen as a chance to raise the Japanese global profile and jump start the economy again (Pellicano 2019; Shimizu 2014).

In the summer of 2019, the Yoyogi Park area was again under renovation or reconstruction; Tokyo Bay was full of cranes preparing new venues for water sports; hotels were popping up left and right, as were new home rentals like Airbnb; and new signage in English, Chinese, and Korean was multiplying throughout the transportation system. The new bullet train, N700 Supreme, began service in July 2020, running along the Tōkaidō route from Tokyo to Osaka with a stop in Kyoto. Furthermore, the JNTO began training new ranks of volunteer guides throughout the nation. In Kyoto, major venues—

from convention halls to the Kyoto Tower building to Kiyomizu Temple—have been under renewal or renovation over the past five years. In 2019 it seemed like there was a new hotel on every corner, and English menus replete with vegetarian, vegan, and halal items could be found easily in the city center. Throughout the course of my research the city has been readying itself for Olympic tourists.

As discussed in the introduction, the 2020 Summer Olympics are a part of Japan's approach to economic recovery through the Tourism Nation Japan strategy. Tourism sits at the intersection of soft and hard power, as it sells cultural experiences in the global economy. The tourism policies crafted in twenty-first-century Japan build on earlier policies through a focus on tourism as both an economic solution and a global asset for Japan's future. The Tourism Nation Japan initiatives aim to increase inbound tourism in both quantity and duration (overall numbers as well as length of stay and number of visits). However, even though tourism brings much needed foreign money and has the potential to smooth international relations—or at least change one's perceptions of a place—it often does so at a cost. As noted, the idea of overtourism is starting to take center stage in conversations about popular tourist destinations like Venice, Rome, Paris, and Kyoto (World Tourism Organization 2019). In Japan, in the past five years news stories of small towns virtually overrun by an onslaught of tourists have become a mainstay in the media; in 2018 the crowds, vandalism, and disruptions by tourists in Kyoto were a regular feature in the news. Just as tourism revitalizes the economy, it taxes local life.

Thus as global tourism events, the Olympic Games are situated at the intersection of the global and the local, prizing international relations through friendly competition and upholding the universal value of national pride on a global stage. A similar logic is at work in world heritage concerns. UNESCO's world heritage discourse emerged out of the devastation of World War II, in which the magnitude of the power to destroy became all too real. As a branch of the United Nations, UNESCO values human diversity through the preservation of natural and cultural places and practices, not merely for national identity or historical memory, but for their universal value for humanity. This line of thinking is also evident in the slogan that opened this chapter, "Experience Kyoto—Making Kyoto the World's Hometown." In this refrain, and in the examples throughout this book, Kyoto represents a kind of timeless Japanese heritage delivered to the world through tourism.

Kyoto Revisited

There is no doubt that Kyoto looms large in images and imaginings of Japan. Established as the capital in 794, it has always been an urban tourism destination. In its early centuries, Kyoto was the center of cultured life; indeed, to be exiled from Kyoto was the height of punishment in the Heian period. As such, domestic tourists have long flocked to Kyoto. In the Edo period, when the political center of gravity was shifting, Kyoto remained renowned for its natural beauty and cultural sophistication. Through the poetics of famous places Kyoto was a part of the earliest tourism booms. With the exit of the emperor in the Meiji period, the city modernized, crafting public spaces shaped by newly imported building styles and technology but keeping its imperial legacy at the fore. The inclusion of school excursions in the beginning of the twentieth century ensured that many Japanese first visited the city as a part of their curriculum. In 1953 Kyoto was declared a world tourist city and was considered a jewel to showcase Japanese culture to international tourists traveling for the Olympics in 1964 and for Osaka's Expo '70. As of 2019, Kyoto has had over fifty million tourists a year for seven years running, and it has been voted a top travel destination by *Travel + Leisure* magazine for several consecutive years as well. Thus urban tourism is a part of Kyoto's history, its landscape and cityscape, its success as a tourist city, and its challenge for the twenty-first century.

Moreover, Kyoto carries the reputation of being "the heart of Japan." Even though this romantic sentiment feels overwrought, Kyoto is seen as the place to go to experience Japanese culture, nature, and history. When asked why they come to Kyoto, time and again tourists respond, "To experience Japanese history and culture," "To feel the historic atmosphere," "You can't understand Japan without going to Kyoto," and the like. These same sentiments kept it from being the target of an atomic bomb in World War II, has driven townscape policies, and is the core of the Kyoto brand. Today, domestic and international tourists alike travel to Kyoto to experience Japanese heritage in the context of a contemporary urban city. It is this confluence of factors—heritage Kyoto, urban tourism, national policy, and the importance of tourism in our global economy—that makes Kyoto a quintessential case study of urban heritage tourism.

This book has focused on unpacking the nuances of heritage tourism in contemporary Kyoto, weaving together particular examples (both material and conceptual) of heritage construction today, Kyoto City tourism promotion plans, and new forms of experiential tourism. As I have argued, heritage is the (re)presentation, commodification, and promotion of history and culture. While both history and heritage seek to tell the stories of past people, places, and things, one aims at accuracy while the other aims at affect. That is, heritage draws on the past to tell stories of import to the present. As the chapters in this book attest, heritage in Kyoto is not understood as a petrification or preservation of the past, even though historic markers pepper the city and its environs. Rather, heritage in Kyoto is living, as seen through examples such as the *machiya* revival; the street renovation of Kōyaku no Zushi; the creation of new seasonal festivals, such as Hanatōro and Kyō no Tanabata, which draw on and extend traditional aesthetics; and even walks through a heritage district in kimono. Across these examples we see the construction of a Japanese-style atmosphere through narratives of the past, architecture and aesthetics, and culinary and sartorial styles—all fostered by a wide range of interlocutors from city officials to citizens to tourists.

This book has traced the shift from "seeing" (*miru*) to "encountering" (*fureau*) to "experiencing" (*taiken*) in tourism. The Kyoto City tourism promotion plans identify experiential travel as an important aim, and slogans such as "Experience Kyoto," "View Kyoto like a local," and "Walk in the ancient capital in kimono" all market both atmosphere and personal or shared experience as much as particular sites or locations. In Kyoto today, personal experience tourism is seen through the ways that history fans find their way to the small-scale Ryōma sites and make personal connections to this modern samurai hero. Furthermore, tourists embody a Japanese experience through a walk through the heritage district in kimono. This I argue, is a quintessential somatic experience as it shapes the body, movement, and comportment, even when wearers are not trying to "be" Japanese. Moreover, this notion of the ways twenty-first-century tourists seek to personalize their experiences is enhanced by our online interconnectedness. Not only do we have images from around the world at our fingertips on screens large and small, but also the distinction between tourist selfies and tourism industry promotions is increasingly blurred as tourists post, share, like, and re-tweet 'their photos; this cycle of peer-to-peer representations shapes tourist imaginaries and experiences of Kyoto today.

At its core, this book set out to revisit Kyoto in the context of the precarity of twenty-first-century Japan, Tourism Nation Japan policies, and current trends toward experiential tourism, attentive to the ways that this heritage city crafts experiences for contemporary tourists. That Kyoto markets itself as historical goes without saying, but the ethnographic analysis of different tourist sites, agendas, and experiences herein highlights the ways that heritage—history and culture—is represented, packaged, and consumed as a means of asserting culture and tradition in today's globalized and interconnected context. In the end, heritage tourism in Kyoto today demonstrates how the past is mobilized in constructing the identity of the city, how that identity shapes understandings of contemporary Japan for domestic and international travelers, and how tourist desires and experiences in Kyoto speak to broader trends in our contemporary moment, in which heritage can feel like an anchor in uncertain times.

Notes

Okoshiyasu

Epigraph. Rowthorn 2005, 5.

1. Each of these slogans is from the Kyoto City Official Travel Guide website for international tourists, available in English, French, Mandarin and Taiwanese, Korean, Spanish, German, Italian, Arabic, Turkish, Malaysian, Thai, and Russian (Kyoto City Convention and Visitors' Bureau). As of this writing, "Kyoto: This place will enrich your life" is centered at the top of the page, where it has been for several years. "Experience Kyoto—Making Kyoto the World's Hometown" appeared on the site beginning in November 2014, followed by the pairing of "Kyoto: The experience here will change you."

2. In the spring of 2020 Japan announced that the Games of the XXXII Olympiad would be postponed to the summer of 2021 due to the global spread of COVID-19. The name "Tokyo 2020" was retained for branding and marketing.

3. Emperor Kanmu (737–806) chose to relocate the capital away from the influence of the powerful Buddhist clergy in Nara, the first capital (710–794). The first such move was to a small town called Nagaoka, just south of Kyoto (784–794). The capital moved again quickly, most likely due to the role of flooding in the low plain, understood as an inauspicious habitat for the capital.

4. There are several excellent histories of the city available in English. For more comprehensive accounts see the following: Brumann (2012); Dougill (2006); Martin and Martin (2014); and Stavros (2014).

5. The Shinsengumi were a group of samurai in Kyoto who were charged by the Tokugawa shogunate with keeping the peace by squelching loyalist plots in the capital during the *bakumatsu* period (1853–1868).

6. *Torii* are gates that mark the entrance to a Shinto shrine.

7. It is important to note that this book was in press as the world was in various stages of lockdown during the COVID-19 pandemic. As I edit

this book, tourism is still down over 90 percent globally. Thus these statistics are all from just prior to 2020, and it is hard to predict exactly how tourism will resume in the coming years.

8. There are important parallels between the features discussed here and earlier twentieth-century tourism policies, including the role of tourism in infrastructural changes and the focus on inbound tourists as sources of revenue. In 1912 the first national tourism agency, the Japan Tourist Bureau (JTB), was established under the auspices of the Ministry of Railroads. Beyond economics, courting international tourists was understood as a way to showcase the newly emerging modern nation of Japan, as well as the country's rich cultural heritage (Leheny 2003, 61). A similar pattern can be seen in the tourism promotion of the high growth years (1960–1970s). In particular, the 1963 Basic Tourism Law was put into place just in time for the Tokyo Olympics in 1964 (Funck and Cooper 2015, 42; Leheny 2003, 92; Soshirodo 2005, 1110). Similarly, in 1964, a new national tourism agency, the Japanese National Tourism Organization (JNTO) was established to promote Japanese tourism abroad.

9. The term "cool Japan" was coined in 2002 by journalist Douglas McGray in an article in *Foreign Policy*. Along with demonstrating the ways Japanese popular culture had become cool in the West, McGray used Joseph Nye's term "soft power" to argue that Japan had a new economic commodity—its cool products—but had not managed to harness it into political or international influence (McGray 2002). Quickly both the media and Japanese officials latched onto the terms "cool Japan" and "soft power," which are foundational for the policies discussed here.

10. https://kyoto.travel/en. Accessed March 9, 2019.

11. https://www.enjoymyjapan.jp/en/about/. Accessed June 20, 2019.

12. While my focus here is on trends in changes to the ways people travel, these are overlapping categories; large bus tours have continued to be offered even as more and more tourists wanted to find their own way; so, too, not all tourists have the time or inclination to participate in the more embodied experiences of the turn to *taiken*.

13. Just as heritage is everywhere, heritage scholarship is likewise ubiquitous. Housed in no particular discipline, heritage studies include both critiques of the discourses, practices, and theories of heritage and the "how to" of preservation work. Emma Waterton and Steve Watson's state of the field volume (2015) provides a good entry point to the understanding of heritage studies.

14. Scholars of heritage have given much thought to the structures, challenges, benefits, and consequences of the global system of World Heritage. In particular, see Di Giovine (2009) and Harrison (2013).

15. The Kyoto City Tourism Office conducts a yearly tourism survey comprised of data collected by Japan National Railway and other transportation groups and hotels, as well as surveys conducted at the tourism information centers or other prime tourist locations. The reports are released on the city's website (in Japanese).

16. The note at the bottom of figure I.1 explains that the survey collection strategies changed in 2011 and 2012, making the numbers hard to estimate; in addition, the Great Eastern Japan Earthquake and Tsunami of 2011 had a significant effect on tourism through 2012.

17. The full name is Kyoto City Industry and Tourism Bureau, Tourism and MICE Promotion Office. I have shortened it throughout the text and references as Kyoto City Tourism Office for ease of use. MICE is tourism lingo for "Meetings, Incentives, Conferences, and Exhibitions."

18. This kind of classification is tricky. The JTB releases monthly tourism reports based on the JNTO official statistics, which include the following countries in the category of "Asia": China, Korea, Taiwan, Hong Kong, Thailand, Singapore, Malaysia, India, Indonesia, Philippines, Vietnam, Macao, Mongolia, Israel, Turkey, and other. In the JNTO statistics Asia, North America, Europe, and "Other" are the regional categories. The Kyoto City documents do not clarify which nations are included in which category, although these documents tend to use the JNTO categories.

19. In addition to eight months in Kyoto from January through July 2012, I returned for follow-up research in the summers of 2013, 2014, 2017, and 2019.

20. The Great Eastern Japan Earthquake and Tsunami was the root of a "triple disaster." First, the earthquake, which took place under water just off the shore of Tohoku region on March 11, 2011, registered 9.0. The second disaster was the tsunami, which devastated the northeastern coast. Third was the nuclear disaster from the meltdown of three nuclear reactors at the Fukushima Daiichi Nuclear Power Plant.

21. The KTA is a nongovernmental organization established as a promotional association by a group of local businesses loosely affiliated with tourism. The KTA, the Kyoto City Tourism Office, and the Convention and Visitors' Bureau are the three main organs of the tourism industry in Kyoto. The three often work closely together.

22. Chinese tourists are the fastest growing sector, and they were visible and on the minds of all the industry personnel with whom I spoke throughout this research. I wish that I had had the chance to speak with more Chinese tourists, but the language barrier prevented it. This topic is ripe for additional research given the historical, political, and economic relationship between Japan and China.

Chapter 1: "The Essence of Travel"

Epigraph: Rakutabi 2009b.

1. Ishimori's work (1989, 192; 1995) is pivotal to the contextualization of the prevalence and evolution of Japanese travel practices.

2. Compiled around 759 CE, the *Man'yōshū* is the oldest extant collection of Japanese poetry. It anthologizes poems in a range of styles dating back to the fourth century. Collected around 905, the *Kokinshū* was the first imperial *waka* anthology. (*Waka* is a thirty-one-syllable poetic form [5–7–5–7–7] that preceded the more widely known *haiku* [5–7–5]). The collection begins with two books of spring poems, one book of summer poems, two books of autumn poems, and one book of winter poems and then moves to themes such as love, travel, celebrations, and miscellany.

3. There is a wealth of research on the creation of national heritage and cultural heritage and their role in solidifying the new nation-state. In the Meiji period, when Shinto was adopted and reimagined as the national religion, Buddhist institutions were under threat. Yet many were able to gain new national importance through the cultural artifacts that they held and that were embraced as national treasures (Aso 2014; Gluck 1985; Ivy 1988, 1995; Tanigawa 2020; Tseng 2018; Vlastos 1998,). Ishimori (1995, 19) discusses the ways that Nara was reconceived as a heritage tourist location through the exhibition of national treasures in the early Meiji period.

4. In the early postwar period, as institutions were disbanded, reorganized, or disassociated from their earlier incarnations, the JTB's name changed from Japan Tourist Bureau (Nihon Kankō Kōsha) to Japan Travel Bureau (Nihon Kōtsū Kōsha), retaining the same acronym in both English and Japanese. At that time, its mission remained the promotion and packaging of Japan for foreigners, but by the 1960s it had turned to domestic audiences as well (Leheny 2003, 92–93).

5. The most famous pilgrimage routes in Japan are the eighty-eight-stage pilgrimage around Shikoku and the Kumano pilgrimage route along the Kii peninsula, just southwest of Kyoto (Funck and Cooper 2015, 11; Hoshino 1997).

6. The number of students in school excursion trips has been declining since the combined economic downturn and decline in birthrates beginning in the early 1990s—from around 6 million in 1990 to 3.4 million in 2015. In the past decade Kyoto has fluctuated at around 1 million students per year (Kyoto City Tourism Office 2018).

7. The structure for such trips is highly organized. The Kyoto City Tourism Office and KTA provide schools with packets of information for

planning, including a DVD and study guides to help students prepare. Mark Oedewald (2009) provides a helpful overview of the aims and practices of such trips.

8. Taking a Western name to make it easier for foreign visitors was a common practice at the time.

9. This test itself is a national standardized test run by the JTA today. Many guides I spoke to discussed it as very difficult, requiring a detailed knowledge of history and culture. As of 2008, a second layer of regional tests was added as a part of the Tourism Nation Japan campaign, which emphasizes the quality and quantity of guide services available for tourists.

10. The first hotel in Kyoto was the Hotel Okura (now Kyoto Hotel Okura), which opened its doors two years earlier, in 1888. The term "hotel" denotes bed and carpet rather than tatami and futon. The typical form of lodging in Kyoto until the late twentieth century were *ryokan,* which are still abundant throughout the city. Today, hotels dominate the lodging landscape. While there is a host of well-known Western brand hotels in Kyoto, most of the hotels in Japan today are Japanese brands.

11. Higashi Honganji, known affectionately in Kyoto as Ohigashi-san, was built in 1602, when Tokugawa Ieyasu split the Shin Buddhism (or New Pureland Buddhism) sect into two. Its counterpart, Nishi Honganji (Onishi-san), is located a few miles directly west and was built by Hideyoshi in 1591. While Higashi Honganji is located just two blocks north of Kyoto Station, it is not a primary tourist site.

12. *Ōkini* is actually native to the Kansai region, but it has become a signature Kyoto word, explained in guides to *Kyoto-ben* (Kyoto dialect) and heard in shops and restaurants throughout Kyoto.

13. The Kimono Passport is offered through the "Kimono matches the town—Kyoto" association, sponsored by a range of textile and tourism associations. The 2018 booklet highlights the fact that the association is trying to register the wearing of a kimono as a UNESCO intangible cultural heritage item. https://kimono-passport.jp.

14. *Ryokan* are considered traditional, but the term was not widely used until the Taishō period (Guichard-Anguis 2009b, 78). While many of the basic features are characteristic of traditional lodging in Japan (i.e., tatami mats, futons, and Japanese features of hospitality), *ryokan* themselves are a modern invention, created to provide a new Japanese-style lodging as Western-style hotels increased in the Meiji period. *Ryokan* continued to evolve over the twentieth century into the current version, which is more like a high-end experience combining Japanese hospitality and nature, food, and bathing (Graburn 1995; Guichard-Anguis 2009b).

15. Trash collection and recycling are taken seriously in Japan. The rules are strict, and most neighborhoods have a community system that is shared to keep the trash collection areas tidy. An influx of transient tenants, and foreign ones to boot, wreaks havoc on neighborhood life.

Chapter 2: A Brand of History

1. Designed by Hara Hiroshi, Kyoto Station is a fete of soaring glass, angles, marble, and steel, and it is still mentioned regularly as an example of a fight over Kyoto's townscape identity. Brumann (2012, 46–67) includes a chapter on this controversy.

2. Throughout the ethnographic chapters of this book, I have included short quotes and comments from various people with whom I spoke across the ten years of this research. As indicated in the introduction, fieldwork on tourism includes many short conversations that don't rise to the occasion of a formal interview. Longer planned conversations and interviews are cited and included in the references.

3. The term "cityscape" might seem more appropriate, but "townscape" is most often used as the translation of the term *machizukuri* in Kyoto city planning and branding materials. More generally, *machizukuri* is a term for city planning, which started as both a citizens' movement and a set of policies to counter the ill effects of urbanization and the depopulation of rural areas in the 1960s and 1970s. Today it is used to refer to a wide range of national or regional city planning initiatives, revitalizations in connection with tourism, beautification, and branding (Brumann 2012; Brumann and Schulz 2015; Evans 2002; Hein and Pelletier 2006; Seaton et al. 2017).

4. The *bakufu*, tent government, refers to the military government under the shoguns from 1185 until 1868.

5. The Kyoto City Tourism Survey provides these categories for respondents to indicate which ones they "were moved by." This tells us what the city thinks is important, but the responses also track with the main features of Kyoto tourism promotion plans.

6. *Hakama* are a traditional trouser-like garment worn over or with kimono. They are traditionally men's dress but were popularized for women in the Taishō period (1912–1926); it is still more common to see men in *hakama* than women.

7. From 1978 until 2001 the World Culture Free Kyoto Declaration/Proclamation (*Sekai buna jiyū Kyoto sengen*) was in place. In 2001 Kyoto sought to take on the challenges of the new century with a plan called the Welcome Plan 21 (Okoshiyasu Plan 21), which was revised and extended to 2010, when the Future Kyoto Plan 2010 went into effect (Kyoto City 2010,

3). In 2015 the Future Kyoto Plan 2010 was replaced by the Yearning for Kyoto Plan 2015.

8. There are two versions of Future Kyoto Plan 2010 available in Japanese on the city's website—a full version and a glossy outline version. My analysis pulls from both. The documents can be found at http://www.city.kyoto.lg.jp/sankan/page/0000098836.html.

9. Like for the Future Kyoto Plan 2010, both a full version and a glossy summary version are available on the City Government Tourism pages: https://www.city.kyoto.lg.jp/sankan/page/0000186495.html.

10. The Kyoto Tour Guide Association was run by Paul Satoh, who was eighty-two at the time and had taken up guiding as a hobby when he retired. It should be noted that in Japan, where retirement age is strictly regulated, a second career is a necessity for many people today. The gig economy provides more options, albeit ones that take a lot of networking and energy to upkeep, like any freelancing job.

11. *Shakkei* (borrowed scenery) refers to the practice of incorporating the views from the surrounding hillside into a garden vista—borrowing scenery from the verdant backdrop.

12. Matthew Stavros's (2014) book on the evolution of Heian Kyoto provides an excellent account of the ways the city center was shaped by grids of varying sizes, depending on the rank and status of the owners. He also discusses the development of *machiya* in early Heian Kyoto.

13. Brumann's seminal book on the townscape of Kyoto (2012, 91–155) has an excellent discussion of the battle over historical buildings in the city center from the mid-1980s to the mid-2000s. He includes a detailed account of the range of *Kyō-machiya* features and their use throughout contemporary Kyoto.

14. The KCCC was set up in 1997 to promote the preservation of *machiya* culture in Kyoto. It has gradually taken on a larger role in city planning and today serves as a clearinghouse, mediator, and collaboration center for community development projects. Its goal is to develop and promote the core character of Kyoto through preservation of the urban landscape. Beginning in 2004 the Machiya Machizukuri Fund was set up to help renovate and restore townhouses throughout Kyoto (Kyoto Center for Community Collaboration 2009).

15. There are five geisha districts in Kyoto today, although their numbers have dwindled significantly since their prewar heyday (Bardsley 2021; Dalby 1983).

16. Yamajō Toru's (2007, 2010) work on Kyoto tourism covers each of these topics in greater detail, focusing on Kyoto's history as a "hub

terminal" for Japanese culture and the attendant cultivation of Kyoto history, tradition, and style (*Kyoto-rashisa*).

17. Brumann's (2009) article is an astute analysis of the ways that heritage has been maintained and renovated in the floats, practices, and performances of the Gion Festival.

18. This name was not posted or used in any of my conversations in 2012; the street was known as Shinkamanza-cho, the name given in 1869. However, the city tourism sign erected since explains that in 938 the Buddhist priest Kuya Shonin established a school in the area. The school became colloquially called Kuya-kuyo, for Priest Kuya and the word for memorial service (*kuyo*); then it was shortened to Kōyaku. *Zushi* means "path." It is worth noting that this is all fairly obscure, not a well-known local legend, although it did occasion an official Kyoto City historical marker.

19. This cobblestone-style asphalt pavement had been used in the Kamishichiken and Kiyomizu historic areas in Kyoto, but the water-retention style was tested at Kōyaku no Zushi for the first time (Kyoto City 2012).

20. "Walking City Kyoto" is what I am calling one thread of the Kyoto city planning and tourism promotion plans. "Arukumachi Kyoto" was used in several of my interviews. It includes a range of projects from widening sidewalks, providing delivery services, making outdoor "no smoking zones," and encouraging domestic tourists not to drive to Kyoto, and the like.

21. See https://kyoto.travel/en/info/enjoy-respect-kyoto/akimahen.html.

22. In 2018 the location became a Tsuruha drugstore, the latest tourist fad, with a traditional beige and brown aesthetic rather than the store's red and yellow branding.

Chapter 3: Seasonal Travel

Epigraph. Kyoto City Official Travel Guide Website 2019.

Epigraph. Shirane (2012, 212).

1. The JNTO provides a cherry blossom forecast on its English-language website: http://www.jnto.go.jp/sakura/eng/index.php.

2. Despite their prominence, *sakura* are not the only celebrated blooms. In fact, celebrations of *ume* (plum blossoms) predate those of cherry blossoms. Plum blossoms in late February, when it is still cold and damp. The vibrant colors of the blossoms (white and dark pink) stand out against gnarled dark wood trunks and branches, and they are a harbinger of spring, assuring that winter is coming to an end. Haruo Shirane (2012, 151, 169–173) notes that in the process of the indigenization of Chinese traditions in

the Heian period, cherry blossoms gradually took central stage over the celebrated plum of China. While most major gardens, tourist sites, and public areas in Kyoto have some plum trees, Kitano Tenmangu Shrine is the most famous place to view plum trees in the city.

3. Generally speaking, *The Pillow Book* has received much less scholarly attention than *The Tale of Genji*. Gergana Ivanova (2018) provides a thorough and engaging account of this classical work, including its reception through the ages.

4. Names are notoriously difficult in the *The Tale of Genji*. The original does not include them, in keeping with the indirectness of classical Japanese. The male characters are referred to by their rank or position, which changes through the course of the novel. To make the text readable to contemporary Japanese and international audiences, many translators use the centuries-old nicknames coined by readers, including Hikaru or *hikaru* Genji. *Hikaru* means "the shining one" or "the blessed one."

5. Christian Tagsold's (2017) book on the cultivation of Japanese gardens in the West provides an astute analysis of these features as they have come to symbolize "Japaneseness."

6. There are two places in the Kyoto area where one can see a replica of Genji's Rokujō mansion, as well Genji-related exhibits: the Costume Museum and the Tale of Genji Museum. The Costume Museum is a textile museum, but it boasts a replica of part of Genji's Rokujō mansion in one-quarter scale. The Tale of Genji Museum is in Uji, just south of Kyoto. The museum is more atmospheric than informational. An excellent example of experiential tourism, it assumes that guests know the basics of the story and want to be able to see, feel, hear, and touch the story's ethos.

7. While some of these features began to be developed in the Heian period, Kuitert (2002, 51–52) is clear that we see just the general contours of these features this early. For more on the development of gardens, see Kuitert's book, *Themes in the History of Japanese Garden Art*.

8. It can be found at https://ja.kyoto.travel/flower/flowermail/ (accessed June 2020).

9. Designed by Ogawa Jihei, the Shin'en Garden is one of the renowned gardens of Kyoto. It is located on the grounds of the Heian Shrine. Despite its name, the Heian Shrine was created in the Meiji period (1895) to commemorate the 1,100th anniversary of the founding of the city in honor of Emperor Kanmu. Thus both the garden and the shrine should be considered modern representations of Heian style, not Heian artifacts (Treib and Herman 2003, 153–155; Tseng 2018).

10. Many of the popular tourist sites offer a small teahouse or area

for tea ceremony for a fee. At most of them, the ritual is shortened to give tourists a sense of it rather than the full ritual. The Shin'en Garden at the Heian Shrine provides a slightly longer version, lasting thirty minutes or so.

11. The word *tōrō* (灯篭) means "garden lantern," but *hanatōro* (花灯路) replaces the final *rō* with the *ro* from *roji* (路地), the name for the narrow, alley-like streets of Kyoto.

12. Kōdaiji is an interesting example of a temple tapping into new tourist trends. Established in 1606 by Nene, Hideyoshi's wife, in his honor, over the past decade it has embraced the theme of love ("You too can have a romance like that of Hideyoshi and Onene"), promoted dragon light-up events, and even hosted an AI robot named Mindar to explain Buddhism to visitors.

13. http://www.kyoto-Tanabata.jp/.

14. *Purikura*, or "print clubs," are a proto-selfie technology popular in Japanese video arcades since the 1990s. They are an important feature of *kawaii* (cute) culture in Japan. An evolution of photo booths—a small booth for taking selfies or small group photos in a strip printed while you wait—*purikura* provide a wide range of backgrounds, messages, and photo enhancements such as makeup and hair color; the images printed are stickers rather than photos.

15. Reports assessing the success of both the Hanatōro and Kyō no Tanabata were made available online after the first few events, and they include information collected from surveys.

16. All of the events have a Twitter, Instagram, and Facebook page where they provide details, share pictures, and reshare visitors' pictures. While there are nearly infinite Kyoto tourism hashtags, #hanatoro and #kyonotanabata elicit a range of visitor photos and comments. As these events cater primarily to domestic tourists, these posts are primarily in Japanese.

Chapter 4: *Bakumatsu* Vacation

An earlier version of the material in this chapter originally appeared as "Meiji Restoration Vacation: Heritage Tourism in Contemporary Kyoto," in *Japan Forum*, 30, no. 4, 564–588, copyright © 2018 BAJS.

1. For a focus on Ryōma tourism, Kyoto is not the first place that comes to mind; Kochi (Ryōma's hometown) and Nagasaki, where he spent quite a bit of time, are more prominent locations. In the context of this book on Kyoto I have focused on the collection of Ryōma sites that commemorate events near the end of his life. For those interested in Ryōma tourism, several articles have been written on the topic in recent years (see Nakamura 2011, 2016; Seaton 2015; Seaton et al. 2017).

2. Given Ryōma's popularity as a *bakumatsu* hero, it is not surprising that much ink has been spent telling his story. My outline of his life here is meant to give the nonspecialist reader a bit more context. In addition to Marius Jansen's (1961) seminal text about Ryōma, the work of Romulus Hillsborough (2004) is widely read.

3. According to the plaque outside the inn, the Teradaya Incident occurred in the spring of 1862, when a group of loyalists was meeting at the inn to solidify plans to seize the imperial palace in Kyoto and restore the emperor to power. Having heard of the plot, Satsuma samurai Shimazu Hisamitsu sent eight men to persuade the loyalists to give up their plans. A fight broke out, and seven loyalists were killed and two later committed seppuku.

4. Between 2013 and 2017 the general layout changed quite a bit. In 2013 only one room on the first floor was open to visitors, but by 2017 several more rooms had been opened and filled with exhibits.

5. As discussed in the introduction, the notion of authenticity is fraught. On the one hand, tourists and industry personnel alike mention its importance in driving visits to historical sites, and yet what exactly constitutes an "authentic" site is widely debated (Bruner 1994; MacCannell 1999, 2011; Harrison 2013; Waterton and Watson 2015). For my purposes here, I simply mark the ways that the notion comes up in the Teradaya materials because it is a part of why people come to see place-based heritage sites.

6. The Ryōzen History Museum is a fascinating site in its own right. It is dedicated to the events and heroes of the *bakumatsu* with a focus on Ryōma and the Shinsengumi. As of 2019, the banner strung across the entrance reads, "Things you are familiar with from drama, Ryōma, Shinsengumi, and Kaishū. . . . A museum to read and understand the *bakumatsu* and Restoration." According to the pamphlet provided upon entry, the museum is dedicated to portraying the *bakumatsu* events and the contributions of those who fought for modern Japan. The museum is renowned for its collection of *bakumatsu* and Meiji Restoration documents and artifacts.

7. Henry Smith (2007) analyzes the youthful atmosphere of the Ryōma Festival a few years before the *yosakoi* performances started. He provides important historical context for the youth demographic at the festival in 2001, tracing its roots back to the 1980s.

8. Alongside Ryōma, the Shinsengumi have attracted a similar fan response in Kyoto. In particular, Mibu Temple, in Western Kyoto, where the group was located, has long garnered fans of the *bakumatsu*. The Shinsengumi make for colorful characters because of their viciousness and their telltale light blue *haori* (short overcoats) with mountain peaks on the trim.

One likely theory is that Ryōma's killer was one of this group. A prominent example of fan-driven heritage contents tourism, Mibu Temple houses a collection of journals where fans spontaneously started writing messages to and about the Shinsengumi (Sugawa-Shimada 2015).

9. *Ryōma ga yuku* was serialized from 1962 to 1966 and was probably the most influential popular account of Ryōma's life (Jansen 1961, 346). According to Henry Smith (2007, 106–107), Shiba was primarily responsible for the strong equation of Ryōma and youth that pervades late twentieth-century accounts of Ryōma's life and deeds.

Chapter 5: Kimono Crowds

Epigraph. JTB Publishing 2010.

Epigraph. Kyoto City Convention and Visitors' Bureau 2016.

1. While the series is now discontinued, in 2015 JTB Publishing's website promoted the *Tabihana* series as perfect for young women travelers: 'Utilizing the voice of real 20-to-30-year-old young women, *Tabihana* tightly packs travel dreams in a small, cute, and very dependable guidebook. It's created in the style of a picture book, so as soon as you look at it, you are in the mood for a journey. In addition, the inclusion of stickers and the 'ready for the trip' appendix allow you to quickly make this your own book. Even before your departure, you can have fun making the most of your journey" (JTB 2015).

2. Higashiyama means "eastern hills," and the term is used in a variety of ways. The contemporary Higashiyama ward spans from Jujō up to Sanjō east of the Kamo River. Further north, the Higashiyama Jisho Temple (home to the Silver Pavilion) was central to the flourishing of tea ceremony and related arts in the late fifteenth century, known as the Higashiyama era of the Muromachi period. Yet in much tourist literature Higashiyama refers primarily to the area east of the Kamo River, from Shichijō up to the Heian Shrine, and sometimes more specifically just to the area from Kiyomizu Temple up to Maruyama Park.

3. Beginning in 2014, Japanese tourists began to show a preference for other, less crowded, locations in Kyoto as international tourist numbers soared.

4. Each year on the second Monday in January, young people across Japan who have turned twenty in the past year dress up, go to local or famous shrines, and celebrate with family and friends for Coming of Age Day, signaling their entry into adulthood. Many kimono rental companies started out catering to this market.

5. There is an important distinction to be made here. Kimono have

been mass produced since the early twentieth century, when printing techniques made the process much quicker (Milhaupt 2016). Ogata (2015) uses Walter Benjamin's notion of mechanical reproduction to make a distinction between an "authentic" craft and the increasingly mechanized cheap kimono that fill the racks at rental shops today.

6. Jan Bardsley (2021) explores the ways that apprentice stories (both fictional and personal) and images have been mobilized as symbols of Kyoto, girlhood, modernity, and tradition.

7. This choice of words is evocative: *henshin* means "metamorphosis" or "transformation," and it is used in popular culture, especially manga and anime, to mean a physical transformation.

8. Because these experiences are crafted for photo ops, a quick search for "*maiko* dress up in Kyoto" or even "kimono rental in Kyoto" elicits a host of tourist photos. Many of the rental shops have Facebook and Instagram pages to display customer photos. See, for example, https://www.instagram.com/kyotokimonorental.wargo/, https://www.facebook.com/yumekyoto/, or https://www.okamoto-kimono.com/gallery/.

9. From 2012 through 2017 these data have been gathered for international tourists. The data reported for Japanese tourists vary a bit each year, and this question showed up in the report for the first time in 2017. The figure that year was 1.7 percent (Kyoto City Tourism Office 2018).

10. In recent years important work has been done by thinking through the ways that reenactment as a popular kind of public history poses both challenges and possibilities for understanding history (Agnew 2004; Katherine Johnson 2015; McCalman and Pickering 2010).

11. *Japonisme* refers to a trend in the late nineteenth century wherein Japanese goods (fans, tea cups, kimono, woodblock prints) were fashionable throughout the West (Miles and Neath 2016; Napier 2007).

12. Cosplay started at Comiket (Comic Market), the longest-running manga convention. Running every year since 1975 in Tokyo, Comiket was modeled on the science fiction fan conventions in the United States. Even in early Star Trek conventions the practice of dressing up in character was common, and this idea carried over into the earliest fan conventions in Japan, where it evolved into a widespread practice among fans from the 1980s on (Yonezawa 2002). Today the World Cosplay Summit, held each summer in Nagoya, is the biggest cosplay event.

Epilogue

1. https://kyoto.travel/en/. Accessed June 2014.

2. *Furusato* connotes much more than "hometown." In the postwar

period, the term has been used to create a sense of home or belonging for the growing suburbs and exurbs through a mobilization of nostalgia for traditional life. Much has been written about this important concept in twentieth-century urban lives in Japan; see Ivy (1995); Kelly (1986); Morris-Suzuki (1997); Robertson (1991).

3. "Flexibility," in this usage, is a double-edged sword. The example of flexible labor is informative. On the one hand, it allows for people to work in ways that fits their schedules—they can decide when they want to drive for Uber and for how long each day; they can fit some hours at a job in around child or elderly care—this is a part of the appeal. On the other hand, there is no security in these forms of income as market demand and sometimes the tyranny of reviews drive the availability of customers. Moreover, job security and larger benefits like health and disability insurance diminish and disappear with flexible labor.

4. The first time Japan won an Olympic bid was in 1936, when it was chosen to host the 1940 Summer Olympic Games. However, due to the outbreak of the second Sino-Japanese War (1937) and the intensification of war in Asia, the games were then relocated to Helsinki, Finland.

5. It is important to note that as of May 2021 decisions about the 2020 Olympics were still in flux, controversies over holding the global games during the COVID-19 pandemic were brewing, and the global tourism numbers were still significantly depressed.

References

Agnew, Vanessa 2004. "History's Affective Turn: Historical Reenactment and Its Work in the Present." *Criticism* 46, no. 3: 327–339.

Allison, Anne. 2013. *Precarious Japan*. Durham, NC: Duke University Press.

Aso, Noriko. 2014. *Public Properties: Museums in Imperial Japan*. Durham, NC: Duke University Press.

Bærenholdt, Jørgen Ole, Michael Haldrup, Jonas Larsen, and John Urry. 2004. *Performing Tourist Places*. Aldershot, Hants, England: Ashgate.

Bardsley, Janice. 2021. *Maiko Masquerade: Crafting Geisha Girlhood in Japan*. Berkeley: University of California Press.

Bauman, Zygmunt. 2000. *Liquid Times: Living in an Age of Uncertainty*. Cambridge: Polity Press.

Beeton, Sue. 2016. *Film-Induced Tourism*, 2nd ed. Buffalo, NY: Channel View Publications.

Beeton, Sue, Takayoshi Yamamura, and Philip Seaton. 2013. "The Mediatisation of Culture: Japanese Contents Tourism and Popular Culture." In *Mediating the Tourist Experience: From Brochures to Virtual Encounters*, edited by Jo-Anne Lester and Caroline Scarles, 139–154. Surrey: Ashgate.

Berry, Mary Elizabeth. 1982. *Hideyoshi*. Cambridge, MA: Harvard University Press.

Bird, Isabella Lucy 1881. *Unbeaten Tracks in Japan*. New York: G. P. Putnam's Sons.

Boston Museum of Fine Arts. 2016. "Kimono Wednesdays: A Conversation." Accessed June 27 2016. https://www.mfa.org/programs/lecture/kimono-wednesdays-a-conversation.

Breen, John, Hiroshi Maruyama, and Hiroshi Takagi, eds. 2020. *Kyoto's Renaissance: Ancient Capital for Modern Japan*. Folkestone, Kent: Renaissance Books.

Brinton, Mary C. 2011. *Lost in Transition: Youth, Work, and Instability in Postindustrial Japan*. Cambridge: Cambridge University Press.

Brumann, Christoph. 2009. "Outside the Glass Case: The Social Life of Urban Heritage in Kyoto." *American Ethnologist* 36, no. 2: 276–299.

———. 2010. "Houses in Motion: The Revitalisation of Kyoto's Architectural Heritage." In Brumann and Cox, *Making Japanese Heritage,* 149–170.

———. 2012. *Tradition, Democracy and the Townscape of Kyoto: Claiming a Right to the Past.* New York: Routledge.

Brumann, Christoph, and Rupert A. Cox, eds. 2010. *Making Japanese Heritage.* London: Routledge.

Brumann, Christoph, and Evelyn Schulz. 2015. *Urban Spaces in Japan: Cultural and Social Perspectives.* London: Routledge.

Bruner, Edward. 1994. "Abraham Lincoln as Authentic Reproduction: A Critique of Postmodernism." *American Anthropologist* 96, no. 2: 397–415.

———. 1995. *International Tourism: Identity and Change.* London: Sage.

Burr, William. 2005. "The Atomic Bomb and the End of World War II: A Collection of Primary Sources." *National Security Archive Electronic Briefing,* Book No. 162. George Washington University. Last modified August 2015. Accessed July 2010. https://nsarchive2.gwu.edu//NSAEBB/NSAEBB162/index.htm.

Cameron, Christina, and Nobuko Inaba. 2015. "The Making of the Nara Document on Authenticity." *APT Bulletin* 46, no. 4: 30–37.

Choo, Kukhee. 2013. "Playing the Global Game: Japan Brand and Globalization." In *Asian Popular Culture: The Global (Dis)Continuity,* edited by Anthony Y. H. Fung, 213–227. London and New York: Routledge.

Cliffe, Sheila. 2017. *The Social Life of Kimono: Japanese Fashion Past and Present.* London: Bloomsbury Academic.

Cohen, Erik. 1985. "The Tourist Guide: The Origins, Structure and Dynamics of a Role." *Annals of Tourism Research* 12, no. 1: 5–29.

———. 1988. "Authenticity and Commoditization in Tourism." *Annals of Tourism Research* 15, no. 3: 371–386.

Coleman, Simon, and Mike Crang. 2002. *Tourism: Between Place and Performance.* New York: Berghahn Books.

Creighton, Millie. 1997. "Consuming Rural Japan: The Marketing of Tradition and Nostalgia in the Japanese Travel Industry." *Ethnology* 36: 239–254.

———. 2009. "The Heroic Edo-ic: Travelling the History Highway in Today's Tokugawa Japan." In Guichard-Anguis and Moon, *Japanese Tourism and Travel Culture,* 37–75.

Dalby, Liza Critchfield. 1983. *Geisha*. Berkeley: University of California Press.
———. 2001. *Kimono: Fashioning Culture*. London: Vintage.
Daliot-Bul, Michal. 2009. "Japan Brand Strategy: The Taming of 'Cool Japan' and the Challenges of Cultural Planning in a Postmodern Age." *Social Science Japan Journal* 12, no. 2: 247–266.
———. 2014. *License to Play: The Ludic in Japanese Culture*. Honolulu: University of Hawai'i Press.
Dallen, Timothy J., and Stephen W. Boyd. 2003. *Heritage Tourism*. New York: Prentice Hall.
de St. Maurice, Greg. 2016. "Edible Authenticities: Heirloom Vegetables and Culinary Heritage in Kyoto, Japan." In *Edible Identities: Food as Cultural Heritage,* edited by Ronda Brulotte and Michael Di Giovine, 67–76. New York: Routledge.
Di Giovine, M. A. 2009. *The Heritage-Scape: UNESCO, World Heritage, and Tourism*. Lanham, MD: Lexington Books.
Dougill, John. 2006. *Kyoto: A Cultural History. Cityscapes*. New York: Oxford University Press.
Elliott, Anthony, and John Urry. 2010. *Mobile Lives*. London: Routledge.
Evans, Neil. 2002. "Machi-zukuri as a New Paradigm in Japanese Urban Planning: Reality or Myth?" *Japan Forum* 14, no. 3: 443–464.
Formanek, Susan. 1998. "Pilgrimage in the Edo Period: Forerunner of Modern Domestic Tourism?" In *The Culture of Japan as Seen through Its Leisure,* edited by Sepp Linhart and Sabine Fruhstuck, 165–193. Albany, NY: SUNY Press.
Freedman, Alisa. 2011. *Tokyo in Transit: Japanese Culture on the Rails and Road*. Stanford, CA: Stanford University Press.
Fujitani, Takashi. 1996. *Splendid Monarchy: Power and Pageantry in Modern Japan*. Berkeley: University of California Press.
Funck, Carolin, and Malcolm Cooper. 2015. *Japanese Tourism: Spaces, Places and Structures*. New York: Berghahn Books.
Germann Molz, Jennie. 2012. *Travel Connections: Tourism, Technology and Togetherness in a Mobile World*. London: Routledge.
———. 2014. *Disruptive Tourism and Its Untidy Guests*. London: Palgrave Macmillan.
Gibson, Sarah, and Jennie Germann Molz. 2007. *Mobilizing Hospitality: The Ethics of Social Relations in a Mobile World*. Aldershot: Ashgate.
Gluck, Carol. 1985. *Japan's Modern Myths*. Princeton, NJ: Princeton University Press.
Graburn, Nelson. 1983. *To Pray, Pay and Play: The Cultural Structure of*

Japanese Domestic Tourism. Rev. ed. Aix-en-Provence: Centre des Hautes Études Touristiques. Les Cahiers du Tourisme 26: Série B.

———. 1987. "Material Symbols in Japanese Domestic Tourism." In *Mirror and Metaphor: Material and Social Constructions of Reality,* edited by Dan Ingersoll and Gordon Bronistky, 15–27. Lanham, MD: University Press of America.

———. 1995. "The Past and the Present in Japan: Nostalgia and Neo-Traditionalism in Contemporary Japanese Domestic Tourism." In *Change in Tourism: People, Places, Processes,* edited by Richard Butler and Douglas Pearce, 47–70. New York: Routledge.

———. 2004. "The Kyoto Tax Strike: Buddhism, Shinto, and Tourism in Japan." In *Intersecting Journeys: The Anthropology of Pilgrimage and Tourism,* edited by Ellen Badone and Sharon R. Roseman, 125–139. Urbana: University of Illinois Press.

———. 2009. "The Past and the Other in the Present: *Kokunai Kokusaika Kanko*—Domestic International Tourism." In Guichard-Anguis and Moon, *Japanese Tourism and Travel Culture,* 21–36.

Guichard-Anguis, Sylvie. 2007. "Pilgrimage, Space and Identity: Ise (Japan) and Santiago de Compostela (Spain)." In *Pilgrimages and Spiritual Quests in Japan,* edited by P. Ackerman, D. P. Martinez, and M. Rodriguez del Alisal, 16–26. Richmond, UK: Curzon Press.

———. 2009a. "The Culture of Travel (*Tabi no Bunka*) and Japanese Tourism." In Guichard-Anguis and Moon, *Japanese Tourism and Travel Culture,* 1–17.

———. 2009b. "Japanese Inns (*ryokan*) as Producers of Japanese Identity." In Guichard-Anguis and Moon, *Japanese Tourism and Travel Culture,* 76–102. Guichard-Anguis, Sylvie, and Okpyo Moon, eds. 2009. *Japanese Tourism and Travel Culture*. London: Routledge.

Guth, Christine M. E. 2000. "Charles Longfellow and Okakura Kakuzo: Cultural Cross-Dressing in the Colonial Context." *Positions* 8, no. 3: 605–636.

Haldrup, Michael, and Jonas Larsen. 2010. *Tourism, Performance and the Everyday: Consuming the Orient*. London and New York: Routledge.

Hall, Jenny. 2015. "Re-Fashioning Kimono: How to Make 'Traditional' Clothes for Postmodern Japan." *New Voices in Japanese Studies* 7: 59–84.

———. 2018. "Digital Kimono: Fast Fashion, Slow Fashion?" *Fashion Theory* 22, no. 3: 283–307.

Hareven, Tamara K. 2002. *The Silk Weavers of Kyoto: Family and Work in a Changing Traditional Industry*. Berkeley: University of California Press.

Harrison, Rodney. 2013. *Heritage: Critical Approaches.* London: Routledge.

Harvey, David. 1990. *The Condition of Postmodernity.* Cambridge: Blackwell.

Hein, Carola, and Philippe Pelletier. 2006. *Cities, Autonomy and Decentralization in Japan.* London: Routledge.

Henderson, Joan Catherine. 2017. "Destination Development: Trends in Japan's Inbound Tourism." *International Journal of Tourism Research* 19: 89–98.

Hendry, Joy. 1987. *Understanding Japanese Society.* New York: Routledge.

———. 2004. "Nature Tamed: Gardens as a Microcosm of Japan's View of the World." In *Japanese Images of Nature: Cultural Perspectives,* edited by Pamela J. Asquith and Arne Kalland, 83–105. London: RoutledgeCurzon.

Hillsborough, Romulus. 2004. *Ryōma: Life of a Renaissance Samurai,* 3d ed. San Francisco: Ridgeback Press.

Hirōka, Hajime, and Shihoko Hirōka. 2012. Interview with author. July 3.

Hobsbawm, E., and T. Ranger, eds. 1983. *The Invention of Tradition.* Cambridge: Cambridge University Press.

Hoshino Eiki. 1997. "Pilgrimage and Peregrination: Contextualizing the Saikoku Junrei and the Shikoku Henro." *Japanese Journal of Religious Studies* 24, nos. 3–4: 271–299.

Ishimori, Shuzo. 1989. "Popularization and Commercialization of Tourism in Early Modern Japan." *Senri Ethnological Studies* 29: 179–194.

———. 1995. "Tourism and Religion: From the Perspective of Comparative Civilization." In *Japanese Civilization in the Modern World IX,* edited by Umesao Tadao, Harumi Befu, and Ishimori Shuzo, 11–24. Osaka, Japan: National Museum of Ethnology.

Ivanova, Gergana. 2018. *Unbinding the Pillow Book.* New York: Columbia University Press.

Ivy, Marilyn. 1988. "Tradition and Difference in the Japanese Mass Media." *Public Culture* 1: 21–29.

———. 1993. "Formations of Mass Culture." In *Postwar Japan as History,* edited by Andrew Gordon. Berkeley: University of California Press.

———. 1995. *Discourses of the Vanishing.* Chicago: University of Chicago Press.

Iwabuchi, Koichi. 2015. "Pop-Culture Diplomacy in Japan: Soft Power, Nation Branding and the Question of 'International Cultural Exchange.'" *International Journal of Cultural Policy* 21, no. 4: 419–432.

Jameson, Fredric. 1995. *Postmodernism or the Cultural Logic of Late Capitalism.* Durham, NC: Duke University Press.

Jameson, Fredric, and Masao Miyoshi, eds. 1998. *The Cultures of Globalization.* Durham, NC: Duke University Press.

Jansen, Marius B. 1961. *Sakamoto Ryōma and the Meiji Restoration.* Princeton, NJ: Princeton University Press.

Japan National Tourism Organization. "Enjoy my Japan." JNTO. https://www.enjoymyjapan.jp/en/about/. Accessed March 20, 2019.

Japan Tourism Agency. 2009. "White Paper on Tourism in Japan: The Tourism Situation in FY2008." Tokyo: Japan Tourism Agency. Infrastructure Ministry of Land, Transport, and Tourism, 56. http://www.mlit.go.jp/kankocho/en/siryou/whitepaper.html. Accessed February 11, 2019.

———. 2016. "Tourism Nation Promotion Basic Law." Japan Tourism Agency. https://www.mlit.go.jp/kankocho/en/kankorikkoku/kihonhou.html. Last modified December 22, 2016. Accessed February 28, 2019.

———. 2017a. Kankō rikkoku suishin honkeikaku—"Sekai ga otozuretakunaru nihon" wo mezashite" (The Tourism Nation Promotion Basic Plan: Aiming for "Japan the World Wants to Visit"). Tokyo: Japan Tourism Agency. Infrastructure Ministry of Land, Transport, and Tourism. https://www.mlit.go.jp/kankocho/en/kankorikkoku/kihonkeikaku.html.

———. 2017b. "The Tourism Nation Promotion Basic Plan." Japan Tourism Agency. https://www.mlit.go.jp/kankocho/en/kankorikkoku/kihonkeikaku.html. Last modified February 16, 2017. Accessed February 28, 2019.

———. 2017c. "White Paper on Tourism in Japan: The Tourism Situation in FY2016." Tokyo: Japan Tourism Agency. Infrastructure Ministry of Land, Transport, and Tourism, 91. http://www.mlit.go.jp/kankocho/en/siryou/whitepaper.html. Accessed March 12, 2019.

Johnson, Eric. 2018. "Let's Discuss Airbnb and Minpaku Laws." *Japan Times,* June 7.

Johnson, Katherine M. 2015. "Rethinking (Re)Doing: Historical Re-Enactment and/as Historiography." *Rethinking History* 19, no. 2: 193–206.

JTB Publishing. 2010. *Kyoto. Tabihana Kansai 1.* Tokyo: JTB Publishing.

———. "*Tabihana* Webpage." Tokyo: JTB Publishing. http://www.rurubu.com/book/recomm/tabihana/. Accessed October 13, 2015.

JTB Tourism Research & Consulting. 2019. "Statistics of Overseas Residents' Visits to Japan (Historical Figures/by Country/by Purpose)." Tokyo: JTB Tourism Research & Consulting Co.

Kadokawa, Daisaku, and Mitsuo Takakuwa. 2010. *Junia nihon bunka kentei tekisutobukku: rekishi toshi, Kyōto kara manabu* (Junior Japanese Culture Official Textbook: Historical City, Learning from Kyoto). Kyoto: Kyoto Shinbun Kaihatsu.

Kawaguchi, Masahiro, Kaite Yusuke, and Oka Natsuki. 2018. "'Minpaku' Lodging Law Goes into Effect, but Complicated Process Thwarts Property Owners." *The Mainichi* (English), June 15.

Kelly, William. 1986. "Rationalization and Nostalgia: Cultural Dynamics of New Middle-Class Japan." *American Ethnologist* 13, no. 4: 603–618.

Kirshenblatt-Gimblett, Barbara. 1995. "Theorizing Heritage." *Ethnomusicology* 39, no. 3: 367–380.

———. 1998. *Destination Culture: Tourism, Museums, and Heritage*. Berkeley: University of California Press.

Kuitert, Wybe. 2002. *Themes in the History of Japanese Garden Art,* 2d ed. Honolulu: University of Hawai'i Press.

Kyoto Center for Community Collaboration. 2009. *Machiya Revival in Kyoto.* Kyoto: Asano Yasuhiro.

Kyoto City. 2010. "Mirai kyōtoshi kankō sōkō purojekutto 2010+5: Iyoiyo ryo he nanatu no purojekutto" (Future Kyoto Tourism Promotion Project 2010+5: Toward the Essence of Tourism—7 Projects in Process). Kyoto: Kyoto City Industry and Tourism Bureau, Tourism and MICE Promotion Office.

———. 2012. "Ishidatami hū hosuisei hosō no seibi ni tsuite" (About the Maintenance of Cobblestone-Style Water-Retentive Pavement). Kyoto: Construction Planning Department, Supervision and Inspection Division.

———. 2015. "Sekai ga akogareru kankō kyōto he: Kyōto kankō shinkō keikaku 2020" (For the World to Yearn for Kyoto Tourism—Kyoto Tourism Strategy Plan 2020). Kyoto: Kyoto City Industry and Tourism Bureau, Tourism and MICE Promotion Office.

Kyoto City Convention and Visitors' Bureau. 2016. "Kyoto City Official Travel Guide Website." City of Kyoto, Kyoto City Convention and Visitors' Bureau, Kyoto Tourism Association. https://kyoto.travel/en. Accessed frequently, 2012–2021.

Kyoto City Landscape Division. 2007. "Kyoto City Landscape Policy: Forming Timeless and Radiant Kyoto Landscapes." Kyoto: Landscape Bureau City Plan Office, 29.

———. 2014. "The Landscape of Kyoto" (Kyoto no keikan). Kyoto: Landscape Bureau City Plan Office, 112.

Kyoto City Tourism Association. 2020. "Kyoto City Tourism Association

Website." City of Kyoto and Kyoto City Tourism Association. https://www.kyokanko.or.jp/. Accessed April 2020.

Kyoto City Tourism Office. 2002–2020. "Kyoto kankō sōgo chōsa" (Kyoto Tourism Survey Report). Kyoto: Kyoto City Industry and Tourism Bureau, Tourism and MICE Promotion Office.

Kyoto Hanatōro Promotion Council. "Kyoto Hanatōro." Kyoto Hanatōro Promotion Council. http://www.hanatouro.jp/about.html. Accessed June 2019.

———. "Kyoto higashiyama hanatōro." Kyoto Hanatōro Promotion Council. Accessed June 2019.

———. 2015. "Kyoto Hanatōro Heisei 27 Hōkokusho" (Report). Kyoto: Kyoto Hanatōro Promotion Council.

Kyoto Handicraft Center. "Kyoto Handicraft Center Concept." http://www.kyotohandicraftcenter.com/concept/. Accessed February 2017.

Kyoto Ryōzen Gokoku Shrine Website. "Sakamoto Ryōma and Shōwa no Mori." http://www.gokoku.or.jp/index.html. Accessed March 11, 2014.

Kyoto Tanabata Executive Committee. "Kyo no Tanabata." http://www.kyoto-tanabata.jp/en/. Accessed June 2019.

Leheny, David. 2003. *The Rules of Play: National Identity and the Shaping of Japanese Leisure*. Ithaca, NY: Cornell University Press.

———. 2006. *Think Global Fear Local: Sex, Violence, and Anxiety in Contemporary Japan*. Ithaca, NY: Cornell University Press.

Lemaire, Raymond, and Herb Stovel. 1994. "The Nara Document on Authenticity." Nara: UNESCO, ICOMOS.

Light, Duncan. 2015. "Heritage and Tourism." In Waterton and Watson, *The Palgrave Handbook of Contemporary Heritage Research*, 144–158.

Lowenthal, David. 1985. *The Past Is a Foreign Country*. Cambridge: Cambridge University Press.

———. 1998. *The Heritage Crusade and the Spoils of History*. Cambridge: Cambridge University Press.

MacCannell, Dean. 1999. *The Tourist: A New Theory of the Leisure Class*, 3d ed. Berkeley: University of California Press.

———. 2011. *The Ethics of Sightseeing*. Berkeley: University of California Press.

Malcolm, Cooper, Radaslawa Jankowska, and Jeremy Eades. 2007. "The Politics of Exclusion? Japanese Cultural Reactions and the Government's Desire to Double Inbound Tourism." In *Tourism and Politics: Global Frameworks and Local Realities*, edited by Peter M. Burns and Marina Novelli, 71–82. Amsterdam: Elsevier.

Martin, John H., and Phyllis G. Martin. 2014. *Kyoto: A Cultural Guide to Japan's Ancient Imperial City*. Tokyo: C. E. Tuttle.

Martinez, D. P. 1990. "Tourism and the Ama: The Search for a Real Japan." In *Unwrapping Japan: Society and Culture in Anthropological Perspective*, edited by Eyal Ben-Ari, Brian Moeran, and James Valentine, 97–115. Honolulu: University of Hawai'i Press.

———. 2004. *Identity and Ritual in a Japanese Diving Village: The Making and Becoming of Person and Place*. Honolulu: University of Hawai'i Press.

Masabuchi, Toshiyuki. 2010. *Monogatari o tabi suru hitobito: Kontentsu tsūrizumu to wa nanika* (People Who Travel the Story: What Is Contents Tourism?). Tokyo: Sairyusha.

———. 2018. *Rōkaru kontentsu to chiiki saisei kankō sōshutsu kara sangyō shinkō he* (Local Contents and Regional Regeneration: From Tourism Creation to Industry Promotion). Tokyo: Suiyōsha.

Masuda, Masuhiro. 2011. "Machi mamoru shikitari-tsukuri" (Making Customs to Protect the Town). *Yomiuri Shinbun* (online), November 22.

Mauss, Marcel. 1967. *The Gift: Forms and Functions of Exchange in Archaic Societies*. New York: Norton.

Mayer, Tara. 2012. "Cultural Cross-Dressing: Posing and Performance in Orientalist Portraits." *Journal of the Royal Asiatic Society* 22, no. 2: 281–298.

McCalman, Iain, and Paul A. Pickering. 2010. *Historical Reenactment: From Realism to the Affective Turn*. Basingstoke: Palgrave Macmillan.

McGray, Douglas. 2002. "Japan's Gross National Cool." *Foreign Policy*, no. 130 (May–June): 44–54.

Miles, Melissa, and Jessica Neath. 2016. "Staging Japanese Femininity: Cross-Cultural Dressing in Australian Photography." *Fashion Theory* 20, no. 5: 545–573.

Milhaupt, Terry Satsuki. 2016. *Kimono: A Modern History*. London: Reaktion Books.

Ministry of Economy, Trade, and Industry. 2014. "Cool Japan/Creative Industries Policy." https://www.meti.go.jp/english/policy/mono_info_service/creative_industries/creative_industries.html. Last modified February 1, 2019. Accessed July 9, 2019.

Ministry of Land, Infrastructure, Transport, and Tourism. 2017. "White Paper on Land, Infrastructure, Transport and Tourism in Japan, 2017." Tokyo: Japan Tourism Agency.

Moeran, Brian. 1983. "The Language of Japanese Tourism." *Annals of Tourism Research* 10, no. 1: 93–108.

Morris, Ivan. 1994. *The World of the Shining Prince.* New York: Alfred A. Knopf.

Morris-Suzuki, Tessa. 1997. *Reinventing Japan.* New York: M. E. Sharpe.

Mr. B—. 2012. "Miyako Westin Hotel Personnel." Interview with author. June.

Mr. I—. 2012. "Kyoto Tourism Association Personnel." Interview with author. February, April.

Mr. K—. 2012. "Kyoto Tourism City Office." Interview with author. May–June.

Mr. Y—. 2012. "Kyo-Navi Staff Member." Interview with author. June.

Mrs. A—. 2012, 2017. "Kyoto Tourism Association Personnel." Interview with author. April, May.

Mrs. H—. 2012. "Tour Guide." Interview with author. April.

Mrs. M—. 2017. "Private Tour Guide." Interview with author. May.

Murasaki, Shikibu, and Royall Tyler. 2001. *The Tale of Genji.* Translated by Royall Tyler. New York: Penguin Classic.

Murasaki, Shikibu, and Dennis Washburn. 2015. *The Tale of Genji.* Translated by Dennis Washburn. New York: Norton.

Nakamura, Yuko. 2011. "NHK taiga dorama wo keiki toshita kochi-shi no kankō no torigumi" (Tourism Initiatives in Kochi City Triggered by NHK Taiga Drama). *Kankō Gakuronshū* 6: 91–99.

———. 2016. "Kochishi no NHK taiga dorama ni yoru kankō shinkō" (Tourism Promotion of NHK Taiga Drama by Kochi Prefecture). *Chiri Kūkan Geospatial* 9, no. 2: 221–232.

Napier, Susan J. 2007. *From Impressionism to Anime: Japan as Fantasy and Fan Cult in the Mind of the West.* New York: Palgrave.

Nenzi, Laura. 2004. "Cultured Travelers and Consumer Tourists in Edo-Period Sagami." *Monumenta Nipponica* 59, no. 3: 285–319.

———. 2008. *Excursions in Identity: Travel and the Intersection of Place, Gender, and Status in Edo Japan.* Honolulu: University of Hawai'i Press.

Nora, Pierre. 1989. "Between Memory and History: Les Lieux de Memoire." *Representations* 26: 17.

NYC & Company. 2017. "NYC Travel and Tourism Overview." New York: NYC & Company. https://business.nycgo.com/research/. Accessed December 2017.

Oedewald, Markus. 2009. "Meaning of Tradition in Contemporary Japanese Domestic Tourism." In Guichard-Anguis and Moon, *Japanese Tourism and Travel Culture,* 105–128.

Ogata, Michimasa. 2015. "Kimono bunka to toshi no gensai: Rentaru to fukusei gijutsu no shigaku" (The Modernity of Kimono Culture and City: The Poetics of Rental and Mechanical Reproduction). *Iichiko: A Journal for Transdisciplinary Studies of Pratiques,* no. 126 (Spring): 114–127.

Okamoto Rental Kimono. "Greetings." https://www.okamoto-kimono.com/. Accessed May 2, 2019.

Okamoto, Takeshi. 2015. "Otaku Tourism and the Anime Pilgrimage Phenomenon in Japan." *Japan Forum* 27, no. 1: 12–36.

———. 2018a. *Anime seichi junrei no kankō shakai-gaku: Kontentsutsūrizumu no media komyunikēshon bunseki* (Tourism Sociology of Anime Holy Land Pilgrimage: Media and Communication Analysis of Contents Tourism). Kyoto: Hōritsu Bunkasha.

———. 2018b. *Junrei bijinesu: Popukaruchā ga kankō shisan ni naru jidai* (Pilgrimage Business: The Age When Pop Culture Has Become a Tourist Asset). Tokyo: Kadokawa.

Pellicano, Elisa Ivana. 2019. "Representing Japanese Hospitality: Takigawa Christel's Speech for the 2020 Olympics." *Journal of International and Advanced Japanese Studies* 11: 89–98.

Pine, B. Joseph, and James H. Gilmore. 1998. "Welcome to the Experience Economy." *Harvard Business Review* (July–August): 97–105.

———. 2011. *The Experience Economy.* Boston: Harvard Business Review Press.

Pitelka, Morgan, ed. 2003. *Japanese Tea Culture: Art, History and Practice.* London: Routledge.

Prough, Jennifer. 2018. "Meiji Restoration Vacation: Heritage Tourism in Contemporary Kyoto." *Japan Forum* 30, no. 4: 564–588.

Rakutabi Bunko. 2007. *Kyō no matchamon* (All Things Matcha in Kyoto), vol. 3. Kyoto: Kotokoto.

———. 2008. *Kyō no rekishi navi—dōran no bakumatsuhen* (Navigating Kyoto's History—The Upheaval of the Bakumatsu edition), vol. 29. Kyoto: Kotokoto.

———. 2009a. *Kyoto yoru kankō navi* (Guide to Kyoto Evening Tourism), vol. 40. Kyoto: Kotokoto.

———. 2009b. *Bakumatsu Ryōma no Kyoto annai* (Ryōma's *Bakumatsu* Guide to Kyoto), vol. 41. Kyoto: Kotokoto.

———.2013. *Kyoto rekishi misuteri* (Kyoto History's Mysteries), vol. 49. Kyoto: Kotokoto.

Rath, Eric C. 2014. "New Meanings for Old Vegetables in Kyoto." *Food, Culture and Society* 17, no. 2: 203–223.

Rickly-Boyd, Jillian, Daniel C. Knudsen, Lisa C. Braverman, and Michelle M. Metro-Roland. 2014. *Tourism, Performance, and Place: A*

Geographic Perspective, edited by Dimitri Ioannides. Surrey, England: Ashgate.

Robertson, Jennifer. 1991. *Native and Newcomer: Making and Remaking a Japanese City.* Berkeley: University of California Press.

Rowthorn, Chris. 2005. *Lonely Planet Kyoto.* London: Lonely Planet.

Saberi, Helen. 2010. *Tea: A Global History.* London: Reaktion Books.

Salazar, Noel B. 2005. "Tourism and Glocalization: 'Local' Tour Guiding." *Annals of Tourism Research* 32, no. 3: 628–646.

———. 2010. *Envisioning Eden Mobilizing Imaginaries in Tourism and Beyond.* New York: Berghahn Books.

———. 2012. "Tourism Imaginaries: A Conceptual Approach." *Annals of Tourism Research* 39, no. 2: 863–882.

Salazar, Noel B., and Nelson H. H. Graburn, eds. 2014. *Tourism Imaginaries: Anthropological Approaches.* Oxford: Berghahn Books.

Schlehe, Judith, Michiko Uike-Bormann, Carolyn Oesterle, and Wolfgang Hochbruck, eds. 2010. *Staging the Past: Themed Environments in Transcultural Perspectives.* New York: Columbia University Press.

Schreiber, Mark. 2018. "Implementation of Minpaku Law Lambasted." *Japan Times,* June 30, 2018.

Seaton, Philip. 2015. "Taiga Dramas and Tourism: Historical Contents as Sustainable Tourist Resource." *Japan Forum* 27, no. 1: 82–103.

Seaton, Philip, and Takayoshi Yamamura. 2015. "Japanese Popular Culture and Contents Tourism Special Issue." *Japan Forum* 27, no. 1.

Seaton, Philip, Takayoshi Yamamura, Akiko Sugawa, and Kyungjae Jang. 2017. *Contents Tourism in Japan: Pilgrimages to "Sacred Sites" of Popular Culture.* Amherst, NY: Cambria Press.

Sei Shōnagon. 2006. *The Pillow Book.* Translated by Meredith McKinney. New York: Penguin Books.

Sheller, Mimi, and John Urry. 2004. *Tourism Mobilities: Places to Play, Places in Play.* London: Routledge.

Shimizu, Satoshi. 2014. "Tokyo—Bidding for the Olympics and the Discrepancies of Nationalism." *International Journal of the History of Sport* 31, no. 6: 601–617.

Shirane, Haruo. 2012. *Japan and the Culture of the Four Seasons: Nature, Literature, and the Arts.* New York: Columbia University Press.

Silverman, Helaine. 2015. "Heritage and Authenticity." In Waterton and Watson, *The Palgrave Handbook of Contemporary Heritage Research,* 69–88. Slade, Toby. 2009. *Japanese Fashion: A Cultural History.* Oxford: Berg.

Slusser, Dale. 2003. "The Transformation of Tea Practice in Sixteenth-

Century Japan." In Pitelka, *Japanese Tea Culture: Art, History and Practice,* 70–96.

Smith, Henry D. 2007. "Sakamoto Ryōma in Kyoto: Getting in Personal Touch with the Past in Heisei Japan." In *Japan and Its Worlds: Marius B. Jansen and the Internationalization of Japanese Studies,* edited by Martin Colcutt, Mikio Katou, and Ronald P. Toby, 103–118. Tokyo: I-House Press.

Smith, Valene L., ed. 1989. *Hosts and Guests: The Anthropology of Tourism,* 2d ed. Philadelphia: University of Pennsylvania Press.

Sorensen, André, and Carolin Funck. 2007. *Living Cities in Japan: Citizens' Movements, Machizukuri and Local Environments.* Hoboken, NJ: Taylor and Francis.

Soshirodo Akira. 2005. "Inbound Tourism Policies in Japan from 1859 to 2003." *Annals of Tourism Research* 32, no. 4: 1100–1120.

Spirou, Costas. 2011. *Urban Tourism and Urban Change: Cities in a Global Economy.* New York: Routledge.

Stavros, Matthew. 2014. *Kyoto: An Urban History of Japan's Premodern Capital.* Honolulu: University of Hawai'i Press.

Stovel, Herb. 2008. "Origins and Influence of the Nara Document on Authenticity." *APT Bulletin* 39, nos. 2–3: 9–17.

Sugawa-Shimada, Akiko. 2015. "Rekijo, Pilgrimage and 'Pop-Spiritualism': Pop-Culture-Induced Heritage Tourism of/for Young Women." *Japan Forum* 27, no. 1: 37–58.

Tagsold, Christian. 2013. "Popular Realms of Memory in Japan: The Case of Sakamoto Ryōma." *Contemporary Japan* 25, no. 1: 41–59.

———. 2017. *Spaces in Translation: Japanese Gardens and the West.* Philadelphia: University of Pennsylvania Press.

Tanigawa Yutaka. 2020. "Buddhism and Society in Modern Kyoto." In Breen, Maruyama, and Takagi, *Kyoto's Renaissance,* 65–91.

Teradaya. *Teradaya Brochure.* Fushimi: Teradaya.

Tokai Seikatsu Kenkyū Purojekuto. 2011. *Kyoto rūru* (Kyoto Rules). Tokyo: Chukei Shuppan.

Traganou, Jilly. 2004. *The Tōkaidō Road: Traveling and Representation in Edo and Meiji Japan.* New York: RoutledgeCurzon.

Treib, Marc, and Ron Herman. 2003. *A Guide to the Gardens of Kyoto.* Tokyo: Kodansha International.

Tseng, Alice Y. 2018. *Modern Kyoto: Building for Ceremony and Commemoration, 1868–1940.* Honolulu: University of Hawai'i Press.

Turner, Victor, and Edith Turner. 1978. *Image and Pilgrimage in Christian Culture.* New York: Columbia University Press.

UNESCO. 1972. "Convention Concerning the Protection of the World Cultural and Natural Heritage." Paris: UNESCO World Heritage Centre.

———. 2020a. "Browse the Lists of Intangible Cultural Heritage and the Register of Good Safeguarding Practices." http://www.unesco.org/culture/ich/en/lists. Accessed May 2020.

———. 2020b. "World Heritage List." http://whc.unesco.org/en/list/. Accessed June 2020.

Urry, John. 1990. *The Tourist Gaze: Leisure and Travel in Contemporary Societies*. London: Sage.

———. 2006. *Consuming Places*. London: Routledge.

Urry, John, and Jonas Larsen. 2011. *The Tourist Gaze 3.0*. London: Sage.

Valk, Julie. 2015. "Research Note: The "Kimono Wednesday" Protests: Identity Politics and How the Kimono Became More Than Japanese." *Asian Ethnology* 74, no. 2: 379–399.

Vaporis, Constantine N. 1989. "Caveat Viator: Advice to Travelers in the Edo Period." *Monumenta Nipponica* 44, no. 4: 461–483.

———. 1995. "The Early Modern Origins of Japanese Tourism." *Senri Ethnological Studies* 38: 25–38.

Varley, H. Paul, and Kumakura Isao. 1989. *Tea in Japan: Essays on the History of Chanoyu*. Honolulu: University of Hawai'i Press.

Vlastos, Stephen. 1998. *Mirror of Modernity: Invented Traditions of Modern Japan*. Berkeley: University of California Press.

Wakita, Mio. 2009. "Selling Japan: Kusakabe Kimbei's Image of Japanese Women." *History of Photography* 33, no. 2: 209–223.

Wang, Ning. 1999. "Rethinking Authenticity in Tourism Experience." *Annals of Tourism Research* 26, no. 2: 349–370.

WaRaiDo Guides. 2017. http://www.waraido.com/index.html. Accessed February 2017.

Wargo. 2019. Kyoto Kimono Rental Wargo website. https://kyotokimono-rental.com/en/. Accessed May 13, 2019.

Waterton, Emma, and Steve Watson, eds. 2015. *The Palgrave Handbook of Contemporary Heritage Research*. Houndmills: Palgrave Macmillan.

Wilson, Sandra. 2012. "Exhibiting a New Japan: The Tokyo Olympics of 1964 and Expo '70 in Osaka." *Historical Research* 85, no. 227: 159–178.

Winge, Theresa. 2006. "Costuming the Imagination: Origins of Anime and Manga Cosplay." In *Mechademia 1: Emerging Worlds of Anime and Manga*, edited by Frenchy Lunning, 65–77. Minneapolis: University of Minnesota Press.

World Tourism Organization. 2018a. “UNWTO Annual Report 2017.” Madrid: UNWTO.

———. 2018b. “UNWTO Tourism Highlights, 2018 Edition.” Madrid: UNWTO.

———. 2019. ‘Overtourism’? *Understanding and Managing Urban Tourism Growth beyond Perceptions,* vol. 2: *Case Studies, Executive Summary.* Madrid: UNWTO.

World Travel and Tourism Council. 2019. “Japan: 2019 Annual Research: Key Highlights.” Wright, Patrick, and Andrzej Krauze. 2009. *On Living in an Old Country: The National Past in Contemporary Britain.* Oxford: Oxford University Press.

Yamajō, Toru. 2007. *Kyōto kankō gaku* (Kyoto Tourism Studies). Tokyo: Hōritsu Bunkasha.

———. 2010. *Kankō no Kyōtoron* (A Kyoto Theory of Tourism). Tokyo: Gakubunsha.

Yamamura, Takayoshi. 2009. “Anime Pilgrimage and Local Tourism Promotion: An Experience of Washimiya Town, the Sacred Place of Anime ‘Lucky Star’ Fans.” *Web-Journal of Tourism and Cultural Studies* 14: 1–9.

———. 2015. “Contents Tourism and Local Community Response: Lucky Star and Collaborative Anime-Induced Tourism in Washimiya.” *Japan Forum* 27, no. 1: 59–81.

Yonezawa, Yoshihiro. 2002. Interview with author. Tokyo, Japan.

Yuzo, Marayama. 2019. *Heritage Culture and Business, Kyoto Style.* Translated by Juliet Winters Carpenter. Tokyo: Japan Publishing Industry Foundation for Culture.

Index

Page numbers in **boldface** type refer to illustrations.

About the Author

Jennifer S. Prough is professor of humanities and East Asian studies in Christ College (the Honors College), Valparaiso University. She is author of *Straight from the Heart: Gender, Intimacy, and the Production of Shōjo Manga* (2011). Her research and teaching center on the ways cultural meanings are produced and managed, experienced and interpreted, through mass culture in contemporary Japan.